How to Think about Religious Schools

How to Think about Religious Schools

Principles and Policies

MATTHEW CLAYTON
ANDREW MASON
ADAM SWIFT

with

RUTH WAREHAM

OXFORD
UNIVERSITY PRESS

OXFORD
UNIVERSITY PRESS

Great Clarendon Street, Oxford, OX2 6DP,
United Kingdom

Oxford University Press is a department of the University of Oxford.
It furthers the University's objective of excellence in research, scholarship,
and education by publishing worldwide. Oxford is a registered trade mark of
Oxford University Press in the UK and in certain other countries

Published in the United States of America by Oxford University Press
198 Madison Avenue, New York, NY 10016, United States of America

British Library Cataloguing in Publication Data
Data available

Library of Congress Control Number: 2024932244

ISBN 9780198924005 (hbk.)
ISBN 9780198923992 (pbk.)

DOI: 10.1093/9780198924036.001.0001

Printed and bound by
CPI Group (UK) Ltd, Croydon, CR0 4YY

Contents

Acknowledgements

This book grew out of a Spencer Foundation funded project on "Faith Schools: Principles and Policies" (Grant #201500102), on which the three of us were principal investigators while colleagues at the University of Warwick. We are very grateful to the Foundation for giving us the opportunity to explore these issues together. Ruth Wareham joined us as a postdoctoral research fellow, providing much valued expertise especially on policy-related issues. After her postdoctoral fellowship came to an end, Ruth worked for Humanists UK as Education Campaigns Manager, and has continued in a part-time role for them as an Education Policy Researcher since taking up a lectureship in the School of Education at the University of Birmingham.

During the early stages of the project, in November 2015, we held a launch event at which Paul Barber (the Director of the Catholic Education Service), Tim Brighouse (Schools Commissioner for London, 2002–7), Ashfaque Chowdhury (Chair of the Association of Muslim Schools), Charles Clarke (Secretary of State for Education and Skills, 2002–4), Simon Goulden (Educational Consultant to the Jewish Community), and Marilyn Mason (former Education Officer, Humanists UK), gave presentations. We would like to thank them for sharing their divergent perspectives on the issue of how faith schools should be regulated.

In June 2017, we held a one-day workshop on "Faith Schools, Social Cohesion and Civic Virtue". We are grateful to Miles Hewstone, Ian MacMullen, Michael Merry, and Carol Vincent, for their insightful contributions. Special thanks are due to Eamonn Callan who acted as an astute summarizer and critic on the day. The papers presented at the workshop were published in a special issue of *Theory and Research in Education* (Vol. 16, no. 2, 2018).

The three of us, together with Ruth, co-authored a pamphlet, *How to Regulate Faith Schools* (Wiley, 2018). This was published as no. 25 in the Philosophy of Education Society of Great Britain's Impact series, *Philosophical Perspectives on Education Policy*. We are very grateful to Michael Hand and the PESGB for including it in that series and for chairing a launch event at University College London in October 2018. We would also like to thank Andrew Copson (Chief Executive of Humanists UK), Emma Knights (Chief Executive of the National Governance Association), and Bhikhu Parekh (Member of the House of Lords and Chair of the Commission on the Future of Multi-Ethnic Britain, 1998–2000) for their thought-provoking commentaries. Material from the pamphlet forms the basis of Chapters 2, 6, and 7. We also draw upon a co-authored article 'The Political Morality of School Composition: The Case of Religious Selection', *British Journal of Political Science*, Vol. 51, 2021, pp. 827–44, especially in Chapter 7. So although Ruth is not a co-author of the book itself, it draws upon material that was co-authored. She also provided invaluable assistance by making us aware of new empirical research and recent developments in law and policy.

Adam published much of the material in his single-authored chapter, 'Parents' Rights, Children's Schools', as 'Parents' Rights, Children's Religion: A Familial Relationship Goods Approach', *Journal of Practical Ethics*, Vol. 8, 2020, pp. 30–65. In addition to Andrew and Matthew, he is grateful to Harry Brighouse, Thomas Douglas, and two anonymous reviewers for comments and discussion. He thanks the editors and publisher for permission to use that material.

Andrew presented the material in his single-authored chapter, 'Religious Schools: A Qualified Defence', at the Philosophy of Education seminar at the University of Birmingham and to a workshop that was part of the GOODINT (Good Integration: Goals and Bottlenecks of Successful Integration and Social Cohesion) research project based at the Arctic University of Norway. In addition to Adam, Matthew, and Ruth, he is especially grateful to Melina Duarte, Andreas Føllesdal, Anca Gheaus, Gina Gustavsson, Michael Hand, Kristján Kristjánsson, Sune Laegaard, Kasper Lippert-Rasmussen, and Annamari Vitikainen, for their comments.

Matthew presented an earlier draft of his single-authored chapter, 'Against Religious Schools' at the Central European University, Dortmund University, University College London, the University of East Anglia, and Pompeu Fabra University, Barcelona. In addition to Adam, Andrew, and Ruth, he is particularly grateful to Giorgia Brucato, Joe Clayton, Andrée-Anne Cormier, Johannes Drerup, Alan Finlayson, Michael Frazer, Anca Gheaus, Dan Guillery, Hussein Kassim, Steve Kettell, Colin Macleod, Chris Mills, Andres Moles, Serena Olsaretti, Tom Parr, David Stevens, John Tillson, Andrew Williams, and Doug Yacek for their comments. Section 2 of the chapter reproduces and adapts material first published in 'Children and Political Neutrality', in Anca Gheaus et al. (eds), *The Routledge Handbook of the Philosophy of Childhood and Children*, pp. 328–38. © Routledge, 2018. He is grateful to the editors and publisher for permission to use that material.

We would also like to thank Peter Momtchiloff, the editor in charge of the book at Oxford University Press, for his support and guidance through the initial stages of the publication process. Three anonymous referees provided us with a diverse set of challenging comments, most of which we have tried to address in the final version of the text. We are grateful to them for their improving suggestions and to Tomás Ljubetic Jaeger for his research assistance in helping us submit a clean manuscript.

Matthew Clayton
Andrew Mason
Adam Swift

PART I
THE TERMS OF THE DEBATE

1
Mapping the Terrain

Religious schools are controversial. Some people think that they should not be an option. If parents want to raise their children as members of a particular faith at home, or by taking them to their preferred place of worship, that may be up to them. But schools should not be involved. Schools are about broadening children's horizons, giving them the skills and information they need to make their own choices about how to live, and helping them prepare for life in a diverse, pluralistic society. If schools are allowed to replicate the messages that children are getting at home, and from their parents' religious communities, then that is dangerous both for the children themselves and for the rest of us. It risks indoctrinating them and depriving us of the opportunity to live in a healthy, tolerant democracy where citizens of many and no faiths understand and respect one another.

Others think it obvious that parents should be free to send their children to religious schools if they want to. Any government that ruled them out would be violating people's rights, either their right to religious freedom, or their parental right to raise their children according to their own lights (or both). According to Article 26 of the *Universal Declaration of Human Rights* (1948), "Parents have a prior right to choose the kind of education that shall be given to their children." This view was consolidated and extended by Article 2 of the first Protocol to the *European Convention on Human Rights* (1952): "the state shall respect the right of parents to ensure such teaching and education in conformity with their own religious and philosophical convictions."[1] Even those who doubt that these important statements are correct as *moral* claims accept that they establish *legal* rights which normally prevent governments from prohibiting religious schools altogether, even if these rights do not require the publicly funded provision of such schools.

With prohibition off the table, two big picture issues remain. One is whether religious schools should be eligible for public funding. Some countries support them with taxpayers' money; others require parents or religious bodies to pay for them out of their own pockets. The other is how religious schools should be regulated. Different countries have different rules about what, how, and who they can teach. These two issues, funding and regulation, are connected. The more public funding such schools receive, the more appropriate it may seem for the state to have a say in how they operate. Perhaps wise choices about funding and rules would enable the state both to respect parents' rights *and* to avoid—or at least to limit—the dangers that critics of religious schools worry about.

Our main aim in this book is to offer readers a clear and systematic way of thinking about these matters. You might not know it from the way they are discussed by politicians or in the media, but religious schools raise deep philosophical questions. Should they be allowed to teach children that particular religious beliefs are true? Should they be allowed not to teach them about other people's beliefs? Should they be allowed to exclude children being raised in other religions? Answers to such questions turn on fundamental principles that sometimes conflict. We will set out a framework for handling the various moral considerations at stake. Whatever your answers, that framework will help you understand the values that underlie them, and the way you are dealing with trade-offs between those values. And it will help you identify where exactly you are disagreeing with others who answer them differently.

We emphasize this point about disagreement partly because the book is rather unusual. We have written it together, but we see the philosophical issues in different ways, and weigh the different moral considerations differently. Indeed, later on we will take it in turn to set out our own particular views, coming at the topic from different angles and reaching somewhat different conclusions. Our proposed framework is our (agreed) way of understanding our own philosophical disagreements. We hope that our articulating the implicit structure of particular views on religious schools will similarly help readers see what is involved in taking, or disagreeing with, any particular position.

But we agree about more than a framework for how to think about religious schools. Despite our somewhat different approaches at the philosophical level, we converge also in our views about policy, about how those schools should be funded and regulated, at least as far as England is concerned. This is another of the book's distinctive features. As well as proposing a structured way of addressing the deeper philosophical issues, we also aim to explain and illustrate a way of moving from philosophy to policy, a way of combining normative and empirical considerations to generate recommendations for policymakers. And, interestingly and importantly (and fortunately!), we show how even those who have different views about how to interpret or weigh different normative considerations may end up endorsing the same policies.

In effect, then, *How to Think about Religious Schools* offers readers not one but several different ways of thinking about them. First, our (shared) way of thinking about how to organize and understand the philosophical questions that they pose. Second, our (divergent) ways of thinking about how to approach and answer those questions. Third, our (shared) way of thinking about how to translate philosophical claims into concrete policy proposals. Fourth, our (shared) way of thinking about how religious schools in England should be regulated.

Different countries handle religious schools very differently. When it comes to funding, there are a variety of models. In England, a substantial minority of children are educated in "faith schools" that receive public money—roughly a third of state schools have a religious character[2]—but parents cannot demand that the state provide them with financial support to educate their children in their preferred religion. In the Netherlands, by contrast, the constitution's guarantee of freedom of education is taken to mean that, provided the numbers make it viable, parents or religious bodies are entitled to set up a religious school and receive public funds to pay for it.[3] The situation in France is very different. The policy of *laïcité*, which requires state education to be free of religious commitments, prohibits the state from running faith schools, but those in the private sector are eligible for public funds provided they teach the same curriculum as state schools, submit to inspections, and do not select pupils on religious grounds.[4] The USA has been even stricter on the separation of Church and state, so that public schools have historically been thoroughgoingly secular while religious schools have received no direct state support.[5] Towards the other end of the spectrum, getting on for 90 per cent of children in the Republic of Ireland attend state-funded primary schools that are not only run by the Catholic Church but devote half an hour a day to lessons aimed at initiating students into, and consolidating their commitment to, Catholicism.[6]

This gives some sense of the range of different funding arrangements, but things are complicated by the fact that it is not obvious what counts as a "religious school" in the first place. In England, for example, even schools that are *not* regarded as "faith schools" are still legally required to hold a daily act of collective worship, which is to be "of a broadly Christian character". And, reflecting England's history of educational provision, and its entangling of politics and religion—the monarch is both Head of State and Defender of the Faith—the Anglican Church is involved in the running of many schools that, officially speaking, have no "designated religious character", including non-religious schools in CofE Multi Academy Trusts. True, many schools effectively ignore the rules about collective worship, and many schools run by the Church of England see themselves as offering an education available to, and appropriate for, members of all faiths. Still, visiting Americans, used to strictly religion-free public schooling, are often shocked by the extent to which Christian elements suffuse schools that do not formally qualify as "faith schools".

Rather than getting bogged down in semantics and trying to pin down what makes something a "religious school", it's more helpful to talk directly about the different ways in which religion might affect a school's characteristics (or, as philosophers might say, its "properties"). At one extreme are schools that are paid for and run by the state, make no attempt to direct students towards any particular religious views, allow no religious elements to affect the character of the school or what and how it teaches, and admit students without any regard to their parents' religious affiliation. At the other are schools that are paid for and run by a religious body (or group of parents), aim to initiate their students into, and instruct them in, their particular religion, allow that religion to affect many aspects of the school and what and how it teaches, and admit only students whose parents are affiliated to that religion. In between those two extremes, many permutations are possible. For example, a school could be paid for by the state and run by a religious body (or group of parents), its religious character could influence its ethos and (some of) what it teaches, but it could make no attempt to instil any particular religious views and could be available to all students regardless of their religious background. We're not interested in what counts as a religious school. We're interested in the various ways in which religion should and shouldn't be allowed to affect what happens in schools and who goes to them.

1. Controversies

We can start to set out the terms of the debate by quickly considering a few recent times when religious schools have become news stories and matters for political debate in the UK. Perhaps the biggest development of the past 10 years was the introduction, in 2014, of a requirement that *all* schools—religious or otherwise, public or private—"promote the basic British values of democracy, the rule of law, individual liberty, and mutual respect and tolerance for those of different faiths and beliefs". This "British Values" agenda was a response to worries about religious extremism, and associated concerns about terrorism and national security particularly in Muslim schools or those with a high proportion of Muslim students. (The schools implicated in the so-called "Trojan horse" scandal in Birmingham, which involved an alleged conspiracy to introduce an "Islamist" ethos, were not designated as faith schools.)[7] Critics were quick to suggest that there was nothing distinctively "British" about the values in question, and indeed the then prime minister David Cameron also advocated the same goals under the perhaps more accurate description of an "active, muscular liberalism". This, for him, contrasted with the attitude of "passive tolerance", which "stands neutral between different values" that had prevailed in recent years.[8] Whatever the label, this was a clear attempt by the state to insist that all schools foster particular—"civic"—values in its future citizens.

Another development, relating to an associated concern with "community cohesion" or "social integration", was less dramatic. In 2016, then prime minister Theresa May announced that the government intended to encourage more new state-supported faith schools by abolishing the cap on religious selection.[9] That cap—permitting new schools to select only 50 per cent of their students on the basis of religious criteria—had been introduced in 2010 as a deliberate attempt to limit the extent of religious segregation and create more diversity within schools. The need for greater diversity in schools was one of the lessons drawn by a government-sponsored report into inter-cultural conflicts that had broken out in 2001 and the cap was widely welcomed by those concerned at the ways in which members of different cultural and religious communities lived "parallel lives".[10] Religious bodies—Catholic and Jewish groups in particular—saw the 50 per cent cap as an obstacle to their opening new schools, which prompted the proposal to remove it. As things turned out, May's government didn't have the votes to get the change of policy through Parliament, so the 50 per cent cap remains in place. But it applies only to new state-funded free schools. In the UK, private schools, and those publicly funded schools that are recognized as having a religious character, continue to be able to use religious criteria to select *all* their students. Critics of the status quo continue to be concerned about the socially divisive, intolerance engendering, effects of religious segregation in the school system.

A different angle on questions of selection concerns the charge that some religious schools are "socially" selective (i.e. that the students they teach are not representative of the wider population in socio-economic terms).[11] It is one thing for them to be disproportionately composed of children being raised in a particular religion, another for them to take less than their fair share of disadvantaged or harder to educate students. The evidence is disputed, but it's easy to see why this matters. One of the reasons the government has given for why it's trying to increase the number of religious schools is that they perform better. But if the reason why they perform better is that they have more of the kind of children who perform better anyway, and would have done so at a different type of school, then the government's reasoning would be undermined. The religious character of the school would turn out to be a spurious variable; a factor that, under inspection, turns out not to do any explanatory work. Suppose, on the other hand, that the government is right and religious schools do indeed perform particularly well. Then we face a problem of distributive justice. Is it fair that children's chances of getting into high-performing schools should depend on their parents' religious affiliation? That question takes on a special significance when one adds in the worry that both parents and schools may cheat: parents by pretending to endorse religious views simply in order to access better schools, schools by prioritizing children from advantaged households.

Sometimes unease about religious schools concerns the danger they pose to the children who go to them. In 2010, the well-known scientist (and atheist) Richard Dawkins made a TV documentary called *Faith School Menace*, which argued that some of them effectively denied their students access to scientific knowledge, and the opportunity to think critically, and for themselves, about the validity of religious doctrines.[12] He filmed a class in which Muslim students were taught about the theory of evolution, so they knew what it was, but they were taught it in a way that portrayed it as false. While defenders of faith schools emphasize parents' rights to raise their children in their religious beliefs, others invoke the UN Convention on the Rights of the Child (1989), which grants children the right to "freedom of thought, conscience and religion" and guarantees them "freedom to seek, receive and impart information and ideas of all kinds…". Humanists UK, a campaign group on behalf of the "non-religious", complains that private faith schools are particularly likely to violate these rights, by allowing their religious ethos to suffuse not only science lessons but also their teaching on gender equality, relationships, and sex education.[13] The complaint here is not only that this kind of schooling indoctrinates children, but also that it fails to respect their rights to know about, and regard as an option, ways of living that do not conform to those favoured by their parents.

Sending children to a religious school is one way that parents might seek to protect their children from messages at odds with their own views. Another is to demand that *non*-religious schools not teach their children things they don't want them to know. In 2019, primary schools in Birmingham were in the news as Muslim parents organized demonstrations protesting at the LGBT content in their children's relationships education.[14] That was a somewhat nuanced case: the objection was that the material, which the school regarded as implied by its requirement to teach about the 2010 Equality Act, was not being taught in an "age-appropriate" manner. But the general issue concerns the state's authority to tell children things that their parents would rather they didn't hear, and to encourage tolerant attitudes in its future citizens. In the UK, parents have the right to withdraw their children from any Religious Education lessons they don't like and, up until three terms from a child's sixteenth birthday, from any parts of the sex education curriculum that is not part of the National Curriculum for science. So it's not only religious schools that raise issues concerning children's autonomy, and their attitudes to those with diverse religious affiliations or sexual orientations. Those issues also arise in schools with no designated religious character, and our book offers ways of thinking about those too. (Really it should be called *How to Think about Religious Schools* **and** *Religion in Schools*...)

Although it rarely attains the level of a news story, one more angle—much favoured by religious bodies—is worth mentioning. This concerns the complaint that, to quote one Church of England report, schools are increasingly "dominated by a secularist viewpoint indicative of an increasingly utilitarian and materialist approach to education in which market economics would become the overriding ethos".[15] From this perspective, religious schools should be seen as offering an alternative to what is in effect a state-sponsored ideology that has no place for the spiritual aspects of life, no acknowledgement of people's need for purpose and meaning. They are pockets of resistance to a form of totalitarianism: the imposition of an entirely secular world view and its associated values, such as individualism, materialism, instrumental rationality. On this view, schools without a religious character are not, as their defenders might claim, neutral or impartial between different traditions. Rather, they promulgate a tradition of their own—secularism—and one that neglects crucial dimensions of what it is to be a human being. Children who are not educated into religious ways of life are not thereby equipped to be autonomous; rather, they are the ones being indoctrinated—into the shallow values of the wider societal, and state-supported, culture.[16] In support of this perspective, it is observed that some parents prefer a religious school to a non-religious one, even if the religion in question is not their own. The thought here is that there is something distinctive about the religious perspective as such, something that "secular" schools do not provide.

That ends our quick introductory survey of the controversies that constitute the terrain we will be covering in the rest of the book. Those who keep reading will be offered a way of thinking clearly about those controversies, and others, and will find out what we think about them. Although the details are complicated, the big picture is straightforward. In different ways, debates turn on views about the correct way to understand, and combine, three sets of rights and interests: those of parents, children, and the state. Or, as we prefer to think of it, of people under three different descriptions: as parents, as children, and as citizens. Parents should surely have some authority over their children's upbringing but should they be allowed to send their children to a school that will reinforce the religious messages they are giving them at home? Children clearly have some interests that must be protected and promoted, even against the actions (and inactions) of their parents, but do those include an interest in being exposed to views that contradict their parents' religious views? The state's job is partly to protect the rights of both parents and children, but to what extent can it also act on behalf of citizens' collective interest, requiring us all to follow rules that will make society fairer, or foster a tolerant, democratic, political culture? Answering these questions involves getting the right balance between competing moral considerations.

2. Getting Clear on the Questions

The next chapter will set out a systematic way of thinking about those considerations—what we think of as an analytical normative framework. That is not as scary as it sounds. "Analytical" comes from "analyse", which means breaking something down into clear and manageable components. Just as a chemist analysing a compound will identify its constituent parts, so we are interested in getting clear about the different elements that combine to form people's views about religious schools. But where the chemists' framework is given by the periodic table, which systematically lists and organizes the discrete and basic constituents of the material world, ours is made up of the various different moral values and principles that people endorse, or disown. Our analytical framework is "normative" (rather than "positive" or "empirical") because it consists of the elements that people use to *evaluate* things—the various ways in which people might regard them as good or bad, right or wrong. It is these elements that combine to generate views about religious schools, with different people holding different combinations, or giving them different weights.

Before we get on to that, let us say something about the different kinds of question that one might ask about religious schools. Different parts of the book will operate at somewhat different levels—and part of it will be about how to move from one to the other—so we need these on the table to map the terrain properly. Although called *How to Think about Religious Schools*, the various questions we have in mind are practical ones; that is, they are questions about what *to do*, not just about what or how *to think*. (Perhaps a better title would have been *How to Think about What to Do about Religious Schools*.) But even with that practical—action-guiding—aspect clearly in focus, it's a further question whose actions we are trying to guide. There are politicians and policymakers, the people who decide what kind of schools are going to be available as options that parents might choose for their children. They make decisions about how the school system should be regulated: they choose the school rules. On the other hand, there are parents, who get to make choices about which of the available schools they want their children to go to: they choose schools given the rules. That makes it sound as if policymakers are more important than parents, and in a sense that's true. Parents only get to make choices between the options that policymakers make available. But of course parents are also citizens and in that capacity can try to influence policy, through campaigning—and voting—for their preferred regulatory regime. It's an interesting question how these two roles or hats relate to each other: the moral questions that confront parents choosing only for their own children play out differently from those that confront policymakers or citizens-as-policy-influencers. For example, most people think that parents are morally permitted to choose the school that will be best for their children but that it would be wrong for policymakers—or citizens-as-policy-influencers—to allow that consideration to affect their decisions about what kinds of school should be generally available.

There are lots of fascinating moral questions one can ask about individuals' choosing schools for their children. These tend to be discussed in the context of elite private schools, or parents opting for an academically selective school, or moving into the catchment area of a "good" school.[17] Some questions look similar when it comes to religious schools. Consider, for example, when parents choose one for reasons that have nothing to do with its religious character but because they think it will be better in other ways. If parents are justified in trying to get their child into a school that is "good enough", in terms of academic results or students' behaviour, and the only feasible good enough option is a religious school, then they may be justified in trying to get their child into that school (though perhaps not in lying about their own religious views in order to do so!). But some questions look different. To choose a religious education for one's child is to exercise a particular kind of control over her formation and development, and the societal effects—and effects on individual children—of religious segregation in the school system differ from those of segregation by class or academic ability. Individual decisions thus take on a different character.

Although some of what we cover may be helpful for parents thinking about schools for their children, we don't try to tackle the micro-level moral questions head on. We're not interested in the question of which schools parents are morally permitted (or required) to choose for their children given the options that the rules make available to them. That is a fascinating and difficult question, but it is not ours. We're interested in the macro-level question. Which rules should govern religious schools (and religion in schools)? That is a question for all who have the opportunity to influence policy.

But we can think about—and answer—questions about policy in different ways, or at different levels. We might, for example, have in mind the rules that would apply in the ideal case, in a perfectly just society—one where people have their fair share of resources, where they respect one another as equals, where, alongside their particular religious commitments, they care about social solidarity and share a commitment to a tolerant democratic culture. The policies appropriate for such a society might well differ from those that would be suitable to more unjust circumstances, such as our own, which is sadly far removed from the ideal. Imagine a society with a long history of amicable relations between different religious groups, or no history of colonialism, or where people's religious identities were entirely independent of their ethnic or racialized identity, or where the different religious groups lived together in mixed neighbourhoods, or where there was no tradition of religious bodies being involved in the provision of public education. The rules regulating the religious aspects of schooling might sensibly be rather different from those appropriate in England in the 2020s. Parents have to choose schools for their children in circumstances that are not of their choosing. Those circumstances are often far from ideal. The same applies to policies.

This book ends with a concrete set of proposals for the regulation of religious schools (and religion in schools) in England. We accept that, at present, these proposals are politically unrealistic. They are too controversial to command a democratic majority and those who oppose them, those with vested interests in the status quo, are too powerful. Nonetheless, we believe that the proposals are feasible in the sense that they would work well if applied here and now. They take into account the various "non-ideal" circumstances that responsible policy proposals must factor in. They are compatible with human rights law, for example. We accept that there are legal constraints on reform, even where we think those constraints misguided because they give people rights that they should not have, morally speaking. We take those constraints to mean that, whatever the rules that regulate state schools, parents will have the option to opt out of state provision and educate their children privately. This possibility makes a difference to the policies that we recommend for the state sector—it leads us to accept some watering down of the policies that we would otherwise support—since it is generally better to have parents sending their children to state schools than opting out altogether.

That is just an example of how the policy suggestions in the last part of the book incorporate real-world considerations, taking into account feasibility constraints and possible unintended consequences that might follow from unrealistically optimistic measures. We mention it now because before that, in Part II, we each—and separately—set out our views at a somewhat more abstract, philosophical level. Those chapters present our individual takes on the macro-question of what the school rules should be. They are not aimed at parents choosing schools for their children. But, unlike the proposals in Part III, they discuss the macro-question in a way that floats fairly free of any particular historical circumstances or social context. They go deeper into the philosophical fundamentals—the different normative considerations at stake—in a way that some might regard as closer to "ideal theory".[18] As we have said, we disagree at that more basic or foundational level. Our visions of the best way to answer the questions about religious schools are somewhat different when we are talking about principles. But having diverged somewhat in Part II, we converge again in Part III.

Because Part II involves delving more deeply into philosophical issues, there is something of a gear change between Part I and Part II. Part II is more abstract, and it involves more nuanced and more detailed discussions of a range of complex issues concerning how we should interpret the different normative considerations at stake and what weight we should give them. As a result, the chapters that comprise it are necessarily harder going. But we hope that they will repay the work involved in studying them. Readers who are more interested in the broader picture, and the way in which our agreed approach can yield surprising and indeed controversial conclusions concerning the regulation of religious schools, are welcome to skip Part II and to move straight to Part III. If you do so, you will miss what we regard as some interesting divergences between us that illustrate the way in which real agreement on how we should approach questions about religious schools is nevertheless compatible with marked disagreement on our fundamental attitudes towards them. But you will nevertheless be in a position to understand the point of the regulatory framework we defend in Part III and the reasons that led each of us to it.

3. Common Ground

Although our philosophical views are *somewhat* different, we didn't get together to write this book because we disagree violently and wanted to fight things out in print. Plenty of people take a very different line from all of us, and from their perspective our individual chapters in Part II may well look like variations on a single theme. In a sense, they'd be right. Our philosophical outlooks are rather similar and we don't pretend that between us we offer anything like the full range of views that are out there. We conclude this introductory chapter by mentioning a few of the big-picture areas where our views coincide.

We converge in rejecting what we regard as three extreme approaches, which we will call "libertarianism", "communitarianism", and "statism". Libertarianism, as we shall use the term, is the view that *parents* have the right to educate their child according to their own lights. If, for example, they want to instil a particular set of religious beliefs and values in her, so that she comes to share their faith, then they are entitled to do so. Communitarianism is the view that a *religious community* is entitled to educate its members in line with its own views. So, for example, it may exercise authority over a child's schooling so that she acquires an unshakeable commitment to a particular religious doctrine—and it may do this even if her parents would prefer her to learn to think for herself, and even if she as an individual has an interest in developing her own views about how she should live. Statism is the view that *the state* is entitled to educate its future citizens according to its own conception of its interests. So, for example, it may cultivate in them a particular national identity—perhaps a quasi-religious devotion to the values, traditions, and practices of a particular national community—even if that involves inculcating national myths that distort the truth.

Why do we reject libertarianism, communitarianism, and statism, understood in the way we have described? The short answer is that they get the wrong balance between the various people whose interests are at stake. (Or, more accurately, between the various interests of the people whose interests are at stake.) Libertarianism gives too much weight to parents' interests. It allows parents to make decisions that may make it hard for their children to flourish and may undermine the prospects of a reasonably just polity. Communitarianism gives too much weight to religious communities' interest in reproducing itself across generations. It allows communities to educate children in ways that may make it hard for their individual members to flourish, especially if they reject the religion of the community into which they are born and, again, may work against a healthy, tolerant society. Statism gives too much weight to the state's interests independently of the interests of those subject to its authority; it allows states to educate children in ways that may fail adequately to respect the rights of parents, children, and communities.

We reject all three partly because we think children's interests are very important, and include an interest in developing the capacity for autonomy. Children have a right to an "open future",[19] which means that they are entitled to an education that cultivates in them a capacity for critical reflection, and precludes the kind of indoctrination intended to instil an unshakeable commitment to a particular set of religious doctrines or national myths. And we reject all three partly because we think that the interests of citizens considered collectively are important and require us to cultivate in children the virtues needed to create and sustain a reasonably just polity. These virtues involve various beliefs that may be incompatible with the doctrines or practices of particular religious or national communities, for example, the doctrine that the proper role for women is to be good wives and mothers, or that homosexuality should not be tolerated.

Another thing we agree about is more controversial. As far as regulation is concerned, we all reject the idea that there is a fundamental difference between the normative principles relevant to publicly funded schools and those that get no support from the public purse. Indeed, we think that the same principles apply also to those who educate their children at home. That is controversial because it is widely held that home education[20] and privately funded schools lie in the private sphere—the realm of voluntary and consensual behaviour—that should not be subject to state intervention. On this mainstream view, it may be legitimate for citizens to make rules that serve their collective interest when it comes to public institutions they are providing for one another. But if people choose not to use those institutions and to educate their children themselves, or through voluntary private associations, then how they educate them is essentially their own business. We mentioned early on that the UK government has recently taken the step of requiring that *all* schools teach "British Values", in our view better described as "civic", or "liberal", or "democratic" values even though (as David Cameron pointed out in defence of his description of them as British) they are anchored in particular traditions and institutions.[21] For us, that is a step in the right direction, but the general idea that the state has less claim to a say over the religious character of private than public (or "state" or "government") schools, and even less when it comes to home education, remains the conventional wisdom. This is true of scholars as well as of popular opinion.[22]

To be clear, the regulatory framework proposed in Part III does not suggest that the same rules should apply everywhere. When it comes to policy for the real world, there are good reasons to give private schools, and those who educate their children at home, more leeway when it comes to religious matters. We've already mentioned, for example, the way that human rights law rules out some policies and makes others less desirable. And even at a more philosophical level, we recognize that attempts to monitor and control what goes on in people's homes might be destructive of important values. Still, none of this involves accepting a simple or sharp distinction between the "public" and the "private". What matters, fundamentally, are the normative considerations at stake. For us, the importance of children's autonomy, on the one hand, and of civic educational goals, on the other, means that there is a legitimate public interest in how children are educated, including in religious matters, wherever that education takes place and whoever pays for it.

Finally, we agree that religion isn't special. That too may sound very controversial, and certainly some will baulk at that thought. Some readers may take it to invalidate our whole approach. Surely it shows that we simply don't "get" religion, so the arguments to come are not worth taking seriously. Other readers may wonder how we've managed to get this far without saying what "religion" is, or what makes a school "religious". Better late than never, we'll end this introductory chapter by explaining how we understand what it is for something to be a "religion" and why, so understood, it isn't special.

For our purposes, religions are bundles of views and attachments about various matters: the nature of the universe (and whether it was created or includes a god or gods, for example), what we ought to believe is intrinsically valuable (such as human life), how we treat each other (whether, for example, we should sacrifice our own interests for the sake of others), and how we live our own lives (such as whether we devote considerable time to prayer, worship, rituals, or meditation).

Of course, a religious life goes beyond beliefs we hold about the big questions of human existence and the meaning of life. People think about their religion as suffusing their way of life in a way that extends beyond the beliefs they hold: their religion gives everything they do a particular inflection. How people dress and structure their daily activities, what they eat, with whom they associate, and much more besides, is often bound up with their religious affiliation and the customs and conventions related to it. Still, these wider commitments and attachments don't stand independently of, but are integrated with and often explained by, beliefs about the universe, how we ought to treat each other, and how we ought to live our own lives. In that sense, they are similar to the non-religious conceptions many hold, in which basic beliefs about morality and ethics explain why these people subscribe to a vegetarian diet, or dress modestly or extravagantly, or pursue particular occupations, and so on.

There is an interesting puzzle about how to tell whether a particular view is religious or not. A view doesn't seem to be religious merely because it addresses *questions* about the origins of the universe, or about how to treat others and live well. Many who are not religious also address those questions: many scientists seek to understand how the universe began, and many non-religious philosophers try to answer questions about what we owe to each other or what a good life consists in. Perhaps a view counts as religious if it offers particular *answers* to these questions. But, if so, it is hard to know what kind of answer qualifies. One might think that a religious conception is one that invokes a deity or deities to explain our world, to evaluate it, or to justify certain kinds of human activity. But that can't be right if we treat atheist Quakers or certain Buddhists as religious. An alternative approach holds that a religious attitude should be understood as holding that human life is objectively valuable and finds the universe awe inspiring.[23] On that interpretation one can be religious without believing in the existence of a deity or deities. No doubt there are many further ways of trying to demarcate a viewpoint as religious.

We needn't delve deeper into these interpretative puzzles. For us, what matters is, first, that the bundle of questions about the universe, how we ought to treat others, and how we ought to live our own lives are important ones, which school children have an interest in understanding and thinking about. And, second, that people disagree about the truth or value of different religions' answers to those questions, and about the truth or value of answers that are commonly regarded as non-religious too. As we know, disagreement about religion is sometimes expressed in the form of terrible violence against those who hold particular views—although we don't treat religion as special in the sense of providing better answers to various important questions, it surely has special historical significance in shaping people's lives and explaining wars and oppression. So, we must address the practical educational issue of how school policy should be framed to ensure that students learn to tolerate or accept those who hold different religious views or views about religion to their own. In addition, we will argue that religious education is part of a more general educational provision that enables individuals to decide for themselves the personal goals and relationships they ought to value and pursue.

In our shared conception of educational justice, then, we argue that students have an interest in living just and autonomous lives. Some people will justify these interests by appealing to world views that encompass ideas about further matters, such as the existence of a deity or deities, or the nature of the universe. That is their moral right. But we believe that the morally important interests that form the basis of our view don't *have* to have a religious basis. That's controversial, because some hold that one can't make sense of our interest in living justly and autonomously without appealing to religious foundations.[24] Though we do not give an argument for the contrary view, it seems clear to us that there could be many sufficient justifications of the core interests we invoke, some of which are religious, some not. Given that belief, in our shared approach to religious schools, we proceed by thinking about school policy without resolving the deeper questions concerning the universe and humanity, which some believe explain why the goods of justice and personal autonomy are so important.

4. Conclusion

We hope that this opening chapter has given readers a sense of the kinds of issue that arise when we start to think about religious schools. Some of them, like admissions policies and "British Values", are political and concrete. Others, like parents' right to choose a religious school and a child's right to an open future, are philosophical and abstract. The former occasionally become news stories that excite controversy. The latter operate more as deep background assumptions that tend to stay under the radar. To make informed judgments about any of them, we need to identify the various moral considerations at stake, to bring the competing values and principles to the surface, hold them up to the light, and think about how best to balance or combine them. In the next chapter, we offer an analytical framework—our nearest equivalent to the chemist's periodic table—that's supposed to help us do just that.

How to Think about Religious Schools: Principles and Policies. Matthew Clayton, Andrew Mason, and Adam Swift, Oxford University Press. © Matthew Clayton, Andrew Mason, and Adam Swift 2024.
DOI: 10.1093/9780198924036.003.0001

2

A Normative Framework

Our first chapter started by quickly running through a number of ways in which religious schools are controversial. The aim was to bring out the complexity and variety of the moral considerations at stake. Sometimes the focus is on what children should learn in school. Sometimes it's on who they should go to school with. Sometimes the question concerns what is due to children themselves—their rights, as individuals, to develop certain skills or capacities. Sometimes it's about the wider effects of religious schooling on our shared social and political life—how our future citizens will come to relate to one another. Sometimes the worry is about which children get to go to better or worse schools. Sometimes—as when attention is on parents' rights to decide these things for themselves—children seem to drop out of the picture altogether.

There are a lot of different things going on here. Our main aim in this chapter is to propose a way of disentangling them, to set out a systematic framework for identifying the different normative elements that feed into these various controversies. With that framework in hand, we—and our readers—will be able to identify the moral sources of disagreement between those with opposing opinions. And, moving beyond analysis and interpretation to argument, we—and they—will be equipped clearly and coherently to form and defend judgments about how the different normative considerations should be combined. Those considerations sometimes pull in different directions, and disagreement about policy with respect to religious schooling is in large part due to people weighing them differently. Often that differential weighting happens unconsciously, or with advocates of particular views only dimly aware of the trade-offs they are implicitly endorsing. Breaking the issues down into their constituent elements helps us understand why we think what we think, as well as why others think differently.

In the final section we shall also present some of our own, shared, views about how some of the different normative considerations we have identified should be interpreted and combined. In this way the current chapter provides a comprehensive overview of the normative basis of our arguments for the regulatory policies that we defend in Part III. Many of those who disagree with us will do so because they do not accept our views about the significance and weight to be attached to two kinds of normative factor: children's interest in developing a capacity to form and revise their own judgments about how to live, and our interests as citizens in living in a society where people share various attitudes and dispositions.

To be sure, not all policy disagreements can be traced back to normative disputes. As we will explain in Part III, people's views about policy nearly always depend not only on their beliefs about values and principles but also on their beliefs about facts. People can share the same moral priorities, and agree about how to weigh the various normative considerations at stake, while disagreeing about the likely effects of a given policy. For example, two people could both think that parents' rights over their children's education are much less extensive than is commonly recognized, and that it is extremely important that children develop the capacity for autonomy, while having different views about how governments might best pursue that agreed goal. One might want to reject all state support for schools with any kind of distinctive religious character, another might favour state involvement in schools that adopt a moderate religious approach. That disagreement would result from their views about what would actually happen under the different policies: which children would go to which schools, what their experience would be like, how that would impact on their developing the capacity for autonomy, and so on. In order to decide what to do, one needs to combine philosophical judgments about where one wants to go, and what paths are morally permissible, with empirical judgments about which is the best route to the preferred destination. Which route is best may well depend on where one is starting from, so different circumstances can easily generate different policy decisions, even where there is no dispute at the level of philosophical principle.

This chapter does not, then, provide all the resources needed to make responsible judgments about policy with respect to religious schools. What it does is offer a clear, accessible and, we hope, manageable framework to structure our thinking about the normative issues that inevitably inform those judgments.

1. Two Ways of Organizing the Issues

As a way in, and starting to sketch the big picture with a deliberately broad brush, here are two distinctions that can help us analyse—break down or cut up—the issues. First, how a society decides to regulate religious schools affects and treats different people in different ways. Indeed, it affects and treats the *same* people in different ways. The first distinction encourages us to look at the issues from different perspectives, and to consider people in different roles: as parents, as children, and as citizens. Second, whether we are thinking of them as parents, children, or citizens, how a society decides to regulate religious schools will affect and treat people in different ways. Policy decisions can have effects that make people's lives go better or worse, but those decisions can also treat people justly or unjustly by respecting, or failing to respect, their moral entitlements, such as their right to make certain decisions for themselves. The second distinction encourages us to separate consequentialist from non-consequentialist considerations.

1.1 Parents, Children, Citizens

The first way of organizing the normative terrain distinguishes between the competing claims of three interested parties: parents, children, and the state. In Chapter 1, we suggested that it was helpful to think of these as identifying people under three different descriptions: as parents, as children, and as citizens. That's partly because we think that what is sometimes called "the state interest" is reducible to the collective interests of people as citizens; there is nothing that can properly count as an interest of the state that is not in some sense an interest of its citizens. And it's partly because the three "interested parties" are not mutually exclusive. All being well, children become adults and, normally at least, adults are citizens. In particular contexts, to be sure, a particular parent might be pitted against a particular child, or against the state (i.e. citizens as a whole). But when we are considering matters of policy for whole populations, and trying to take into consideration all relevant interests, we think more clearly if we recognize that what we're looking for is the right balance between the interests of the same people at different stages of life, or in different roles, rather than the right balance between the interests of different people.

We can illustrate the merits of this "parent, child, citizen" frame by seeing how it copes with one of the controversies identified in Chapter 1. Parents sometimes have religious reasons for not wanting their children to be taught certain beliefs. Sometimes those beliefs are about facts, such as how the planet Earth came into being. Sometimes they are about values, such as whether gay or lesbian sex is wrong. Those who give a lot of weight to parents' interest in raising their children as they think best may believe that they should be free not to send their children to a school where they will be taught beliefs—whether factual or evaluative—with which those parents disagree. Others may insist that it is children's interests that should come first. Perhaps that interest is in knowing what science tells us about the world we inhabit, or in living our sexual lives without guilt or shame. Perhaps it is more fundamentally in developing the capacity to decide for oneself what to believe about those things. On any variant, there is a conflict between what some claim to be valuable for us as parents and what some claim to be valuable for us as children. Still others may see the issue from the citizen's perspective. Whatever the proper balance between our interests as parents and our interests as children, as (current or future) citizens we share social and political institutions and collectively make decisions about how those institutions should be. From that angle, too, as third parties affected by decisions about how children are educated, we may all have an interest in living in a society in which children are taught the difference between beliefs about the natural world that are supported by scientific evidence and those deriving from religious texts, or in which they learn to tolerate and respect people living a wide range of different kinds of sexual life.

Of course, setting out the issues in this framework does not take us all that far. There remains plenty of scope for disagreement about the best way to understand the content of parents', children's, and citizens' interests, and that's before we get to the question of how to deal with conflicts between them. Still, when you come across a debate about religious schooling, or indeed about education more generally, it's a useful first step to see how the various positions affect people as parents, children, and citizens, and how they strike the balance between them.

1.2 Consequentialist and Non-Consequentialist Considerations

The second big picture distinction is a bit harder to get, and a bit harder to explain. We're now talking about a philosophical issue that unfortunately can't easily be captured in ordinary language. The "consequentialist" side of the divide is reasonably straightforward. As we will soon explore, readers may well disagree about *which* consequences matter, or at least about how to weigh them against each other when we have to make trade-offs. What exactly should policy be trying to achieve? Happy parents, autonomous children, tolerant citizens, or fair distributions? But the general idea that policies can and should be assessed in terms of their consequences is fairly obvious. "Consequentialist considerations" are simply those reasons for favouring or rejecting a policy that involve appealing to its expected consequences—the good or bad outcomes it will produce. Compared to the alternatives, will the policy generate benefits, or will it make things worse?

But consequences are not the only things that count. There are moral constraints on the ways in which good outcomes can be produced, non-consequentialist considerations that must be also be taken into account in our overall evaluation of a policy. People are entitled to be treated in certain ways, and not to be treated in other ways. We cannot regard them simply as means to good outcomes. Indeed, we can't do that even if those outcomes would be good not only for us but for them. For example, people have rights to make some choices for themselves, and to make choices that will be worse, in terms of consequences for themselves and others, than other choices they might have made. Perhaps, then, religious groups are entitled to set up, and parents have the right to choose, schools that select all their students according to religious criteria, even if other admissions policies would produce better outcomes.

We will shortly explore both consequentialist and non-consequentialist considerations in a lot more detail, but this example of parental choice nicely illustrates the distinction between the two. Arguments supporting parental choice and making it easier for organizations to enter the education "market" typically slide between—or, more charitably, combine—two different claims. On the one hand, there is the non-consequentialist thought that we have just mentioned: parents are entitled to exercise choice over their children's schooling. On the other hand, there is the consequentialist variant: requiring and allowing schools to respond to parental demand can be expected to improve standards, especially standards at the bottom. This mixture of different kinds of reasoning arises in argument about markets quite generally. Some people defend market mechanisms on the ground that they respect individual rights of free exchange, others because they are productive, efficient, and tend to benefit everybody in the long run.

Both considerations are particularly salient in the case of religious schools. On the one hand, parental choice with respect to religious education is widely regarded as especially important—more, say, than choice with respect to a school specializing in science or music. So policy should aim to allow parents to exercise their right, and there is a problem of fairness if members of some religions can do so while others cannot. On the other hand, schools with a religious character are often claimed to be "better" than their non-religious equivalents, so encouraging faith organizations to open new schools can be expected to increase the number of "good" school places.[1] The debate around parental choice involves both considerations. There are arguments about outcomes, about what makes a school "good", and about which children have the most pressing claims to better schools. And there are arguments that aren't about outcomes at all but rather about parents' rights to decide what kind of schooling their children should receive.

Again, as with the three-way distinction between parents, children, and citizens, getting clear on the difference between consequentialist and non-consequentialist considerations is only a first step in the analytical process. The real argumentative action starts when people offer their views about which outcomes matter, or about who is entitled to what kinds of treatment. But, again, when you come across someone saying something for or against religious schools, it's helpful to think from the start about where their point falls in terms of the broad distinction. Are they appealing to judgments about which consequences should be considered good, and about how best to produce—or perhaps distribute—those good consequences? Or are they invoking rather claims about people's entitlements to be treated in some ways rather than others?

These two ways of organizing the issues are set out in Table 1. Combining the two distinctions, we can see that there are six different cells in relation to which the argumentative action might take place. Table 1 is useful because it makes explicit the full range of factors that are relevant when thinking about religious schools from a normative perspective.

It is common for politicians and those who write about these issues in the media to focus on some of these and ignore others. Simplifying some-what, the debate is usually conducted as if the only issues at stake were in cells 1B and 2A. The focus is typically on either what kinds of school are

Table 1 Organizing consequentialist and non-consequentialist issues

	(A) Parents	(B) Children	(C) Citizens
(1) Consequentialist	Good for parents	Good for children	Good for citizens
(2) Non-Consequentialist	Respecting parents' moral entitlements	Respecting children's moral entitlements	Respecting citizens' moral entitlements

good for children or what rights parents have to decide for themselves the kind of school their children should go to. Political philosophers, by contrast, are as likely to be interested in questions about the moral entitlements of children (2B), or about our relevant interests and entitlements as citizens (1C and 2C).

2. Unpacking Consequentialist Considerations: Goods and Distributions

With this basic analytical apparatus in place, we can now set out our normative framework in more detail. We start by unpacking the various consequentialist considerations raised by religious schools. Our aim is to offer a comprehensive and systematic way of thinking about the value of the different kinds of outcome that might guide decisions about how to regulate those schools. Indeed, the approach we propose is intended to be *so* comprehensive and systematic that it could guide decisions across the full range of education policy. But as well as mapping the relevant conceptual space, we will focus particularly on the outcomes most pertinent to those debates about religious schools—and religion in schools—that we set out in Chapter 1.

2.1 Educational Goods

The claim that religious schools tend to be good schools, or that a new way of regulating them would be an improvement, supposes a particular view about what it means for a school to be "good", or what counts as "improvement". When politicians make such claims, they typically have in mind exam results, or test scores, of the kind reported in published "league tables". These are presumably indicators of a good thing that our society wants schools to produce—call it cognitive capacity or human capital—which in turn might be valued partly because of its importance for children's labour market prospects, or for the country's economic future. But we might want schools to aim at other goals too. Perhaps, even from a labour market perspective, "soft skills" are important factors we want schools to develop in children. A human resources website lists no fewer than 15 such skills, among them teamwork, time management, stress management, creativity, adaptability, and openness to criticism.[2] Presumably it is also valuable that schools produce children with certain democratic competences or liberal attitudes, such as tolerance of other religious traditions, and that they equip children to think for themselves. And so on.

One can express this idea that we want schools to pursue a number of different educational goals through the concept of "educational goods".[3] These are not goods like washing machines or cars, nor can they be equated with economic resources or money. They are *goods* in the abstract philosophical sense that they contribute to well-being. What makes them *educational* is that they are the kind of goods that educational processes distinctively produce; goods that inhere in adults as a result of their education. Educational goods, in our sense, are the knowledge, skills, dispositions, and attitudes that help their adult lives—and typically those of others—go better. It matters that children learn how to read, write, do maths, and so on. But if we think about schooling in broader terms, these cognitive skills and knowledge are only part of the story. Good schools will equip their students with a much wider range of attributes that are conducive to those students, and the rest of us, living good lives.

Brighouse et al. identify six capacities that one might plausibly want schools to develop in children. They also list, amongst other non-educational values by which schools might be evaluated, "childhood goods"—such as creativity and play—which are valuable for children in ways independent of their developmental benefits. Doubtless, creativity and play do have educational value, but that is not the only kind of value they have. They are things that we want schools to foster—or at least not to obstruct—because they are good for children qua children, not only because they are formative for the adults that their students will become.

Brighouse et al. aim to cover the full range of educational, and indeed non-educational, goods relevant to the assessment of school policy in general. To keep things focused, we combine their "capacity for democratic competence" and "capacity to treat others as moral equals" into a single category which we call "civic and moral capacities". For us, then, five types of educational good are particularly relevant to the assessment of policy concerning religious schools.

- Economic productivity
  The knowledge and skills necessary to participate in the economy and to sustain oneself and one's family financially.

- Personal autonomy
  The capacity and confidence to make and act on one's own, independent, reasoned and well-informed judgments about what kind of life to live.
- Civic and moral capacities
  The knowledge, skills and understanding required to participate in the political life of one's society, and the disposition to use them in appropriate circumstances; the capacity to regard others as having equal moral status and to treat them accordingly, respecting and tolerating differences.
- Healthy relationships
  The emotional and psychological capacity to form a range of healthy relationships with others, including intimate and loving relationships.
- Personal fulfilment
  The capacity to undertake projects that engage one's physical, aesthetic, intellectual and spiritual faculties.

The understanding of each of these goods would be improved by further discussion, but in order to keep things under control we are going to restrict our commentary to personal autonomy, for it plays a particularly important role in our argument. As we have said, personal autonomy is the capacity and confidence to make and act on one's own, independent, reasoned and well-informed judgments about what kind of life to live. It is a matter of degree and can only be acquired gradually. It involves learning how to identify sources of information that are reliable for the effective pursuit of one's goals, including how to determine whether a person should be treated as an expert on a subject, whether the evidence contained in a publication should be treated as a reliable basis for making a practical decision, and whether the claims made in an internet blog should be given any weight in one's thinking. What methods and techniques will be conducive to the development of these abilities will vary depending on the maturity of the child, but the aim should be to ensure that by the end of their formal education, children can assess whether a source is reliable in a way that enables them to make properly informed judgments about how to lead their lives and what social and political policies to support; for example, whether to receive a particular vaccination and whether to back a national vaccination programme.

Once we make explicit the range of different values that might guide education policy, the problem with a narrow focus on academic results immediately becomes apparent. Even if, by the official criteria, religious schools are more likely than their non-religious counterparts to be designated as "good", that tells us only about schools' performance on those criteria. It tells us little about how well those schools are promoting the good of students' personal autonomy or fulfilment, or their civic and moral capacities.

There is, in fact, considerable disagreement about whether religious schools do actually perform better, even with respect to test scores and exam results, than their non-religious counterparts. Several studies have found that the better outcomes achieved by such schools are entirely due to the (non-religious) characteristics of the children who attend them. They are not being compared with genuine equivalents and their better results should be attributed to their socially selective composition rather than their religious character.[4] In light of our list of educational goods, the most striking thing about that empirical controversy is the narrowness of its terrain. What children learn at school, and who they go to school with, affect the kind of people they become in many different ways.

Looking back at the various controversies that we surveyed in Chapter 1, we can now see that many of them involve competing views about the various kinds of educational goods—the knowledge, skills, dispositions, and attitudes—that schools should teach, instil or develop in children. The legislation introduced in 2014, whereby all schools have a duty to "promote the basic British values of democracy, the rule of law, individual liberty, and mutual respect and tolerance for those of different faiths and beliefs" seems to sit squarely under the "civic and moral capacities" heading, despite its nationalistic overtones. Our lives go better, as citizens, if we live alongside others committed to liberal democratic values. The same applies to the debate about whether schools should be allowed to select all their students on the basis of religious criteria. Those who worry about the effects of high levels of selection, and hence segregation, on community cohesion are appealing to the claim that contact between children from different religious groups is important for the development of tolerance and mutual understanding.[5]

Other objections, like those about religious schools' denying children the opportunity to think critically about their parents' religious views, or to learn about same-sex relationships, put personal autonomy centre stage. The issues here concern the value of children's developing the capacity to make and act on their own judgments about what kind of life to live, and what kind of schooling is conducive to its development. Learning about same-sex relationships is relevant also to the capacity for healthy relationships. Those who think that parents should not be permitted to withdraw their children from the relevant lessons are partly worrying about the impact on those children, some of whom will themselves be gay or lesbian, whose relationships may be harmed if they are denied the opportunity to hear and talk about homosexuality from a non-religious perspective. (Those Muslim parents in Birmingham who protested against the LGBT content in their children's lessons on the grounds that it was not "age-appropriate" might have been invoking a claim not about educational goods but about childhood goods.[6] Sexual innocence is sometimes regarded as one of the distinctively valuable constituents of a good childhood.)

Finally, we noted that some defences of religious schools present them as bastions of resistance to an increasingly dominant utilitarian and material-ist educational ethos in which education becomes subordinate to market economics. This view—that religious schools attune their students to the spiritual aspects of life, giving them a sense of meaning and purpose not available from "secular" schools—appeals to the value of the capacity for personal fulfilment. The worry is that denying children access to a religious education—like denying them access to art or literature—may inhibit their opportunity to enjoy a distinctive source of well-being that is not taken seriously enough elsewhere.

Many debates about religious schooling can helpfully be analysed in terms of the various different kinds of educational good we have identified. Those who make the arguments may not conceive the issues in quite these terms, and are unlikely to use the language of educational goods. But, implicit in their views, and discernible to the normative analyst, will almost certainly be claims about which of these goods are particularly important, how best to understand what each of them amounts to, and about what schools need to be like to produce them.

To offer this list of goods as part of an analytical framework is in no way to endorse any of the claims made in terms of those goods. It's simply to identify the *kind* of claim that people (implicitly) make when they are argu-ing about religious schools. The fact that they appear on our list does show that we think they are good—they wouldn't count as "educational goods" otherwise. But it tells you nothing about whether we think it's the job of schools to develop them. It's perfectly coherent, for example, to think that schools should not get involved in fostering students' capacity for healthy relationships, or personal fulfilment. Nor are we saying anything about the relative importance of the different educational goods that appear on that list. And we're certainly not taking any view about which of these goods religious schools, however regulated, are and are not likely to produce. In

Part III we will explain how our framework, in combination with empirical social science, might be used to make arguments for and against particular proposals for the rules that should apply to religious schools. That will involve weighing the different goods against each other, accepting that there are trade-offs between them, and judging which policies will produce the best combination overall. At this stage, we're just identifying some of the elements that will go into that process.

Notice that many of the controversies mentioned in Chapter 1 are about more than one educational good. We've had one example of this already: LGBT education can be valued for the sake of children developing both the capacity for personal autonomy and the capacity for healthy relationships. But that kind of education is valuable also for reasons that fall under the "civic and moral" heading. Its supporters claim that it's good not only for those who develop their own capacities but also for the rest of us, who will live alongside them. We all benefit if children are taught to respect and tolerate differences, including differences in sexuality. So one news story—about Muslim parents wanting to withdraw their children from PSHE (personal, social, health, and economic) lessons—turns out to be analysable into at least three different goods (and, if you interpret those parents as motivated primarily by childhood goods, one non-educational good). Sticking with the periodic table parallel, we can think of real-world controversies as analogous to chemical compounds. Just as the chemist analyses substances into their constituent elements, so that baking soda ($NaHCO_3$) turns out to be a mixture of sodium, hydrogen, carbon, and oxygen, so the political theorist analyses arguments into their various components.

2.2 Distributive Principles

When thinking in consequentialist terms—about valuable outcomes—we cannot consider issues of cultivation alone. Governments should not aim simply at maximizing the production of educational goods, not even if they have made good judgments about how to weigh and make trade-offs between them. It matters also how educational goods, and access to those goods, are distributed. While parents are often concerned only with whether benefits accrue to their own children, policymakers must take the wider view. For example, a school turning out students with very high levels of all the goods discussed so far might be doing so by selection procedures that make it harder for other schools to do the same. Those procedures might distribute access to those high levels in an unfair way. They might even prevent other schools providing their students with an adequate level of those goods.

Recall, from Chapter 1, the government's claim that religious schools tend to perform better than non-religious schools, which they have invoked in support of their goal of increasing the number of schools with a religious character. Critics suggest that this justification is flawed. The evidence shows that the real reason why religious schools get better results is because they are socially selective. Such schools admit, on average, more children who are easier to educate, and fewer who are hard to educate, than non-religious schools. Those who present this challenge to the government's rationale are sometimes motivated by a distributive worry as much as by a concern to understand properly what kinds of school are most productive of educational goods. The problem is that, as things stand, religious schools do not provide fair access to all who want to go to them. They discriminate in favour of the more advantaged and do not take their fair share of poor children. Here the normative issue concerns not the production of educational goods but the distribution of access to them.

Suppose that these critics are wrong and the government is right. Suppose that religious schools really do perform better, and they perform better *because* they are religious. That looks like a good reason to be in favour of such schools, or at least it would if we believed that the better performance—in the form of higher test scores—did not come at the expense of other educational goods. But even if religious schools performed better in every way, one might still worry about fairness in the way they select their students. When it comes to admissions, those schools are typically allowed to prefer children whose parents are members of a particular religion. The recent debate has been about how many of their students they should be allowed to select on that basis, not about whether they should be allowed to do so at all. But—and here is the fairness worry—why should one child have a better chance than another of going to a good school just because her parents have particular religious views? There might be good answers to that but either way the distributive concern needs to be taken into account.

There is a substantial philosophical literature on what distributive justice requires with respect to education, with theorists debating the merits of educational equality, adequacy, and the idea of prioritizing benefits to the less advantaged. For some, it matters that children have equal opportunity to achieve educational goods, while others care more modestly that all children receive an adequate level of—or, perhaps, adequate opportunity for—those goods. Characterized in these very broad ways, both views leave a lot up for grabs. Equality of educational opportunity is amenable to widely differing interpretations.[7] Whose opportunities should be equal? Are we talking about equalizing the opportunities of similarly talented and motivated children from different social backgrounds? Or should all children have equal opportunities, irrespective of their natural ability? The answer to that may well depend on what exactly the opportunities are *for*.

The same applies to so-called "adequacy" views, which hold that equality is not the right distributive principle. What matters, from this perspective, is not that children enjoy equal opportunities with one another, but rather that all children have *enough*. Equality might require us to level down—depriving some children of valuable opportunities simply so that they don't have more than others—which seems counterintuitive. In any case, the urgent problem at the moment, adequacy theorists argue, is not inequality, which is about comparisons or relativities between different children. The real issue is that so many children are so badly served by the school system in absolute terms, falling below an acceptable threshold. Here too, we will soon find ourselves asking "enough for what?"[8]

A third distributive principle—priority to the worse off—also asks us to think particularly about those at the bottom, but for a different reason. For so-called "prioritarians", we should worry about those children with the worst opportunities not because they fall below an acceptable minimum but simply because it's more important to benefit the least advantaged than to benefit others. (Some readers may be familiar with Rawls' famous difference principle, according to which inequalities are justified if they serve, over time, to benefit the least advantaged. That is a variant of prioritarianism.) That would remain true even if the least advantaged were receiving an education that was "adequate" in absolute terms. Those who hold that benefits to the less advantaged matter more must decide how much more they matter, and whether benefits should be conceived as "educational goods" or in wider terms.[9]

Each of us has explored these distributive issues in more detail elsewhere, and it would take us too far afield to get into the weeds, interesting though they are. The important point is that, when thinking about consequences, we must have in mind not only the production of educational goods but also their distribution. Although very important in other contexts—for example, in debates around private, or academically selective, schooling—the differences between these various distributive principles tend not to be crucial to debates about religious schools. True, we have just seen that such schools do indeed raise an issue of fairness, which is naturally put in terms of the value of equality. Why should some children have better opportunities than others just because their parents endorse a particular religious view? But, on the whole, the arguments for and against religious schools, and about how such schools should be regulated, involve claims that would apply on any of the three distributive principles that we have identified. The typical worry is that such schools might deny some of their students—or, perhaps, some of the students attending other, non-religious schools—the basic minimum of educational goods that they should be getting as a matter of justice.

Two more points conclude this section unpacking consequentialist considerations. First, the benefits that result from the production of educational goods can accrue to people other than the educated person. We conceive those goods as "the knowledge, skills, dispositions and attitudes to which children are entitled or that help their adult lives—and typically those of others—go better" precisely in order to leave open both possibilities. Consider, for example, the benefits achieved by educating children to be democratically competent, or to be tolerant of one another's religious views. Here the good consequences accrue at least partly to those with whom the children do, or will, interact; positive externalities or "spill-overs" result from the goods in question.

Second, notice that the benefits in this last example are not themselves "educational goods", or at least not exclusively so. They include all kinds of advantage that are enjoyed by people who live alongside democratically competent, tolerant, fellow citizens. Add to these the observation that how religious schools are regulated affects not only their character but also that of all the other schools with which they co-exist and it becomes clear that policy decisions affect society as a whole. The impact of those decisions extends far beyond the students who attend them.

3. Unpacking Non-Consequentialist Considerations: Parents, Children, and Citizens

3.1 Parents

For some readers, our discussion so far will seem to have missed the point. We have been talking about the outcomes that might result from different policies: which goods are produced and how they are distributed. But much thinking about religious schooling focuses not on these consequentialist considerations but rather on parents' rights to determine the content of their children's education. As we mentioned when introducing the distinction, those rights are sometimes conceived in instrumental terms, so that granting parents the right to choose a school for their child is justified by appeal to its beneficial impact on educational outcomes. If so, the argument is ultimately consequentialist in character. Typically, however, a parent's right to choose a religious school for her child is understood as deriving more directly from her own moral standing: the thought is simply that parents' right to freedom of religion, or perhaps to freedom of association, entitles them to raise and educate their children as members of a particular faith.

That right is formulated in non-consequentialist terms. The thought is not that granting the right makes parents' lives—or anybody else's—go better. It is simply that, within certain boundaries, parents are entitled to engage their children in educational activities or forms of schooling even if they fail to produce the best educational (or other) outcomes. For example, it is widely held that, as members of a religious community, parents are entitled to choose a school that selects pupils on the basis of religion, or offers a certain kind of religiously inspired curriculum, even if allowing them to do that has worse consequences than would denying them that option. On this view, parents' rights operate as constraints on the way good outcomes—such as those concerning the production and distribution of educational goods—can permissibly be brought about.

The view in question sees a parent's right to choose a religious school for her child as an instantiation of a more general right, such as the right to freedom of association or the right to freedom of religion. However, in the paradigm cases of these rights, what is protected is association between *consenting adults*, or an individual's freedom to decide the religion according to which she will live *her own* life. Schooling raises more difficult issues because it involves some (i.e. adults) deciding how others (i.e. children) are educated. Even if parents should indeed have the authority to decide how their children are schooled, that conclusion cannot plausibly be derived simply from claims about their rights over themselves. Non-consequentialist considerations can be invoked in favour of different policies because there are different views about who are the ultimate bearers of the rights in question.

3.2 Children

Parents are not the only ones who might be thought to have rights that constrain policymakers in their pursuit of desirable outcomes. Children also may be the bearers of non-consequentialist rights in education in ways that limit adults' freedom to choose their schools. Various versions of what we might call child-focused non-consequentialism are available, depending on the particular rights ascribed to children. On one familiar version of this view, it is morally wrong for anyone—parents as well as the political community—to force children to become a part of an association by sending them to schools that obstruct the development of their capacity for personal autonomy. Here the thought is that, simply in virtue of their standing as prospective agents, children are entitled to an education that will give them the capacity and confidence to make and act on their own, independent, reasoned and well-informed judgments about what kind of life to live. They have a right to live their own lives, and only if they have chosen it autonomously, on this view, will their life be truly theirs.

Attentive readers may be puzzled by our now presenting the capacity for personal autonomy as the object of a non-consequentialist right of children (i.e. as something to which children are entitled for reasons that have nothing to do with the consequences). In the previous section that same capacity was listed as one of our proposed educational goods—as something to be valued and produced—because it makes people's lives go better (i.e. as a *consequentialist* consideration). So it appears in both 1B and 2B of Table 1. This may look suspicious but there is no sleight of hand here. The fact that the capacity for personal autonomy comes up in both categories simply shows that there are two kinds of reason for thinking it important, two routes to the conclusion that we should do what we can to ensure that children get the kind of education that will develop it.

From a consequentialist perspective, autonomy matters because it either promotes well-being or is a component of it. One thought here is that children's lives are more likely to go well if they are able to choose for themselves how to live, if they are authors of their own lives. People are different. A way of life that works very well for one—a straight, stay-at-home mother, say—may not be valuable for another. On the plausible assumption that, generally speaking, people are the best judges of which ways of life will be good for them, it makes sense to give them what they need to make the choice for themselves. From a non-consequentialist perspective, however, the case for personal autonomy—for authorship of one's own life—does not rest on the purported link between autonomy and well-being. Simple respect for children's moral independence—for their status as separate individuals with their own lives to lead—means that they are entitled to an education that will give them the capacity for autonomous agency—for authorship of their own lives—whether or not that will be good for them. They may make bad choices, but at least the choices will be theirs. If, like many, you find both arguments plausible, then you might think the case for personal autonomy is overdetermined. It is valuable, instrumentally, as a likely means to people living lives that go well or, intrinsically, as a component of a flourishing life, *and* it is something to which people are entitled simply in virtue of their moral status as separate individuals.

But the capacity for personal autonomy is not the only thing that might appear in 2B. On another view, children's rights to moral independence are violated whenever they are directed towards controversial religious belief systems.[10] The particular worry here concerns adults *intentionally enrolling* their children into controversial conceptions of the good (i.e. conceptions of the good that they may reasonably come to reject). Plainly, parents and adults act in countless ways that affect the beliefs, desires, and prospects of children. However, many in the non-consequentialist tradition argue that, while it is often morally permissible to affect others as a side-effect of one's conduct, it is often morally wrong to make others perform acts that they are not morally required to perform or to impose harms on them they are not morally required to incur.[11] Non-consequentialist arguments for parental choice assume that parents have a moral right to determine (at least provisionally) the religious or occupational ends that their child pursues; but if everyone is entitled to set their own ends, then parents do not enjoy that right over their children.[12] Indeed, respect for children's independence requires that parents do not treat their children in that way. According to this variant of child-focused non-consequentialism, then, governments should deny parents the opportunity to send their child to a school that is run in accordance with their convictions about religion, even if those schools would not obstruct the child's development of the capacity for autonomy.

3.3 Citizens

We have just seen that the capacity for personal autonomy can be conceived in both consequentialist and non-consequentialist terms. On the one hand, it is an educational good to be valued for its contribution to well-being. On the other hand, it is something to which individuals are entitled, in virtue of their moral standing, irrespective of the consequences. Similar points apply to the civic and moral considerations in column C of Table 1.

Look again at the capacities we introduced as "civic and moral": the knowledge, skills, and understanding required to participate in the political life of one's society, and the disposition to use them in appropriate circumstances; the capacity to regard others as having equal moral status and to treat them accordingly, respecting and tolerating differences. These count as educational goods because they make people's lives go better as adults. In the case of the distinctively civic or political capacities, it is educated people themselves who most obviously stand to benefit. Participating in the political life of one's society is an important way to stand up for one's interests, and it is easy to see why people are likely to suffer if they lack the relevant civic competences. In the case of the capacity to regard others as moral equals, and to respect and tolerate differences, it is the people with whom the educated person will interact, rather than that person herself, that more naturally come to mind as the beneficiaries. We all benefit from living alongside, and sharing our social and political institutions with, tolerant fellow citizens who regard and treat one another as equals, without prejudice or discrimination.

It's widely recognized that the state may legitimately act to inculcate the civic and moral capacities required for a just society and a healthy liberal democracy, and its reasons for doing that are typically framed in consequentialist terms. But, like personal autonomy, one can also argue for the importance of those capacities from a non-consequentialist perspective. For some, the main reason to educate children to be good citizens is that others are entitled to be regarded and treated according to those standards. The point, from this perspective, is not that educating children to endorse liberal and egalitarian norms makes anybody's life go better. It is rather that those norms express a view about people—about the ways they should and should not be treated, about their equal claim to respect and consideration—which properly reflects their moral standing. Educating children to tolerate members of other religions, or not to be sexist, racist, or homophobic, is doubtless good for those who would otherwise be on the wrong end of hostility, discrimination, and prejudice. Their opportunities in life will probably be better, they may feel safer, and so on. But, for the non-consequentialist, these well-being considerations are not the whole story. Religious intolerance, sexism, racism, and homophobia do not only harm their targets. In failing to accord them the respect and recognition they can rightfully claim as moral equals, those attitudes and dispositions also treat them wrongfully.

4. Balancing Normative Considerations

We have presented a systematic framework that identifies the various normative elements that feed into a range of controversies about religious schools. As we have noted, these different elements can be interpreted and weighted differently. This leads to different conclusions concerning how, if at all, religious schools should be regulated and whether they should receive public funding. Although, as readers of Part II will discover, we disagree on some points, we converge on some key views about how these elements should be interpreted, and which are the weightiest. That convergence helps us, in Part III, to reach agreement on a particular regulatory framework. And the fact that others will reject our key shared views about how to interpret and weigh the elements explains why our conclusions are likely to be controversial.

The headline here is that we all give considerable weight to children's interests or entitlements and less weight to parents'. Although we disagree about whether and why parents' preferences or wishes should be taken into account when deciding education policy, we share the belief that there are powerful reasons to develop children's capacities to live autonomously and to act in ways that display concern and respect for others. We agree, further, that these child-focused reasons generally override competing parental claims to decide how their children are educated.

This balancing pitches us against a prominent perspective in public debates—the view that parents have powerful interests or claims to have the option to educate their children in ways that do not promote their personal autonomy. Much public debate about education proceeds as if school policy should largely be responsive to the demands of parents. Perhaps that is because people believe that parents want what's best for their children and are the best judges of their interests. Unfortunately, the latter belief is mistaken in many cases. There may be very good reasons for parents to be consulted and involved in school decisions about how to educate their children, but identifying what matters fundamentally—what educational goods schools should be promoting, for example—does not depend on having intimate knowledge of particular children. Regardless of whether one is attracted to the ideal of personal autonomy because it is in itself or instrumentally valuable to lead such a life, or because it is fitting for people to make their own reflective and informed decisions about what to believe about religion and how best to live, children are entitled to a schooling that develops their capacity for autonomy. We know this by reflecting quite generally on the consequentialist and non-consequentialist considerations that apply to educational decisions.

Of course, some defences of parental rights over education deny that autonomy is valuable, or at least that it is sufficiently valuable to outweigh the claims of parents.[13] Those views, however, struggle to explain why some people (parents) have a fundamental right to shape the lives of others (their children) in ways that fail to enable those others eventually to make free and informed choices about their own lives. The consensus of a liberal society is that citizens generally have the right freely to change and pursue their own religious convictions. In the light of that consensus, it's hard to believe that children aren't similarly entitled to an education that enables them to reflect on the truth or value of the different religions and non-religious practices that are available for adoption and pursuit.

We have similar thoughts about the relationship between moral and civic education and parental influence, but here the argument is a little different. The kind of education we have in mind with respect to morality and citizenship is not merely about the development of skills and knowledge (though it is partly about that). It also involves the shaping of children's dispositions and motivations: school students should receive an education that enables them to appreciate the equal moral status of others and to become motivated to treat them accordingly by showing them concern and respecting differences in belief or lifestyle. Children have no reasonable complaint against having their beliefs and desires shaped in these egalitarian ways because they have a duty to view and treat each other as equals.

Some parents object to their children receiving the educational good of civic and moral education interpreted in the "equal respect" way we propose. On one side of the argument, some believe that parents should be free to send their children to schools that encourage them to be intolerant towards particular differences: for example, by suggesting that children campaign to change the law so that same-sex marriage is legally prohibited. Our policy proposals would not allow schools that encouraged such intolerant and disrespectful attitudes. On the other side of the argument, some argue that schools should go further than we propose and steer their students not merely to embrace the view that each is entitled to pursue the conception of sexuality or marriage they affirm, but also to reject religious doctrines that claim that same-sex sexual relationships are sinful.[14] Our proposals for religious schools are designed with the educational good of equal respect in mind, so they don't require schools to be dismissive of religious doctrines that regard LGBTQ+ lifestyles as sinful. But we do emphatically reject the view that parents should be free to select schools that steer children towards those religious doctrines that disrespect or are intolerant of difference in gender or sexuality.

In these ways, then, our liberal proposals for the regulation of religious schools are informed by a shared understanding of the priority of children's interests in the design of educational institutions. We attach great importance to the realization of the educational goods we described earlier and, particularly, to the promotion of students' autonomy and moral and civic capacities. Others will doubtless weigh the competing considerations differently. Some will insist on parents' entitlements to educate their children as they wish, despite the cost in terms of other considerations. Some, while like us in regarding the civic goal of "equal respect" as very important, will interpret it differently, and in ways that yield differing policy implications. In Chapters 3–5 we will give our own particular detailed reasons for the views on which we converge. The point here is simply to highlight those balancing judgments that we share, and that help to explain the regulatory framework that we propose in the final part of the book.

5. Education Policy: Perfectionist or Neutral?

We have highlighted several different consequentialist and non-consequentialist considerations as tools that enable us to make sense of debates about religious schools. The distinctive focus of this book is the *government's* regulation of schools rather than how parents make choices for their children's schooling within the legal framework that applies in their country. For many, the focus on government policy makes a difference to how we should interpret and combine the different consequentialist and non-consequentialist considerations we have outlined. This is for two reasons. First, education policy is often part of the law, thereby placing citizens under a legal obligation to obey the requirements enshrined in it. For example, parents have a legal duty to obey laws that are intended to make sure their children get at least basic levels of certain educational goods; and every citizen is obligated to pay taxes that, among other things, are used to fund the school system. Second, education policy is often implemented through coercion or force. Parents who fail to send their children to school, or to give them an appropriate education at home, are fined or subject to intervention that, at the extreme, might lead to their losing custody of their children. Similarly, education policy forcibly prevents those with no formally recognized role in the education or upbringing of children from having control over their schooling, even those who want to take charge of a particular child's education and would do so effectively. When trying to identify the right approach to the government's regulation of schools, then, we need to select and interpret the consequentialist and non-consequentialist considerations in a way that is sensitive to the fact that we are proposing politically authoritative and coercively administered policies.

Political philosophers disagree about the values and principles that ought to inform government policy. Indeed, they disagree about the *kinds* of values and principles that ought to do so. One fundamental dividing line is between so called "political perfectionists" and "political neutralists". There are several ways of understanding the debate between these philosophical camps, but the basic disagreement is over whether governments should try to identify and promote the right view of what it means to live well or to have a good life. Perfectionists think that this is a proper aim of government and, by extension, one that citizens ought to attend to when electing their representatives—they often say that a government's exercise of authority or coercion over citizens is justifiable when and because it enables them to live good lives.[15] Neutralists disagree. They argue that in contemporary societies there are multiple disagreements among citizens about the nature of human flourishing and it is not the business of the state to get involved in these disputes by aligning itself with particular controversial views. Governments should seek to justify their policies on the basis of values and principles that all citizens can accept regardless of their particular conception of the good. They shouldn't take a stand on further matters, such as whether particular citizens are making mistakes about religion or human flourishing. To do so, neutralists argue, would be disrespectful because it would involve officially questioning the religious or ethical judgment of certain citizens or it would damage the relationship between state and citizen.[16]

Disagreements between perfectionist and neutralists are hardly mentioned in debates about the regulation of religious schools that occur in political forums or newspapers. Nevertheless, the difference of approach can illuminate the issues at stake. For example, many advocates of religious schools make a point of saying that an education that promotes religious values and practice is good for children. At the heart of that argument is a perfectionist conception of politics, together with the particular belief that religious lifestyles are good ones. On the other side, many critics of publicly funded religious schools appeal to the neutralist view that the government should enact policies that are acceptable to citizens regardless of their particular conception of the good.

Note, however, that the perfectionism–neutralism distinction doesn't always align with the distinction between pro- and anti-religious schooling. Some who are perfectionist about politics also believe that a religious life is a bad one because it rests on false beliefs. Holding that particular combination of beliefs inclines them to be sceptical about the value of religious schools. And, taking the opposite starting point, many neutralists argue that the right way for the state to be neutral about religion is to make available various schools—some religious, some not—and allow parents to choose between them.[17]

The distinction between political perfectionists and neutralists doesn't only shed light on how and why people disagree about religious schools. It is also a useful starting point for developing and defending our own views about education policy in general and the regulation of religious schools in particular. The distinction helps us to interpret and combine the consequentialist and non-consequentialist considerations outlined earlier. For example, it is natural for perfectionists to interpret the value of personal autonomy and fulfilment in consequentialist terms, as aspects of a flourishing or successful human life. On that interpretation, schools have a role in enabling students to think carefully and rationally about the alternative lifestyle options available in society because doing so is good for children. Perfectionists might also recognize other ways of promoting valuable ways of living, such as children and parents' participating in activities together. If they hold that combination of views, then they might favour allowing parents to choose the religious character of a school, within certain limits, because, overall, such a policy enables everyone to live better lives than the alternatives.

By contrast, if you're attracted to political neutrality, your defence or critique of religious schools will start by bracketing questions about human flourishing. You will interpret the goods set out earlier in ways that do not depend on judgments about what makes one's life go well. It's likely that you will appeal to the non-consequentialist claim that children or parents (or both) have rights to make decisions and, indeed, the right to make poor or unwise decisions. Interpreted in neutralist terms, the educational good of personal autonomy isn't valuable because it enables individuals to identify and pursue *worthwhile* ends. It's valuable because it enables them to exercise their right to set and pursue *their own* ends.

The perfectionism–neutralism debate illustrates a further feature of our framework. We might agree that schools ought to be evaluated by their success in helping children develop the list of educational goods set out earlier. But we can disagree over *why* the educational goods in question have the status of "goods". Perfectionists tend to interpret goods by referring to what it means for individuals to have flourishing lives or personal well-being; neutralists tend to interpret them as capacities, motivations, and attitudes that are helpful in terms of individuals' exercising their own agency and treating each other justly. And, as will become clear in the individual chapters of Part II, one's overall judgment about whether religious schools should be allowed and funded by the state may depend on one's position within this more general philosophical debate between neutralists and perfectionists.

6. Conclusion

This chapter has identified and distinguished the various normative issues that arise when thinking about religious schools. Our analytical framework—our way of decomposing views into their constituent elements—may seem complicated. If so, that's because arguments about religious schools *are* complicated. They unavoidably raise a variety of different considerations and, though not always conscious of the fact, advocates of particular views are inevitably making judgments about the relative importance of those considerations. So what we're offering here is just what is needed to think clearly about the full range of issues at stake. For us, it's helpful to be explicit about the different elements that combine to form particular positions in the debates, and we're hopeful that the framework we propose won't prove unmanageable.

That concludes Part I—The Terms of the Debate. In it we have set out our shared way of thinking about religious schools. We will come back to the things we agree about in Part III, where we discuss how to combine values and evidence in order to get From Principles to Policies. In Part II, however, we go our separate ways, offering our own individual perspectives on some of the more abstract, foundational, and philosophical issues at stake.

How to Think about Religious Schools: Principles and Policies. Matthew Clayton, Andrew Mason, and Adam Swift, Oxford University Press. © Matthew Clayton, Andrew Mason, and Adam Swift 2024.
DOI: 10.1093/9780198924036.003.0002

PART II
THREE VIEWS

3

Religious Schools

A Qualified Defence

Andrew Mason

Schools can have a religious character in many different ways.[1] Some may bear a very light religious imprint. Imagine a state-funded secondary school that is run in accordance with Christian values interpreted in a specific way. Teachers are expected to display these values in their interactions with children and each other; school rules, including disciplinary procedures, are designed in accordance with them, for example, these rules require students always to strive to forgive those who behave badly towards them and to avoid aggression even in self-defence, and more generally to display the virtues of a pacifism that is committed to non-violence. Students thereby come face to face with a particular tradition of Christian thought and are required to conform to its values.

The school doesn't aim to inculcate these values, however. Academic subjects are selected for inclusion in the curriculum without reference to them and are taught in a way that does not presuppose any allegiance to them. Other religious traditions, Christian and non-Christian, are taught respectfully, as are atheist world views, and students are encouraged to behave tolerantly towards people who live in accordance with religious or secular doctrines that differ from their own. The school does not in its admissions or employment policies give priority to children or teachers who are Christians or from Christian families, but students are expected to obey the school's rules devised in the light of its specific interpretation of Christian values, parents are expected to support the school in its application of these rules, and teachers are expected to behave at school in accordance with its interpretation of these values even if they are not Christians or interpret Christian values differently.

The school aims to equip children not only for successful working lives and finding personal fulfilment, but also for democratic citizenship: they are taught that being a good citizen requires impartial reasoning about matters of public concern, giving equal weight to each citizen's interests regardless of his or her religious beliefs, and the school seeks to cultivate the capacity and disposition to think and debate in this manner. Let us also suppose that the school realizes its aims: generally speaking, the children educated at it develop well-rounded characters, achieve excellent exam results, and emerge with the capacities and dispositions required to be good citizens. In consequence, it recruits children from different backgrounds and is diverse in terms of both the composition of its student body and of its teaching staff. Not only those parents who endorse the school's specific interpretation of Christian values send their children to it, but also parents who are committed to similar values on secular grounds or who adhere to other religious traditions, whether Christian or non-Christian, that share related values. The school even attracts children from families that don't adhere to that many of the school's values, but nevertheless are happy to send their children to it because of its achievements.

The school I have described can be characterized as one with a particular religious ethos. It seems to me that there is no reasonable objection to it, provided there are suitable publicly funded alternatives available for the children of parents who do not share its values or for other reasons do not want to send their child to it. Some might object to it on the grounds that its rules and policies embody values with which they disagree, for example, they might think that there are some acts that are unforgiveable, or that it may be permissible and even sometimes morally required to use violence in self-defence. But that seems a weak objection when parents who disagree with its values do not need to send their children to it, for example, when there are spaces available in neighbouring schools that are run in a way that does not involve conformity to any particular religious or non-religious moral doctrines (and if parents want their child to be educated in a school that is run accordance with their own specific religious or non-religious values, then public funds are made available for a school of this kind when this would be an efficient use of educational resources.) Even childless adults who think that the religion which informs the school's ethos is deeply mistaken do not seem to have a reasonable objection to it all things considered, or to their taxes being used to fund it, provided that in a tolerably efficient way it nurtures good citizens who do not become a burden on the state as a result of their education. Even if we concede that they have a reason to object to their taxes being spent in this way, it is insufficiently strong to defeat the case for publicly funding such a school.

The moral issues with schools that have a religious character arise when their practices or their composition depart from those described in my imaginary example. There are five potential divergences that are especially troubling. First, when a school of this kind aims to instil a particular set of religious beliefs and values. Second, when it does not seek to provide what with good reason might be regarded as an adequate civic education on the grounds that this would be corrosive of the religious beliefs and values they are seeking to instil. Third, when in selecting students it gives priority to children from families that share its religious outlook in order to sustain its ethos, with the result that those who do not share that outlook have less chance of being admitted and the school concentrates together those with a similar religious background. Fourth, when even though it does not select on religious grounds, it ends up being homogenous in terms of the religious background of its students because parents who are not sympathetic to its ethos send their children elsewhere. Fifth, when in selecting teachers (or indeed other employees, such as administrators, caretakers, cooks, and cleaners) it gives priority to those who share its religious affiliation, again in order to sustain its ethos. In what follows I shall focus on the first four of these departures from the imaginary example in which a school's religious character manifests itself solely in its ethos.[2]

1. Religious Indoctrination, Personal Autonomy, and Children's Interests

Suppose that a school aims to form in its students an unshakeable commitment to a particular set of religious doctrines by instructing them in the importance of blind faith and by not cultivating in them capacities for critical reflection. The school teaches them that it is through the exercise of these capacities that the devil does his work, and it denies them access to the intellectual and material resources that would motivate them to question what they are taught; for example, they are told that the world was created less than 10,000 years ago, they are not introduced to the theory of evolution, and there is no book in the school library that mentions it. For good measure let us also suppose that the school aims to instil religious doctrines in a way that would make it very costly emotionally for its students to abandon them, just in case that after their schooling they are left able to do so; for example, it aims to make sure that they would be wracked by feelings of guilt, or by fear of the consequences of abandoning their faith as a result of being taught that the hottest part of hell is reserved for those who do so. Let me define an approach to instruction that has this character, and that has some degree of success in closing children's minds in the way described, as *indoctrination*.[3]

Indoctrination, characterized in this way, is an extreme and perhaps relatively rare approach to moulding children's minds, at least in societies that are, or aspire to be, liberal-democracies, but it is nevertheless illuminating to consider why it is objectionable. One plausible explanation is that by closing children's minds in this manner, indoctrination prevents them from acquiring *personal autonomy*, or "autonomy" for short. In Chapter 2 we identified autonomy as an educational good, that is, as something valuable that schools should cultivate and promote. But what is autonomy and why is it valuable? There are extensive scholarly debates concerning the nature of autonomy that I do not want to get drawn into here.[4] Let me simply adopt the definition we gave earlier, namely, that autonomy is the capacity and confidence to make and act on one's own, independent, reasoned and well-informed judgments about what kind of life to live. At the very least, autonomy requires a person to possess the ability to reflect upon how she should live, including the ability to form and revise her own conception of how she should do so. It also requires her to be in an environment in which she is free from certain kinds of coercion and manipulation, and that provides her with an adequate range of options from which to choose and the knowledge necessary to make informed choices from them. Why does autonomy, so understood, matter and why is it important that a child should come to acquire it? More specifically, why is it important that a child should acquire the knowledge required to make informed choices, the ability to form and revise a conception of how she should live, and perhaps also the *disposition* to exercise this ability?

There are a number of possible answers to these questions, several of which appeal to the idea that the child's interests are best served by her developing and exercising autonomy but differ in terms of their explanation of why this is so. Some maintain that the exercise of autonomy is an *intrinsically valuable constituent* of a flourishing life, that is, it is an ingredient of such a life. The most radical version of this view holds that autonomy is such a vital ingredient of a flourishing life that it is impossible for anyone to achieve an adequate level of flourishing unless she regularly exercises autonomy, at the very least when important choices are being made.[5]

Note that this claim goes beyond what might be called *the endorsement thesis*, that is, the thesis that it is impossible for a person to flourish unless she *believes* she is leading a valuable life. If someone is to flourish, it is surely important that she leads her life "from the inside", as it were, in accordance with her beliefs about what is valuable, rather than being forced against her will to act in accordance with someone else's judgments about what is valuable.[6] But a person's belief that her way of life is valuable might itself be inculcated through indoctrination, or be acquired unreflectively; holding this belief does not require her to possess personal autonomy or to have exercised that capacity if she has it. In contrast, according to the view I am considering, it matters that she forms this belief through the exercise of her autonomy.

The claim that it is impossible for a person to achieve an adequate level of flourishing unless she comes to judge that her way of life is valuable as a result of exercising her autonomy would, if true, provide a powerful reason for opposing indoctrination. But it seems highly implausible. Surely there are many people who do not exercise autonomy but lead lives in which they engage in a range of valuable activities and (quite justifiably) believe their lives to be well lived. For example, some simply do what their parents or community expect of them, without giving much thought to whether living a different life might be more fulfilling for them or make better use of their capacities. What reason do we have to deny that they may achieve an adequate level of flourishing?

A less radical version of the view under consideration might hold that even though the exercise of autonomy can be an intrinsically valuable ingredient of a good life, there are other such ingredients that may be just as important to a person's flourishing. As a result, a person may achieve high levels of flourishing even if she does not lead her life in a way that involves even the intermittent exercise of autonomy, for example, by simply conforming to the customs and practices of her community, or by doing what a religious leader says she should.[7] This moderate claim is more plausible, but it does not provide a powerful argument against indoctrination. This is because it leaves open the possibility that those who are indoctrinated may nevertheless achieve adequate (perhaps even high) levels of flourishing because their lives contain enough other intrinsically valuable ingredients. Of course, a large range of intermediate claims are possible; for example, it might be argued that autonomy is an intrinsically valuable ingredient of the good life that is of sufficient intrinsic importance that it is difficult to achieve a high level of flourishing in its absence. But intermediate claims of this kind face a dilemma that is difficult to overcome: either they are dubious because they make questionable claims about the way in which the immense intrinsic value of autonomy makes it hard to flourish in its absence regardless of what kind of life a person leads in other respects, or they do not show that indoctrination is especially harmful since they allow that people can flourish even though they have been successfully indoctrinated to prevent them from becoming autonomous.

An alternative argument would appeal to the *instrumental* value of autonomy rather than its intrinsic value. This argument claims that in practice the possession of autonomy, and the disposition to exercise it, facilitates flourishing or is a means to achieve flourishing. It is hard, perhaps often impossible, for a person to lead a flourishing life without possessing autonomy because, generally speaking, we need to exercise autonomy in order to be able to find a life that is fulfilling for us.[8] John Stuart Mill captures some of the plausibility of this "instrumental argument" when he writes:

> A man cannot get a coat or a pair of boots to fit him unless they are either made to his measure, or he has a whole warehouseful to choose from: and is it easier to fit him with a life than with a coat, or are human beings more like one another in their whole physical and spiritual conformation than in the shape of their feet? If it were only that people have diversities of taste, that is reason enough for not attempting to shape them all after one model. But different persons also require different conditions for their spiritual development; and can no more exist healthily in the same moral, than all the variety of plants can in the same physical, atmosphere and climate.[9]

The instrumental argument provides a particularly powerful case against indoctrination when it is combined with the thesis of value pluralism. At a minimum, value pluralism maintains that there is an irreducible plurality of values. It can also be extended to incorporate the idea that different values may be realized in different ways of life, that very different ways of life may each have value, and that different individuals may have natures that suit them to different ways of life that each have value. When deployed against indoctrination, the instrumental argument gains support from value pluralism in this extended form because, given our fallibility, it is often the case that in practice we need to exercise autonomy in order to identify what ways of life are valuable and then to find one that fits, to use Mill's metaphor.

The instrumental argument makes an empirical claim that ideally requires evidence to support it, but it is not easy to formulate it precisely or gather evidence that bears upon it. In fact, there are many different versions of it that can be generated from the following formula: there is a probability x that a percentage y of the political community will not achieve a level of flourishing z unless they possess, and exercise, autonomy. The instrumental argument seems plausible even when reasonably high numbers are substituted for x and y, and z is specified as an adequate level of flourishing. Perhaps most people can achieve an adequate level of flourishing in a variety of different lives—rather like the average person can find clothes that fit reasonably well straight "off the peg" in a range of shops—and do not need to exercise autonomy to find a valuable life in which they can achieve that level of flourishing. But there may still be a sizeable minority who can flourish to an adequate extent only in a small number of ways of life. (These people are the ethical equivalent of men taller than 6' 6", with feet that are size 13 or larger, who struggle to find clothes and shoes that fit unless they have them made to measure.) They might not be able to flourish simply by conforming to their family or community's conception of how to live—and indeed might be seriously damaged if they were indoctrinated to accept its tenets and the assumption that it is the only valuable way to live.[10] Perhaps this is true of many gay men and lesbians who are born into homophobic communities.

There is another way of explaining the importance of respect for autonomy that does not appeal directly to the interests of the child, and which draws upon the idea mentioned in Chapter 2 that autonomy may matter not only from a consequentialist perspective, in terms of its role as an educational good, but also from a non-consequentialist perspective. The child-focused non-consequentialist argument I have in mind maintains that indoctrination, both at school and in the home, is morally objectionable because it fails to respect the child's potential to develop autonomy by treating her as a mere means, as a mere vehicle for furthering her parents' or teachers' conception of how to live. Although this approach requires more development and clarification, it strikes me as forceful. The problem with indoctrination is not simply that it is harmful because it makes it harder for some children to flourish when they become adults. The treatment of a child can be morally objectionable even if it is harmless because it is a violation of her *independence*.[11] Suppose, for example, that a child is sexually molested but remarkably it has no harmful effects on her of any sort. We would still regard it as morally objectionable because she lacks the capacity to consent and is being treated as a mere means to another person's gratification. And we might want to say something similar about the indoctrination of a child even when it is harmless: even if she goes on to flourish, it is objectionable for parents or teachers to treat her as a mere means to furthering their conception of how to live by trying to prevent her from acquiring the capacity to make her own decisions on that matter.

When combined, the instrumental argument and the child-focused non-consequentialist argument seem to provide a powerful case against permitting any school with a religious character, even a private school, to engage in indoctrination. If there is a fear that this would prompt some parents to home educate their children, then the response should surely be that even home education needs to be regulated in a way that tries to prevent parents from indoctrinating their children in the tenets of a particular religion.

2. Shaping the Child's Beliefs and Values but without Indoctrination

The child-focused non-consequentialist argument I have described is potentially very radical in its consequences, however. Indeed, it seems to provide an objection not only to indoctrination in my narrow sense, but also to "directive" teaching even when that falls some distance short of indoctrination as I have characterized it; for example, when it aims to form a child's religious beliefs and values so they come to be held in a manner that is partially independent of the arguments or evidence that bear upon them, but without closing her mind or making it costly for her to abandon these beliefs and values in later life. In what follows when I refer to *shaping a child's religious beliefs and values*, it is this attempt to form her beliefs and values in a way that falls short of indoctrination that I shall mean.

Someone who endorses this child-focused non-consequentialist argument need not deny the obvious truth that a child's beliefs and values, including her religious beliefs and values, are inevitably going to be influenced by her social interactions. But from the point of view of the version of this argument with which I am concerned, it matters whether those who interact with her do so with the intention of forming in her a particular set of religious beliefs and values or whether her acquisition of these beliefs and values is the unintended (though perhaps foreseeable) consequence of her various encounters with them. Indeed, from this point of view, the religious indoctrination of children is morally problematic in part because it involves intentionally instilling in them beliefs and values in relation to matters over which reasonable people may disagree, not only because it involves intending to close their minds.[12]

But it is not clear that there is anything problematic from the point of view of respecting the child's *right to autonomy* when her parents or the school she attends shape her religious beliefs and values in such a way that they are not properly grounded in an appreciation of the available arguments and evidence, provided that her capacities for critical reflection are developed to an adequate level and she is encouraged to exercise those capacities in some important contexts. In response, it might be said that when parents or teachers shape a child's religious beliefs and values, they treat her as a mere means for furthering their conception of how to live, even if they are altruistically motivated, and even if they also cultivate her capacity for critical reflection. When religious beliefs and values are instilled in a child so that they come to be accepted at least partially independent of the arguments and evidence for them, doesn't that involve a form of manipulation that treats her as a mere instrument and therefore violates her right to autonomy?

The idea that children should not be treated as a mere means, instrument, or vehicle is vague. What matters from the point of view of respecting the child's right to autonomy is that her independence, the fact that she can be put on a path to acquiring autonomy so that she will become capable of forming and revising her own conception of how to live and be disposed to do so, should be given sufficient weight. And my claim is that this is done when her religious beliefs and values are shaped provided that her capacities for critical reflection are developed to at least an adequate level, she is encouraged to exercise these capacities in some important contexts, and it is not made costly for her to abandon those beliefs and values in the future when she reaches adulthood.[13] When these conditions are met, her right to autonomy has been respected; even if she has been manipulated she has not been treated as *merely* a means to furthering someone else's conception of how to live.

Suppose, for example, that a school teaches that sex before marriage is morally wrong, contraception is a morally impermissible form of birth control, and that abortion is murder, and does so by giving religious and non-religious reasons. It introduces students to alternative arguments, but teaches that these arguments fail to undermine the case for the immorality of pre-marital sex, contraception, and abortion. Indeed, on a range of issues, secular and religious, the school acquaints children with diverse perspectives and encourages them to consider the various arguments and evidence that bear on the choice between them, even though it sometimes brings the discussion to an end prematurely by simply encouraging the children to believe that a particular claim or doctrine is true or by insisting that it is true. They may do so by appealing to religious authority, for example, by claiming that this is what it says in the Bible or the Qur'an. Or

they might appeal to religious or non-religious reasons in favour of the doctrine and then maintain that the counter-arguments against it fail, perhaps
drawing a line under the discussion by asserting "this is what we as
Catholics (or Protestants, Muslims, etc.) should believe". Instructing in this
way would seem to involve manipulation and to some extent discouraging
critical reflection. But from the point of view of respecting the child's right
to autonomy, what matters is that her capacity for critical reflection is developed to a level that is adequate for her to be able to form and revise her own
conception of how to live, that she is encouraged to exercise this capacity in
at least some important contexts, and that abandoning the beliefs she has
acquired as a result of the manipulation she has experienced would not be
very costly for her.

It might be said that it is incoherent to suppose that a child's capacities
for critical reflection could be cultivated whilst shaping her religious beliefs
and values in such a way that they are not adequately grounded in the arguments and evidence. Perhaps there is a tension here in practice. No doubt it
will be hard to shape a child's religious views in this way whilst cultivating
in her a capacity for critical reflection, even if that capacity only needs to be
developed to some adequate level. And if in one part of the curriculum children are taught in a way that they are expected to subject ideas to full critical scrutiny, then that is likely to spill over into those parts of the curriculum
where children are expected to accept ideas to some extent uncritically. But
the relevant question here is not whether a school can pull this off, but
whether it is morally permissible for them to try to do so provided that they
avoid contributing to indoctrination. My claim is that the child's right to
autonomy does not provide a basis for objecting to such an attempt.

In response it might be argued that whenever children's religious beliefs
and values are shaped in school, there is a danger that their minds will be
closed in a way that would constitute a violation of their right to autonomy.
When schools with a religious character reinforce what is taught informally
at home, it might be thought there is a high risk that a significant number of
children who go to them will find that their capacities to think for themselves are reduced to the point at which they cannot be described as having
the kind of open future that the right to autonomy demands. It is hard to
deny that there is a risk that some children will suffer in this way, but the
question is whether this risk is sufficiently high in relation to a large enough
number of them. We know, for example, that one of the risks of collecting
together children in schools is that some will suffer bullying from their fellow students. But this is a side effect of pursuing a permissible goal, and the

harm caused is not sufficiently great, at least when protections are put in place, to cast doubt on the defensibility of bringing children together in schools to educate them. So too we might think that in many circumstances the risk that shaping children's religious beliefs and values might contribute to closing their minds is not sufficiently high in relation to a sufficiently large number of children to justify banning schools that do so, or refusing them public funding. Indeed, placing a regulatory requirement on schools, both private and state-funded, to ensure that they do not contribute to closing their children's minds might in most cases provide a sufficient barrier against that happening. Judgments about whether we should in practice go further are sensitive to an assessment of the specific risks involved at particular times and places. (In Chapter 7, we favour prohibiting religious instruction in schools in England because of the risk we think it poses, but the argument I defend in this chapter does not logically compel me to move in that direction more generally.)

It might be thought that there is nevertheless a residual moral problem with shaping children's religious beliefs and values without indoctrinating them. We don't generally think that it is permissible for one adult to shape, or attempt to shape, another's religious views. So what's special about a parent's relationship to her children that means she is entitled to shape her children's religious beliefs and values? It's not the specialness of the relationship one has to one's children that matters primarily here (though there may indeed be ways in which it is different from the relationship one has to fellow adults); it is rather that respect for independence places different constraints on one's treatment of fellow adults. In the case of adults, respect for their independence rules out shaping their religious beliefs and values since (normally at least) they have developed a capacity for critical reflection, whereas children have not yet developed such a capacity, so respect for their independence permits such shaping, provided it is accompanied by an attempt to cultivate that capacity.

This might seem ad hoc. I maintain that shaping of a person's religious beliefs and values is morally problematic sometimes but not always. I maintain that respect for a child's right to autonomy—in particular respect for her independence—sometimes prohibits shaping her religious beliefs and values but sometimes doesn't. It doesn't follow from this alone that my account is ad hoc, however. In claiming that some but not all shaping of a child's religious beliefs and values is morally impermissible, I am appealing to morally relevant differences. It matters, morally speaking, whether the child's capacity for critical reflection is being cultivated alongside the shaping, and it matters, morally speaking, whether her religious beliefs and values are formed in such a way that they are put beyond the reach of this capacity or it is made costly for her to abandon them when she reaches adulthood. In other words, there are morally relevant differences between indoctrination and mere shaping that matter when it comes to determining what it is permissible for parents or teachers to do in educating children. Indeed, it is not unusual to think that principles and values are conditional in various ways on the circumstances. We believe that killing is sometimes wrong but not always, and in making discriminations here we appeal to morally relevant differences. We believe that pleasure is generally valuable but not always; for example, not when it is gained from torturing children or animals.[14]

3. Parents' Interests, Children's Interests, and Family Life

Even when a child's religious beliefs and values are shaped without violating her right to autonomy, that shaping may nevertheless damage her interests. Indeed, sometimes it might serve to limit her access to various valuable opportunities to gain personal fulfilment, one of the educational goods identified in Chapter 2, for example, by inadequately preparing her for public examinations and in effect excluding her from the possibility of going to an elite university or being selected for jobs when the competition for them is strong. An education that shaped a child's beliefs so that she came to accept the Bible as the literal truth and to think that the world was created less than 10,000 years ago with a complete fossil record might have this consequence, even if somehow her capacity for critical reflection was at the same time developed to an adequate level, because it might damage her performance in science exams. The importance of personal fulfilment provides a powerful argument for not permitting parents or teachers to educate children in a way that would limit their access to it. That argument applies not only to state-funded schools but also to private schools—and indeed to home education—giving a reason to regulate each of these to ensure that they do not have this effect.

Even when shaping a child's religious beliefs and values does not limit her access to personal fulfilment, we might think that it goes against her best interests. The potential damage to her interests is not simply a consequence of the manipulation she has suffered. We manipulate children all the time in ways that seem perfectly consistent with promoting their interests, for example, when we make sure that they don't know about the chocolate in the cupboard when there is fruit on offer, or we lead them to think that the internet connection has been lost when they need to wind down before going to bed. But manipulating a child's beliefs concerning religion might be thought to be different, on the grounds that it is generally in her interests to acquire these beliefs in the light of a proper appreciation of the arguments and evidence that bear upon them (taking into account what is accessible to her in the light of her current educational development). Many will reject that thought, perhaps on the grounds that it is generally in a child's interests to be inducted into a religious world view because otherwise she will not be able to come to appreciate fully the value and significance of a religious or spiritual life. But let us suppose for the sake of argument that it is generally against the interests of children to have their religious beliefs and values shaped by others. Would parents nevertheless have a right to send their child to a school that does so?

The idea that parents have a right to send their child to a religious school that shapes its students' religious beliefs and values is sometimes thought to be grounded in a more fundamental non-consequentialist right, either a right to practise one's religion, or a right of free association. But without further argument it is hard to see how a right to practise *one's own* religion could justify one's having an entitlement to take steps to induct *another person* into that religion without her consent. For some religious adherents, part of what it is to lead a good religious life is to instil religious beliefs in one's child, but we mustn't forget that children do not yet have the capacities required to give consent. And without further argument it is hard to see how the right *of parents* to associate with whom they choose could justify an entitlement to send their *child*, again non-consensually, to a school in which she will be part of an association that has as one of its purposes the shaping of her religious beliefs.

The most plausible way of making the connection between freedom of association and the freedom to send one's child to a school of one's choice is by appealing to the idea that parents are entitled to make associational and educational choices on behalf of their child because she does not yet have the capacity to do so herself and they are in general the best judge of her interests, even if they sometimes make mistakes about those interests. This would be a very different sort of argument because it seems to ground the right to make associational and educational choices on behalf of one's child in the good consequences for her that will generally flow from doing so, rather than in some right that is justified independently of its consequences.

Perhaps such an argument could justify allowing religious communities to set up schools that shape their students' religious beliefs, and justify permitting parents to send their children to them, but it is hard to see how it could justify publicly funding such schools if it is the case that the process of shaping children's religious beliefs and values does generally go against their interests.

Even if the public funding of religious schools that shape their students' beliefs and values is hard to justify by appeal to a non-consequentialist right of free association, we might nevertheless think that it can be justified when it is in the interests of *parents* to have their children educated in such a school. Even if the interests of a child are to some extent set back by having her religious beliefs and values shaped, we should not exaggerate the damage that is done to her provided that her capacity for critical reflection is nurtured to an adequate level, she is encouraged to exercise it in some important contexts, and this process of shaping does not make it costly for her to abandon those beliefs and values in later life. Under these circumstances the adverse impact on her interests is usually relatively minor. It needs to be weighed against the damage to the interests of parents that may occur when they are unable to send her to a school that would make it more likely that she will come to share their beliefs and values. It can be burdensome for parents when their child acquires beliefs and values that they think are deeply mistaken. In most cases parents are strongly committed to the flourishing of their child and they may think she will do so only if she lives in a particular way and holds the beliefs and values that are required in order to do so. When parents care deeply about their children and feel a special responsibility towards them—as they generally do—it can be upsetting for them to see their children acting in ways, which by their lights, involve going seriously astray with potentially momentous repercussions.

This is especially true in the case of religion, though it could be true of non-religious world views as well. The burdens that parents experience, or would experience, as a result of their child rejecting their beliefs and values, should be given some weight in assessing whether schools that shape their students' beliefs and values should receive public funding. The point here is not that the satisfaction of parents' desires in relation to how their child should behave, and what she should believe and value, matter in their own right.[15] It is rather that it is burdensome for parents to see their child develop in ways that they regard as deeply harmful to her, and that these burdens should be taken into account because of their detrimental effect on parents' well-being.

There are other, perhaps more important, reasons for publicly funding schools that shape students' religious beliefs and values that do not appeal simply to the burdens that parents would experience were their child to go seriously astray by their lights. The shaping of a child's religious beliefs and values may be one way in which mutually beneficial relationships are forged within families, involving the formation of what Harry Brighouse and Adam Swift call "familial relationship goods".[16] Sometimes it may be possible for religious parents to realize the distinctive kind of goods that are involved in a healthy parent–child relationship, such as the particular kind of intimacy and emotional sharing that is distinctive of it, without shaping her beliefs and values about matters of religion. It may be possible for parents to give her insights into their world view, and to follow her lead and respond to her evolving concerns and the values expressed in them, without any attempt to do so.[17] But that may not always be feasible in practice, and even when it is possible to cultivate the intimacy and emotional sharing that are part of the value of parent–child relationships without shaping her religious beliefs and values, it may be much more difficult to do so. It may be much easier to experience that intimacy and emotional connection when one's child shares to a greater extent one's beliefs and values. In that case, if I am right in thinking that shaping the child's religious beliefs and values does not involve any necessary violation of her right to autonomy, then the value of familial relationship goods may be sufficient on its own to justify doing so, and more generally, may justify parents making choices *with the purpose of* increasing the likelihood that she will come to accept their own religious beliefs and values, as a means to realize these goods. This sort of argument appeals to the way in which the interests of both parents and children may provide a reason for permitting and publicly funding religious schools that shape the religious beliefs and values of their students.

Does it make any difference whether the school that is shaping its students' religious beliefs and values is a primary school or a secondary school? There are strong grounds for preventing both primary and secondary schools with a religious character from indoctrinating their students. But it might be argued that there are grounds for permitting primary schools to shape their children's beliefs and values, and to provide them with public funds, that do not apply to secondary schools. It may be that schools are a confusing place for younger children when the formal education they receive in them differs markedly from the informal education they receive at home. If at home, for example, they are constantly given religious reasons for how they should behave but at school they are given non-religious reasons, then this may be perplexing for them and a source of distress.[18] If this is the case, then primary schools that shape children's religious beliefs and values may be able to avoid this undesirable consequence.

In response it might be pointed out that this argument, if successful, appears to give a reason for funding a variety of schools with different perspectives, religious and secular, so that each child can attend a school that appeals to the reasons she is given at home and the values she has learned there. (Indeed, if a child is given only reasons of justice at home because her parents refrain from enrolling her in any comprehensive moral doctrine, then it gives a reason for providing a school for her that does the same.) But in countries such as Britain the danger of a distressing schism between home and school is greater for children coming from religious homes since the background culture is largely secular and dismissive of religious commitments, and most students will come from families that are non-religious.[19] Furthermore, the problem might be exacerbated for some children from religious families when a hostile view of their particular religion prevails in the wider culture, as is arguably the case with Islam in Britain (and elsewhere in Europe and North America) at the moment.[20] Indeed, this can make it harder for them to acquire a positive sense of their identity, that is, a positive attitude towards the moral commitments they have acquired at home and that they regard as central to who they are—even if schools attempt to counteract this negative view by presenting that religion in a positive light. A positive sense of one's identity might be a condition of acquiring self-respect and self-esteem, which in turn seem to be a condition of acquiring autonomy. These are largely empirical matters that cannot be settled by philosophical argument alone, but if the conjectures I have described are correct, then there would be an additional reason for permitting and publicly funding primary schools with a religious character that appeals to the interests of the child.

4. Citizens' Interests and Civic Education

The imaginary school with a religious ethos that I began by describing provides an effective civic education. But what if a school with a religious character was opposed to an education of this kind? In this section, I shall explore the grounds for thinking that civic education is important but explain why schools with a religious character might nevertheless have reason for not wanting to provide it. In doing so I aim to lay bare a potential conflict between the interests that may be served by shaping the religious beliefs and values of children and the interests of citizens considered collectively.

Civic education seeks to cultivate in children the capacities and dispositions necessary to be good citizens of the state to which they belong. In other words, it helps to cultivate the civic and moral capacities and dispositions that we identified in Chapter 2 as important educational goods. These goods are valuable in part because they help to create or sustain a reasonably just society or, at least, help to create or sustain a more just society than would exist without them. When civic education plays a role in realizing these goods, it promotes the interests of citizens considered collectively. Whether civic education can be valuable in this way is partly an empirical matter. There is no systematic evidence available concerning the effectiveness of formal civic education, so some of the claims I make in this section have a speculative character.[21] There is, however, a reason to worry about leaving the cultivation of these civic and moral goods solely to families and civil society. Some families or communities may bring up their children to be intolerant or to give greater weight to the interests of their own members in matters of public policy, and there is no guarantee that their children's involvement in civil society will counteract learnt tendencies of this kind, especially if their participation in it is centred on religious groups that share these tendencies. As a result, there is some reason to suppose that schools should prepare their students for citizenship, and be required to do so, irrespective of whether they are privately funded or state-funded, at least in the absence of solid evidence for thinking that civic education is doomed to be ineffective.

Some parents might object to their children receiving a civic education. They might want to foster an unshakeable religious commitment in their children, or at least to foster a commitment that it will be costly for their children to abandon, and they might believe, with justification, that civic education would work against that aim. But I have already argued against the moral permissibility of religious indoctrination, so there is no need to consider this ground for opposing civic education. There is, however, a more powerful challenge to civic education that grants the impermissibility of religious indoctrination. This challenge maintains that in some cases the shaping of children's religious beliefs (in a way that nevertheless cultivates their capacity for critical reflection to an adequate level and encourages them to exercise this capacity in at least some important contexts) is hindered by civic education and that, when it is, religious schools should be exempted from the requirement of providing one, or should be allowed to offer only a limited form of it. In what way might it be thought that civic education could work against an autonomy-respecting imparting of faith? Before we can answer that question we need to explore in more depth what an adequate civic education would involve.

An adequate civic education requires at the very least cultivating in children a set of closely related capacities and dispositions that constitute educational goods of the civic and moral kind we identified in Chapter 2: the capacity and disposition to think impartially about matters of public concern, the capacity and disposition to treat others as equals, and the capacity and disposition to behave tolerantly. A civic education oriented towards cultivating these capacities and dispositions would need to draw upon a set of arguments for why they are valuable that can be understood and digested by children. Even though there need be nothing morally objectionable about the non-rational shaping of a child's beliefs about what she owes to her fellow citizens when her capacities for critical reflection are also developed to an adequate level, it would seem that these beliefs are more likely to be held in a stable manner if she is presented with powerful arguments for them, at least in a rudimentary form. So the arguments for why it is important for children to acquire various civic virtues are also arguments that need to be employed as part of civic education, even if they are presented in a simplified form.

Consider the virtue of tolerance. What arguments could be presented in an accessible way to school children, at least those who have reached secondary school level, that could persuade them to regard it as important? It seems to me that a key part of the case for the importance of toleration is provided by the instrumental argument for the value of autonomy, together with the extended form of value pluralism that I suggested in Section 1 of this chapter it should incorporate. According to this overall view, it is hard (perhaps impossible) for people to flourish unless they possess and exercise autonomy, because unless they do so it will be hard for them to find valuable lives that fit. This provides an argument for toleration that is readily digestible by secondary school age children and can be vividly illustrated by Mill's metaphors about clothes and plants, and by historical examples.

There is also an analogue of the child-focused non-consequentialist argument, considered earlier in this chapter, that strengthens the case for toleration in the way mentioned in Chapter 2. This argument is harder to make accessible even to secondary school age children, but it has a potential role to play in cultivating an appreciation of the importance of toleration as part of civic education. It could be illustrated by cases in which a person's independence is violated, that is, when she is treated as merely a means to the satisfaction of others' desires or the promotion of their conception of how to live.

The case for toleration can also be supplemented by two further arguments, the first of which I shall call "the argument from peaceful coexistence", and the second "the argument from the burdens of judgment". The argument from peaceful coexistence can be presented very simply by appealing to the way in which, throughout history, deep disagreement over how we should live, especially religious differences on this matter, has had a propensity to lead to violent conflict when tolerance has been in short supply. It can be illustrated by historical examples of religiously motivated wars that have torn countries and communities apart, and by emphasizing the way in which peace is a condition for the successful pursuit of most of the activities we value. The argument from the burdens of judgment draws upon John Rawls' observation that there are a variety of sources of disagreement between reasonable people. He emphasizes in particular the way in which evidence can be hard to assess because it is complex and conflicting; even when people agree about what considerations are relevant, they may disagree about what weight to give them; and our differing past experiences may affect the judgments we make.[22] These "burdens of judgment", and the way in which divergences in people's conceptions of how to live can emerge from the sincere and reasonable exercise of their rational capacities, in a way that merits respect, could readily be grasped by secondary school age children.

A robust civic education would need to cultivate in children a commitment to toleration in part through a rudimentary appreciation of the full range of arguments and doctrines I have described. However, some schools with a religious character may with good reason regard a civic education of this kind as hampering the realization of their goals, since these arguments and doctrines might be corrosive of certain types of religious belief. Several of the ideas I have mentioned potentially go against an aspect of faith: some religions (or traditions within them) hold that there is only one way in which a person will flourish, namely, by acting in accordance with its tenets; some religions hold the view that a person flourishes more by being forced to conform to it than by being allowed to live in accordance with their own conception of how to live; some religions deny the burdens of judgment and claim that reason is univocal in its implications, and that people fail to see this because of their flawed natures.

Acceptance of the burdens of judgment might be regarded as especially corrosive of faith, for it entails acknowledging that these burdens apply to one's own religious views.[23] Given the importance of cultivating tolerance, it might seem that if bringing up children to accept a particular set of religious beliefs and values is incompatible with acknowledging the burdens of judgment, then so much the worse for those beliefs and values. But some concessions may be justifiable here. For example, we might think that a religious school should be permitted to operate with a form of civic education that cultivates in children the disposition to be tolerant, but without offering the full range of arguments for the importance of toleration that would rightly be part of a more robust form of civic education but which would be corrosive of the particular faith taught within that school. So it might teach the importance of toleration, and of a high degree of separation of Church and state, by presenting and illustrating the argument from peaceful co-existence, by appealing to the endorsement thesis (namely, that a person will find it hard to flourish if she is not allowed to live in accordance with her judgment of how she should do so, no matter how mistaken), and by drawing upon religious ideas (such as the idea that it is important for people to find their own path to God), but without appealing to the burdens of judgment or to value pluralism.[24]

The scope for permitting an attenuated civic education of this form may be greater when a society is reasonably just than when it is seriously unjust, for in the latter it may be more important to cultivate robust and extensive civic virtue in the next generation in order to give a polity the best chance of tackling successfully the injustices currently present in it. And even when a society is reasonably just, one might think that although privately funded religious schools should be permitted to offer an attenuated form of civic education when a full-blown version of it would threaten their ability to shape their students' religious beliefs and values, state-funded schools should not be allowed to do so. If a school is to be publicly funded, it should wholeheartedly serve public purposes, even if it serves other purposes (such as religious ones) as well.

That might be objected to on the grounds that it simply favours wealthy parents who can afford to pay school fees over poor parents.[25] This counter-argument, which is of the distributive kind identified in Chapter 2, has force when a society is seriously unjust, that is, when some parents have much more resources than they are entitled to and others much less, but no force when all parents have the resources to which they are entitled and no more. Under these circumstances, whether parents send their child to a private school that teaches in accordance with their religious beliefs and values may turn in part on whether they can afford to do so; however, they have no reasonable complaint if they have the resources to which they are entitled but cannot afford to do so.

Could they make a reasonable complaint *on behalf of their child*—that she was being deprived of an education that would sustain her faith without which she would suffer eternal damnation, and that as a result she lacked equality of opportunity with those children whose parents could afford to pay for such an education? At most, this might give reason to favour assisted places for parents who could not afford to send their child to such a school. But it is not clear that it even warrants that response. The complaint here is no more reasonable than, say, a complaint mounted on behalf of a child that she could not go on some religious pilgrimage that her parents deemed to be important for her spiritual development because they could not afford to take her on it even though other parents were able to do so. One of the inevitable consequences of just inequality, in combination with the division of children into different families and the different values and talents of parents, is that these will affect what opportunities are available to one child compared to another. There are difficult issues here concerning what the ideal of equality of opportunity requires in this context, but it would be implausible to think that differences in opportunity that arise in this way necessarily undermine equality of opportunity. The ideal of equality of opportunity places limits on the character and extent of morally permissible differences in children's opportunities that result from variations in their parents' values and the economic circumstances of their families, but not all of these differences threaten the ideal of equality of opportunity.[26]

5. Selecting on the Basis of Religion and the Composition of the School

Let us return again to the imaginary school with a religious ethos that I described at the beginning of this chapter. Suppose that its success means that it is over-subscribed. It decides to change its admissions policy so that it will now give priority to the children of practising Christians. Would this be morally justifiable?

There will of course be practical difficulties in applying any such policy. We know that using religious criteria in admissions is ripe for abuse: when a school with a religious character is successful, some parents will manipulate whatever rules it uses for giving preference to religious families; for example, they will attend church for the minimum period required to meet the selection criteria. That is not the most important problem with such a policy, however. There are two other potential problems with it that are more damaging in my view.

The first potential problem is that selection on religious grounds may violate equality of opportunity, one of the three distributive values we identified in Chapter 2. When a school with a religious character is successful in terms of its exam results because of better teaching, smaller class sizes, peer-group effects, or the ethos of the school, students who study there are advantaged relative to others in the competition for jobs and places in higher education. Under these circumstances, giving priority in admissions to those of a particular religion seems to give members of that religion an unfair advantage. (And if, independently of religious affiliation, middle-class parents are more skilled at securing places at the school, then selection on religious grounds may have the effect of benefitting children who are already materially advantaged.) When a school with a religious character is academically successful—more successful than other religious and non-religious schools in the same area—and uses religious criteria for selection, it is hard to deny that there is a real and important threat to equality of opportunity, one that may damage the interests of those children who are excluded and threaten the just distribution of benefits and burdens within a society. And that threat exists whether the school is run on a private basis or is publicly funded.

The second potential problem is that one likely effect of selecting on religious grounds is that a school will concentrate together children from families that share the same faith, leading to fewer encounters between children from families that have different faiths. This would seem to provide a less effective environment for cultivating civic virtues such as toleration and mutual respect, which are educational goods that citizens have an interest in collectively as well as individuals. Although it is ultimately an empirical issue, there are at least two mechanisms that seem to be important for cultivating these virtues that have a more limited role in a school that has very little, or no, religious diversity. First, it might be thought that virtues such as toleration are acquired, or at least most effectively acquired, by habitual practice. Within the Aristotelian tradition, it is argued that virtues, understood as settled dispositions to behave in particular ways in particular circumstances, are acquired by acting as if one possessed the virtue:[27] one becomes tolerant or respectful by acting as if one were tolerant or acting as if one were respectful, by curbing any inclinations one has to act intolerantly or disrespectfully until those inclinations dissipate. If this is true, then schools in which children encounter those from different faith backgrounds are likely to be more effective at cultivating civic virtues such as toleration and respect.

Second, there is a body of empirical evidence that suggests that, under certain conditions at least, contact between those from different religions, and different ethnic groups, undermines prejudice, which might be thought to be one of the bases of intolerance and lack of respect. According to this hypothesis—first presented by Gordon Allport in the 1950s but now well-confirmed—when people from different ethnic and religious groups encounter each other on a re-occurring basis, engage together in cooperative activities in a way that is supported by institutional authorities, and have equal status in these activities, then this tends to reduce prejudice.[28] It might be thought that schools in general are one of the best potential sites for realizing these conditions and generating this beneficial result, but schools with a religious character that admit selectively on the basis of religion are less well-equipped to do so when they concentrate together those of the same faith.

Both the contact hypothesis and the Aristotelian account of how virtues are acquired provide reasons for worrying about over-subscribed schools with a religious character selecting on religious grounds. (Indeed, both raise concerns about any school in which the students are predominantly or exclusively drawn from families that adhere to the same religion, irrespective of whether it selects on grounds of religion.) Taken on their own, they provide the basis for a strong but not overwhelming argument against permitting religious schools to select on grounds of religion. Of course, schools *without* a designated religious character may also be religiously homogenous because they are located in, and draw children from, a geographical area that is itself religiously homogenous. But the special problem with religious schools is that, potentially at least, they act as siphons for children from a particular faith background, with the result that schools without a religious character in the same area become much less diverse than they would otherwise be. In this way they reduce the capacity of the educational system as a whole to cultivate educational goods such as tolerance and mutual respect.[29] As a result, the contact hypothesis and Aristotelian moral psychology provide a strong but not overwhelming argument against the existence or public funding of religious schools that concentrate together those from the same faith background.[30]

The argument these theories provide against religious schools that are homogenous in terms of religious background is inconclusive because the children who attend them may be able to overcome prejudice and acquire civic virtues such as tolerance through interactions outside of school contexts, or indeed without coming into direct contact with those from other religious groups.[31] Furthermore, a school in which students are drawn from the same faith background might be able to forge links with other schools that have a different religious composition, thereby providing opportunities for their students to encounter those of another faith or no faith and to practise toleration.[32]

We should also be wary of assuming that schools that are diverse in terms of religion will necessary involve contact of the sort that leads to a reduction in prejudice and the cultivation of tolerance. When these schools are structured in the right way and possess the right kind of ethos, then they will provide *opportunities* for members of different groups to have contact of the relevant kind with each other, but for various reasons these opportunities may not be taken up. Rather than integrating children from different ethnic and religious backgrounds, schools that are diverse in these respects may even contain within them informal practices of separation as a result of children being drawn to those who share the same outlook or have had similar experiences.[33]

Furthermore, even if religious schools that are homogenous in terms of the religious background of their students provide a sub-optimal environment for acquiring civic virtues compared to *an ideal* school that is both diverse in terms of its religious composition and well-integrated, the environment they provide may be no worse in this respect than the available or feasible alternatives, and they may be better for their students in other respects. In our imperfect world, the existing religiously diverse schools may not satisfy, even approximately, the conditions under which Allport claimed his contact hypothesis applied. Michael Merry points out that when schools without a designated religious character are rife with religiously motivated bullying, religious schools, especially those that serve victimized minorities, may do a better job of reducing prejudice and cultivating civic virtues. These religious schools may provide a safe environment in which their students can acquire a confident sense of their own identity—one that they can regard positively and that therefore provides a basis for self-respect and self-esteem.[34] The force of this argument in practice depends in part upon the feasibility of reforming schools that are diverse in terms of their composition so that they do a better job of fulfilling Allport's conditions. It also depends in part on whether contact of a kind that does not fulfil those conditions, or that does so only partially, may nevertheless have beneficial effects in reducing prejudice. (The evidence is that it does, and that the conditions he specifies are *facilitating* rather than necessary.[35])

Even though allowing schools with a religious character to select on the basis of religion may threaten equality of opportunity, and may lead to the creation of schools the composition of which is sub-optimal for reducing prejudice and cultivating civic virtues when compared to other feasible alternatives, there may still be an argument for allowing them to do so, and to receive public funding, if it is the case (as I argued in Section 3 of this chapter) that parents' interests should be given some weight. It might be hard for a school to sustain its religious ethos, and therefore its religious character, unless a reasonably high percentage of the students who attend it (and, perhaps even more importantly, of the teachers who teach there) share that faith. If so, the imaginary school I described at the beginning might be unsustainable over time. This may even have a levelling down effect: if, contrary to the available evidence, the religious character of a religious school may contribute to its success, then the loss of its religious ethos may lead to its decline, with the consequence that its students no longer achieve the same levels of academic excellence.[36]

So there are reasons for *permitting* schools to select on religious grounds. Selecting on these grounds may be necessary under some circumstances for sustaining a successful school with a religious character, of a kind that benefits the children who attend it; these schools may be better able to protect parents' legitimate interests in bringing up their child to share their religious beliefs and values or, at least, not to reject those beliefs and values; under some circumstances these schools may provide an environment that is as good as the feasible alternatives for cultivating civic virtues and also help to provide students with a secure sense of their own identity. But there are also reasons for *prohibiting* schools with a religious character from selecting on religious grounds. Selecting on these grounds may violate equality of opportunity; the resulting composition of the school may provide a significantly sub-optimal environment when compared to the feasible alternatives for the cultivation of civic virtues; it is likely that it will be possible to manipulate the selection rules. These various considerations need to be weighed against each other in the particular circumstances that prevail. When there are already significant inequalities of opportunity within a society, the considerations that count against permitting an over-subscribed school to select on religious grounds may win the argument, even if that would mean that the school would eventually lose its religious ethos. But in some circumstances at least, the best balance between these reasons may point towards a system of regulation that requires an oversubscribed school to adopt a selection policy in which some places are reserved for children from families who share its faith, whilst the other places are allocated on some other basis, for example, by lottery or proximity to the school.[37]

6. Conclusion

The school with a religious ethos that I began by describing is unobjectionable provided certain conditions are met, and indeed there are positive arguments for allowing such schools to exist and for them to be given public funds, provided there are suitable alternatives available for the children of parents who do not share its values that can be sustained in an efficient way. The problems with schools with a religious character arise when these schools aim to indoctrinate their students, or run a high risk of doing so even if that is not their aim; or when their curriculum involves no civic education or only an attenuated form of it; or when they select students on religious grounds or end up being homogenous in terms of the religious background of their students even though they do not select on religious grounds.

I have argued that religious indoctrination is impermissible because it violates the child's right to autonomy. This is a weighty and complex right that is justified by both consequentialist and non-consequentialist considerations. I have suggested that there need be no problem with a school shaping its students' religious beliefs and values so long as they acquire the capacity to subject those beliefs and values to critical scrutiny, are disposed to exercise that capacity in at least some important contexts, and are able to abandon the beliefs and values in later life without that being costly to them. But I have left open the possibility that the importance of not closing children's minds may, in some circumstances, justify not permitting schools to shape their students' beliefs and values, even if they do not intend to indoctrinate them. The risks of closing children's minds may be sufficiently great that the best way of avoiding this outcome is to regulate schools in order to prevent them from trying to instil religious beliefs and values even when they are not seeking to indoctrinate their students.

A civic education that fosters civic and moral educational goods, such as tolerance, is important—sufficiently important in most circumstances to impose it as a requirement on both private schools and state-funded schools—but when a society is reasonably just there may be grounds for permitting more limited forms of civic education when it would otherwise be hard for an autonomy-respecting school with a religious character to cultivate its particular faith.

Even though selecting students on religious grounds may threaten equality of opportunity, and create a sub-optimal environment for promoting civic virtues such as toleration, sometimes it may be permissible for a school with a religious character to do so when maintaining its ethos is at stake, in the light of parents' legitimate interest in sending their children to a school with an ethos of a particular kind. Furthermore, in a seriously unjust society, religious schools that serve victimized religious minorities, and that are homogenous in terms of their religious composition, may protect their students against bullying and harassment, and may provide an environment that is no worse than that provided by existing schools with no religious character (even when we take into account how they might feasibly be reformed) for reducing prejudice and cultivating civic virtues.

How to Think about Religious Schools: Principles and Policies. Matthew Clayton, Andrew Mason, and Adam Swift, Oxford University Press. © Matthew Clayton, Andrew Mason, and Adam Swift 2024.
DOI: 10.1093/9780198924036.003.0003

4

Against Religious Schools

Matthew Clayton

Is the public funding of religious schools morally acceptable? Is it morally right that private religious schools paid for by parents exist? I believe the answer to both questions is a qualified "no". I favour the phased abolition of religious schools where they exist. That doesn't mean that I believe that schools should be anti-religious or promote humanist values. Rather, schools should generally not take a stand on the merits of religious or non-religious views about the existence of gods or the projects and relationships we ought to pursue in our lives. This is the view I defend in this chapter.

My approach rests on the thought that to arrive at a judgment about the moral acceptability of religious schools we need to identify the principles that should guide citizens in how they vote and the principles that ought to guide parents in raising their children. First, then, I set out why I believe we need to address issues concerning religious schooling by engaging with debates in moral and political philosophy. Second, I describe what I take to be an attractive political ideal that should guide how citizens vote, which is developed from the widely supported idea of the separation of Church (and other religious institutions) and state: the ideal of anti-perfectionist liberalism. Our question is whether the public funding of religious schools can be justified within such a liberal society. In Section 3, I argue that it cannot. That conclusion leaves open the possibility that religious schools are acceptable if they are paid for by parents or religious organizations rather than the taxpayer. In Section 4, I offer further arguments, this time against private religious schools, which trade on the thought that parents are like states because they exercise nonvoluntary coercion over children. I argue that if anti-perfectionist liberalism applies to states it should also apply to parents, and I defend the claim that private religious schooling is also unjust.

Having offered principled reasons for the non-existence of religious schools in an *ideal* society, in Section 5 I turn to consider the place of religious schools in the *unjust* world in which we live where we need to identify what is the best response to various kinds of injustice. Non-ideal considerations complicate the moral picture, I argue, and suggest that the campaign for the prohibition of religious schools needs to be qualified and attentive to various valuable roles currently played by religious schools.

1. Schooling and Political Morality

As discussed briefly earlier, debates about religious schools can't be resolved without identifying what are the right principles of morality and political morality. This claim is controversial. For example, some believe that education ought to be governed by distinctive principles that are *apolitical*. They claim that we can identify what it means to be taught to understand and know about different subjects and to develop various skills. On the basis of that kind of inquiry, they argue, we can identify what counts as good or bad education. If that view were right, then our task would be to evaluate whether different kinds of religious schools provide their students with a good education. We wouldn't need to ask more general questions about how individuals or citizens ought to treat one another. All we would need is an understanding of the enterprise of education.[1]

Apolitical conceptions of education are mistaken.[2] I do not deny the importance of being able to identify good or bad teaching. But, as we noted in Chapter 2, in every society schooling is administered *coercively* in several ways. First, children and parents are coerced by laws requiring compulsory schooling or laws mandating that certain educational outcomes be realized. Second, because children—at least young children—can't choose rationally for themselves they need more mature citizens to choose the education they receive, and the political community must allocate the legal right to determine their schooling to particular adults. This right might be given to parents, teachers, others, or shared between several agents. As James Dwyer observes, whatever allocation is selected, the upshot is that certain adults enjoy rights that involve the state's forcibly preventing others from interfering with the education they choose for the child in question.[3] For example, if the state gives *parents* rights of school choice, those who are not parents but who want to choose the character of a particular child's schooling are legally prohibited from doing so. Third, every citizen lives under the coercively administered laws of her society. For example, with respect to economic matters certain citizens enjoy more or fewer rights to wealth compared to those they would enjoy under alternative tax and expenditure arrangements—high earners benefit from a low-tax economy that devotes few resources to the education of children; those unable to work benefit from tax and transfer arrangements that redistribute income from the lucky to the unlucky through health and educational arrangements that benefit every family. These arrangements are coercive because the state forcibly prevents individuals from enhancing the opportunities they enjoy by acting contrary to what the law requires—it forces citizens to pay tax and prevents them from taking the wealth that others possess, for example.

The fact that publicly funded schools are part of this coercive regime makes a difference to the principles that ought to guide their regulation. When, as citizens, we assess whether we ought to vote for a particular education policy we must ask whether the policy is *a morally permissible exercise of coercive force* over children and other citizens. Thus, when questions arise about a society's education policy we need to turn to political philosophy for answers.

Imagine a country without an education policy: a society that doesn't tax its citizens to fund schools and one that doesn't legally require children to be educated or to attend particular schools. In such a society, suppose, all decisions concerning the education of children are taken by the children's parents. If you like, you can think of an island that is otherwise deserted on which a single family lives. The point I want to make is that even this imaginary society may not be free of coercion. Even if educational arrangements lacked the involvement of third parties, children would still be coerced—by their parents: for example, they may well be forced to be educated in a way that aligns with the parents' religious views.[4] So, we also need to know whether parents are morally permitted to instruct their children in a particular religion and, in addition, whether they have a right not to be prevented from educating their children according to their own convictions.

I turn to moral questions about parent-directed education in Section 4. First, in Section 2, I set out what I take to be the most attractive conception of political morality, which identifies the principles that ought to guide citizens when they vote—directly or indirectly—for particular coercively applied laws. Once that is in place, in Section 3 I explain why publicly funded religious schools would not exist in a fully just society.

2. Anti-Perfectionist Liberalism

Ethics, religion, and morality deal with several evaluative, normative, and metaphysical questions. Is there a god and, if there is, must we obey its commands? How ought we treat others? What are the properties that make one's life successful or good? People disagree profoundly about what are the right answers to these questions. Given that fact, may citizens adopt particular answers to these questions that do not command universal assent and vote for policies that use the coercive powers of the state to promote the conception they endorse? There are plenty of powers that might be used: citizens could vote to enact laws that criminalize and punish those who follow moral or religious practices that they take to be mistaken or harmful; they could use the state's power to tax and spend resources in order to penalize the pursuit of certain activities and subsidize others; and they could promote approved conceptions through state-initiated educational campaigns administered through schools or various media. Our question is whether citizens have the moral right to vote for policies that involve the state using these powers to promote particular conceptions of morality, religion, and ethics.

Anti-perfectionist liberalism—at least the version I shall discuss here—holds that citizens are under a duty to vote for a government that enforces certain controversial *moral* ideals, but they are not permitted to vote for policies that make other citizens serve particular *conceptions of the good*.[5] In what follows, for the sake of simplicity, I frame my remarks in terms of the what "the state" may or may not do, but it should be noted that I mean this to be shorthand for the rights and duties of citizens with respect to their use of the coercive power political institutions exercise over every citizen. So, according to anti-perfectionist liberalism, the state must uphold the rule of law and criminalize certain wrongs such as murder, various kinds of bodily harm to others, theft, fraud, and so on; it must also force citizens to pay taxes to fund a legal system that protects important civil rights and socioeconomic arrangements that distribute various goods such as education, health, and wealth fairly. The state is morally permitted to adopt and pursue these policies even when some citizens believe that the ends it pursues are misguided or morally wrong. With respect to certain questions about what we owe to each other, then, the state's task is to enforce certain very weighty moral duties that apply to every citizen. However, with respect to conceptions of the good, questions about religion, sexuality, and occupation, anti-perfectionists argue that the state must not take a stand. It shouldn't have a view of which religion, if any, is true, and it may not use its powers to promote a particular conception of human flourishing.[6]

Anti-perfectionist liberalism is sometimes expressed as the idea, outlined in Chapter 2, that the state should remain *neutral* between conceptions of the good. However, the language of "neutrality" needs to be used with caution because there are different understandings of that term. In the field of international relations, for example, the term "neutrality" is often used to describe the position of a country that does not favour a particular side in an international dispute or war—Switzerland during the two World Wars being the classic case. The idea is that the neutral country must not act in ways that benefits one of the warring parties more than another: if a country sells arms to one country then neutrality demands that it sells to other countries involved in the war. According to this interpretation, the neutral country mustn't act in ways that help or hinder one side more than another.[7]

But the ideal of political neutrality proposed by anti-perfectionist political philosophers is rather different. It doesn't say that the *consequence* of state action must not set back or advance the interests of one religious group, say, relative to others. Rather, the proposal is that the state's laws and policies mustn't be *justified* by reference to the intrinsic merits of any particular conception of the good. So, for example, when deciding what laws to enact or policies to pursue, the government mustn't take a stand on whether there is a god. Even supposing that it could correctly identify that there is a god, it may not act on that fact by taking steps designed to encourage citizens to form theistic beliefs. For this reason, it is common to distinguish between *consequential* neutrality (the kind of neutrality discussed in international relations) and *justificatory* neutrality (sometimes called "neutrality of aim"), which is how anti-perfectionist political philosophers understand the idea.[8] In what follows, when I use the language of political neutrality, I mean political agents excluding from consideration certain values that animate other parts of their lives: a committed Muslim who steadfastly pursues her religion in her non-political life must set those convictions aside if she is a voter or politician deciding whether a particular piece of legislation should be passed.[9]

To summarize, the ideal of political neutrality, at least as I shall understand it here, requires political actors to set aside their convictions about human flourishing and religion. Political decisions ought to enforce important moral requirements so that individuals' civil and political rights and claims to resources are satisfied. But it isn't the business of the state or citizens to try to identify and use the available levers of political power to promote the correct religion or view about what makes a life a success. In a sense, the idea of neutrality is an extension of the idea of the separation of Church and state. As it was initially conceived, the separation idea was the belief that political institutions should stand above disagreements between different religious groups. Political neutrality extends that requirement to other controversies, such as those concerning occupational choice, sexuality, and other goals people adopt in their personal lives.

Different arguments for political neutrality have been developed.[10] Perhaps the most influential defence is offered by John Rawls whose argument in *Political Liberalism* goes roughly as follows. Suppose citizens live in a political community that protects various important rights, such as the right to practise and express their religion, the right freely to associate with others, and to participate as equals in the political process. Rawls notes that the inevitable consequence of legal institutions that protect such rights is that citizens will disagree about various evaluative and normative matters, including questions concerning what we owe to each other and questions about which religion, if any, is sound.

A political community that protects various freedoms and socio-economic opportunities that enable citizens to make effective use of those freedoms is already committed to a certain way of living together. It has already taken a stand on the importance of certain educational goods, such as personal autonomy and civic and moral capacities, and particular non-consequentialist considerations, such as the right to freedom of conscience, expression, and association. And it is committed to a particular conception of distributive justice, because it insists that economic interactions must be regulated so that the interests of the least advantaged are protected.

Nevertheless, the issue arises whether the state ought to take a stand on other matters, such as those concerning religion and how individuals ought to use their freedoms. Rawls argues that it shouldn't, because if it did it would jeopardize individuals' political autonomy.[11] It is important for free and equal citizens to be able to understand and affirm the institutions and laws that profoundly affect their life chances and shape how they understand themselves, and it is important that they endorse the justifications the political community offers in defence of those institutions and laws.[12] If the state were to recognize as true a controversial conception of religion or successful living then, given the inevitability of disagreement about those questions, it would jeopardize that important interest in political autonomy, because those who dissent from the officially recognized view would be incapable of fully affirming the institutions that govern them.

Suppose, for example, that in addition to protecting important civil and political liberties the government sought to advance Christianity by using tax revenues to subsidize activities to encourage people to adopt that religion. That would violate political autonomy, because citizens who follow a different, or no, religion would not agree with the aims for which taxes are coercively levied. Of course, the same result would obtain if the government promoted atheism or a different religious doctrine. Thus, for the sake of individuals' political autonomy, the government must not take a stand on the truth of different religious views and promote them in society. Rather, principles of political morality should be ones that can be shared by people who hold different conceptions of the good, conceptions of religion and well-being that guide them in their choice of occupation and how they use their leisure time.

The political autonomy argument for anti-perfectionism obtains even when the government merely recognizes, but does not promote, a particular religion. Suppose the government does not use its powers to promote a specific religion or conception of the good by trying to get citizens to adopt and practise it. Suppose it merely recognizes the religion as true by, for example, conducting its official ceremonies in the rites and traditions of the religion in question—by reading from its central text during the investiture of a government or by requiring witnesses in court to promise not to lie by touching a particular book. Although these recognitional practices do not aim to promote a particular religion, they nevertheless fall foul of the ideal of political autonomy because citizens who reject the officially recognized religion cannot fully accept the legal and political system that rules over them. For that reason, the deeper ideals to which a political community appeals to justify its institutions and laws must be ones that do not take a stand on questions about the good life or religion that divide citizens.

In the context of education, anti-perfectionist or neutralist liberalism is comprised of a particular bundle of normative considerations discussed in Chapter 2. It also offers a distinctive interpretation of them by explaining why they matter. By viewing citizens as "free and equal", it asserts that individuals are entitled to an education that enables them to discharge their duties of concern and respect for others, which is interpreted by reference to a list of liberties and socio-economic opportunities everyone should enjoy. So, everyone has a claim to be educated to develop their civic and moral capacities. Citizens are also assumed to have distinctive views about religion and about what it means to live well, which may well diverge from other citizens' views. They're entitled to a schooling that enables them to form, reflect on, and to pursue such views—personal autonomy. They're also entitled to an education that enables them to understand and participate in the different options regarding the relationships and pursuits that are available in society. And they have a right to the conditions that ensure that they have opportunities to participate as equals in the marketplace—what we've called "economic productivity"—a claim to fair opportunity to develop the skills and capacities to take advantage of the occupational opportunities society makes available.

So, neutral liberals can endorse the list of items described in Chapter 2 as "educational goods". But a distinctive feature of this approach to political philosophy is that we don't justify these "goods" by saying that having them makes citizens happier or facilitates their leading more flourishing lives. It's important for neutralists to avoid those kinds of arguments because there is widespread disagreement in society about the nature of human flourishing and its relationship to religious belief. For the sake of securing political autonomy for everyone it is important for the state not to align itself with a particular controversial conception. To avoid those disputes, then, neutralists pare back the claims we make by relying on the basic and widely endorsed view that citizens are entitled to set and pursue their own religious or ethical ends. This means that they have a moral claim to educational and other institutions that facilitate their setting and pursuit of ends involving religion or well-being, provided the ends involve attending to the claims of others.

More generally, it is worth noting that anti-perfectionists typically appeal to non-consequentialist considerations as we have characterized them—the bottom row of Table 1—and stress the moral importance of respecting people's claims or entitlements to treatment. Political autonomy, understood as a claim to legal and political arrangements that are acceptable in the light of each citizen's conception of the good, is one such consideration, which provides a particular interpretation of citizens' (and, I'll argue later, children's) moral entitlements that carry considerable importance within this view.

3. Against the Public Funding of Religious Schools

As noted in Chapter 1, many countries have education systems that permit religious groups to run state-funded schools. As things stand in England, for example, while receiving funds from the central government or local authorities, such schools have qualified rights to use religious criteria in their selection decisions: by giving priority in admissions to children of practising Christians, for example. They may also teach *directively*, that is, with the aim of encouraging their pupils to embrace the merits of the religion endorsed by the school.[13] And they are free to hold assemblies that include collective worship in accordance with the rites of the religion in question.[14] In this section, I offer an anti-perfectionist case against the existence of such schools.

First, let us consider a simple neutrality-based argument against state-funded faith schooling. As we shall see, the simple argument is incomplete and needs buttressing with further arguments. Nevertheless, it is useful to have it stated, because it conveys the basic worry anti-perfectionists have about faith schools that are funded through general taxation and enforced coercively. The argument is as follows.

The simple argument: If anti-perfectionist liberalism is sound, then it is unjust for the state to impose on citizens schools that serve or promote controversial religious views, or to support such schools by forcing citizens to fund them through taxation.

According to the simple argument, a state-financed school should not endorse a particular view of the good or religion in its curriculum or ethos. Instead, it should develop its students' capacities to think for themselves and to deliberate about the different ethical and religious views that people find attractive. Of course, it should also develop their sense of justice so that they can show appropriate concern and respect for others. But that kind of moral direction is compatible with a neutral education with respect to religion and what constitutes a good life. True, there might be certain aspects of religious views that are in tension with children's developing a sense of justice and respect for others—parts of religious texts, for example, that recommend inferior civic status for women or violence towards heretics. Plainly, in those cases schools may need to challenge the religious views in question. However, doing so is compatible with remaining neutral with respect to the rest of the religious doctrine.

The simple argument is too simple, because it overlooks the fact that advocates of religious schools might be able to give *non-religious reasons* for the state funding that do not fall foul of the ideal of neutrality or anti-perfectionist liberalism more generally. It assumes that citizens and legislators who favour state-funded religious schools do so because they believe their religion is right or a route to the good life and promoting it through schools is justified for that reason. But that might not be the case. It might be that the case for religious schools rests not on the truth or value of religion, but on the fact that parents want their children to attend such schools, or the beneficial effects of having different kinds of school, or the developmental advantages to children of having a school curriculum or ethos that conveys similar messages to those they receive from their parents. In short, then, there might be neutral—what Rawls calls "public reason"—justifications for having an educational regime that includes religious schools funded out of general taxation.[15]

So, the simple argument needs buttressing with further responses to defences of state-funded religious schools that, at least at first sight, do not appeal to the intrinsic value of religion or some other contested view of human flourishing. Accordingly, the remainder of this section is devoted to an examination of what I take to be the most prominent neutral defences of religious schools.

3.1 Parents' Claims

One reply to the simple argument appeals to parental choice. It is not a violation of neutrality, some argue, if the state allows and funds parents to send their children to a school that engages in directive religious education; the state is not, thereby, endorsing any particular religion. Under this educational regime, the kinds of schools that are available would reflect the choices that parents make on behalf of their children. There would be schools that practise and promote Christianity, Judaism, Islam, Hinduism, Buddhism; there would also be schools animated by atheism and different humanist viewpoints. A regime of parental choice, then, permits the existence of a variety of different types of schools and escapes the charge that the state is aligning itself with a particular conception of the good. The appeal to the claims of parents is a feature of many arguments that seek to reconcile state-funded religious schools and political neutrality.[16]

To test whether an argument for state-financed religious schools represents a genuinely neutral justification, one that everyone can endorse in the light of her own conception of the good and consistently with regarding others as free and equal citizens, it is helpful to think about whether or not an individual who rejects religious views—an atheist, for example—can reasonably object to the argument offered for her being constrained by the policy. An initial objection she might make is that she is being forced to pay taxes to fund schooling that promotes (religious) doctrines she believes to be mistaken or, perhaps, ethically dangerous. But that objection would not work here, because although the policy does indeed allow the promotion of religious doctrines in state-funded schools, it is defended not on that basis but rather because it is good or right to satisfy the preferences parents have concerning how their children are educated.

In general, an anti-perfectionist critic of state-funded religious schools might offer two replies to arguments that purport to be neutral. First, she might argue that, contrary to appearances, the justification of such schools does after all rely on controversial claims about religion or the good life and, therefore, violates the requirement of neutral justification. Or, second, she might accept the anti-perfectionist credentials of a particular defence of such schools but argue that, nonetheless, the argument is unsuccessful for some other reason: for example, it might be that the reasons given for taxing citizens to fund religious schools are not reasons at all or are insufficiently weighty reasons to justify taxation. In what follows, I shall deploy both kinds of response.

3.1.1 Parental Preferences

The question we confront is whether an appeal to parents' interests is both neutral and gives us decisive reasons to favour the state-funding of religious schools. Let us review a couple of versions of the appeal to parental interests. First, consider an appeal to the good of satisfying parents' preferences. Some parents want their children to believe in and worship a particular god and, for that reason, it is valuable to make religious schools available through public finances. Is parental preference-satisfaction a successful neutral reason that cannot reasonably be rejected by our atheist taxpayer? I don't think it is.

It is worth noting that preference-satisfaction has received a bad press from anti-perfectionist liberals. The objection here is that the appeal to preference-satisfaction appears to rest on a controversial conception of the good. To see this, we ask: why should we judge how well off or disadvantaged an individual citizen is for the purposes of identifying just social policies by measuring the degree to which her preferences are fulfilled? One natural answer is that preference-satisfaction just is what makes one's life go well. But if that answer is given it is clear that the mooted justification is not neutral.[17] The view that preference-satisfaction constitutes human flourishing, or is indicative of it, is very controversial; many people deny that a life in which one's preferences are fulfilled more rather than less is to that extent a better or more successful life. Our atheist tax payer as well as many who have religious convictions can reasonably reject this defence of publicly funded religious schools.

Suppose the advocate of state-funded religious schools appealed to parental preference-satisfaction, not because preference-satisfaction is good for individuals but because it is a suitable reference point for judging how fairly the state is treating different citizens. According to this view, those with lower preference-satisfaction have a claim of justice to have opportunities redistributed from those who have greater preference-satisfaction. But now the argument has become entirely mysterious. It is unclear why the reference point for judging the justice of social policies should be preference-satisfaction, rather than something else, such as opportunities for education, health, and monetary resources at individuals' disposal, or certain capabilities to perform certain activities, or live a particular kind of life, or some mixture of these different conceptions.[18] There are very many problems with parental preference-satisfaction defences of state-funded religious schools.

3.1.2 The Right to Pursue One's Conception of the Good

Second, consider the view that a liberal society protects the freedom of individuals to pursue their particular conceptions of the good. One feature of many religious conceptions is that they claim that their followers ought to become parents who enrol the children in their custody into the religion in question. Thus, it might be thought that denying parents the right to choose a school that supports them in their enrolment mission violates religious adherents' right to practise their conception of the good.[19]

This seems to be the kind of argument anti-perfectionist defenders of publicly funded religious schools are looking for, because it doesn't appear to rest the argument on the fact that they promote particular religions, but rather on the state's reason to protect everyone's freedom to pursue her conception of the good. Of course, if the argument were successful, it would have to be generalized to fund the establishment of schools that enable non-religious parents to induct their children into their conceptions of the good. We might see the establishment of a raft of humanist schools, or schools that encourage pupils to pursue economic, sporting, or artistic success. But we can ignore these issues, I think, because notwithstanding its neutral credentials, the argument is suspect.

To see why, consider a society that distributes freedoms and resources to enable individuals to pursue their own conceptions of the good. Now add children to the picture. Children have a right to an education funded through general taxation. The argument from freedom to pursue one's conception of the good now needs to explain why parents, and only parents, are entitled to use the funds earmarked for children's schooling in pursuit of their conception of the good. Suppose taxpayers put in place an educational regime of the kind I have proposed, one in which schools are non-directive with respect to conceptions of the good. Might parents reasonably complain that such a regime violates their right to practise their conception of the good? It seems not. The political community owes educational provision to children, not parents, and, in fulfilling that requirement, it should proceed on the basis of norms that can be endorsed by everyone committed to freedom and equality. The right to pursue one's conception of the good does not imply a *parental* right to control some portion of the education resources the political community owes to children.

One reply to this argument trades on the observation that, in many societies, education is compulsory: religious parents' right to practise their conception of the good is violated by the legal requirement to give up their child to the state for many hours a day to conform with the requirement of compulsory schooling. Other individuals, those who have no children, suffer no similar loss of opportunity to practise their conception of the good.

In the next section, I shall address the more general issue of whether parents are morally permitted to enrol their child into their religious doctrine or conception of the good. I don't believe they are, but, here, I don't rely on that argument. Here, it is sufficient to note two things. First, the arrangements I am defending in this section do not necessarily legally require children to attend a neutral school; the requirement of compulsory education can, in principle, be satisfied by parents educating their child at home with their own resources. My argument against religious schools here relies on the thought that the political community's fulfilment of *its* educational duties to children need not be fulfilled on terms that enable parents to pursue their conception of the good more effectively. Second, even if, for some reason, a liberal society did require children to attend a state-funded neutral schools for a part of the day, that requirement would be justified by reference to the interests of the child in having the educational goods specified earlier, alongside the requirement that public funds be justified on the basis of ideals that are acceptable to everyone. Individuals—parents and non-parents alike—would remain legally free to use their just share of resources to pursue their conception of the good in ways consistent with the requirements of justice. So, the kind of neutralist liberalism I'm advancing involves respecting *adults'* right to pursue their conception of the good, but no special *parental* claim to public funds to direct children's lives.

I have suggested that arguments for the public funding of religious schools that appeal to parents' claims, either their right to pursue their conception of the good or their preference-satisfaction, are not likely to succeed. Perhaps there are other arguments that need to be assessed for a complete rebuttal. Nevertheless, I am confident that the considerations I have noted will generalize. These are: first, the child has independent moral status and claims against the community in virtue of that status; second, because the community's response to these claims constrains the activities of citizens, any policy it adopts must rely on reasons that can be shared; third, the claims of parents to control publicly provided educational funds will either rest on a controversial conception of the good (e.g. the first version of the argument from preference-satisfaction) or fail to justify the need for state-funded religious schools (e.g. the right to practise one's conception of the good does not imply a parental right to control public funds earmarked for children's schooling).

3.2 Children's Claims

I turn now to consider what I take to be more promising arguments for the state-funding of religious schools—those that rely on the claims that might be made on behalf of children.

3.2.1 The Value of Consonance between School and Home

Some have argued that children's interests are best satisfied if the conception of the good of the child's parents also animate the school—its composition, ethos, and curriculum, for example. This might be true for certain schools but not all schools. For example, MacMullen argues that there should be religious or ethical "consonance between school and home" in *primary* schools—until the child is about 11 years old—but not necessarily thereafter.[20] Advocates of the consonance argument typically appeal to a bundle of considerations: the thought that the child needs to be given some kind of "provisional identity" on the basis of which she can deliberate and learn what it is to have and pursue a conception of the good, and that identity-formation should be part of the school's remit; and the claim that to avoid the problem that the child might become disoriented, it is better if the school's identity-formation of the child does not compete with the formation that is offered within the family.[21]

According to this argument, then, the educational interests of children within religious families are damaged if they are denied at least an infant and junior school experience that matches the religious upbringing they receive within the home. Before assessing this defence of religious schools, let me make a few comments about it. First, it should be noted that at least certain versions of the consonance argument have good anti-perfectionist credentials—they appeal to values such as the child's development into an adult who possesses liberal civic and moral capacities and enjoys personal autonomy.

Second, notice that although these arguments are typically used to defend parental *choice*, it is not clear that they succeed in that respect. If it is genuinely important for a child's development that the messages she receives in school about religion should be the same as those within the home, then, putting aside issues concerning the difficulty of enforcing the policy, this is a reason to deny religious parents the option of sending their child to a school that is religiously neutral, or which promotes a religious or comprehensive conception different to the one they endorse.

Finally, as should be obvious, any final resolution of this dispute will rely on an investigation of the social and psychological facts about the need for consonance between school and home with respect to the conception of the good that is promoted. In that investigation, it is important to eliminate noise generated by variables that would be absent in a just society. For example, as we'll note in more detail later, some have argued that religious consonance between school and home protects or fosters a sense of self-respect in children who live in a society that generally discriminates against those who practise the particular religion in question.[22] At best, such arguments support the retention of religious schools in non-ideal circumstances, but they are insufficient to justify the existence of religious schools in an ideal society free of discrimination.

I don't know of any noise-free study of the consonance hypothesis, so cannot give a knock-down case against it. Still, it is worth clarifying the argument and stating my hunch that it is mistaken. First, it is worth clarifying the meaning of "identity-formation". For the defence of religious schools to work, it needs to be established that to develop the capacity to reflect on, revise, and pursue a particular conception of the good, the child needs to be initiated into a particular conception of the good. It is also worth noting that the society advocated by anti-perfectionist liberals is not hostile to every kind of identity-formation. Indeed, we want children to become deeply committed to quite specific norms of justice—to comply with and support a raft of laws that protect civil, political, and socio-economic rights. To the extent that the argument from consonance relies on the thought that children must know what it is like to be committed to a set of values and norms on the basis of which they can learn to evaluate others they encounter, it is unclear why initiation into liberal democratic values is not enough.

Second, there are stronger and weaker interpretations of what counts as consonance between school and home. A strong interpretation holds that the child's development suffers if her school *fails to reinforce* her parents' religious values. A weaker interpretation holds that the school *must not gainsay* her parents' religious convictions. Now, the weaker version is of no help to the advocate of religious schools, because it's fulfilled by schools that teach about different religious views and direct children towards various political virtues, but refuse to direct its pupils towards any particular religion or conception of the good. If home–school consonance is compatible with non-direction, then this argument for religious schools fails because neutral schools are not in tension with it.

The strong interpretation seems mistaken. There are countless parents who go out of their way to choose schools that expose their child from a very young age to religious and ethical viewpoints that are different to those they affirm, not only to give her the opportunity to learn to respect individuals who live life differently, but also to develop an awareness that their (the parents') conception is one she should reflect on and accept or reject on the basis of her own evaluation. The consonance argument for religious schools needs to claim that children who go through that kind of schooling are less well served than those who attend schools that reinforce the directive religious teaching they receive in the home. I would like to see the evidence that sustains such a strong claim.

3.2.2 The Benefits of Diversity in Schooling
Following J. S. Mill's ideas, a different public reason argument for religious schools appeals to the benefits of diversity in schooling. Children are entitled to the educational goods we've listed: the capacity to sustain themselves economically, various moral and political virtues, and the capacity to engage in independent reflection and pursuit of a conception of the good. The diversity argument for religious schools is that an educational regime that includes multiple independent providers pursuing different experiments in schooling, alongside parental choice between the various schools, will tend to promote these educational outcomes better than a regime that prohibits schools that instruct students in a particular religion. As Mill suggests, encouraging experiments in living and allowing individuals to choose between them is our best bet for exchanging "error for truth".[23] Similarly, we might learn from our own and others' educational successes or mistakes. A society that lets "a thousand flowers (schools) bloom" will deliver what we want from education better than an educational regime without publicly

funded faith schools. Thus, advocates of religious schools can appeal to the good consequences that follow from there being diverse providers of education.

In the next section, I elaborate an argument that appeals to the child's claim to a neutral upbringing, which challenges this defence of religious schooling. According to that argument, notwithstanding the society-wide educational benefits of religious schools, it constitutes a non-consequentialist wrong to the child to enrol her into a controversial conception of the good. But, as before, I put that argument aside for now.

Like the consonance argument, the success or failure of the diversity argument for religious schools turns on certain non-normative facts. We need to know whether more, rather than less, diversity in schooling is beneficial with respect to the production of good educational outcomes and, in particular, whether the right kind of diversity would be sustained by the involvement of religious organizations in the provision of schooling. In the first place, we might worry that the involvement of influential religious organizations might diminish educational diversity compared to alternative arrangements. In the UK, for example, the Church of England and the Catholic Church are major suppliers of publicly funded schools. Comparing different Church of England schools, for example, the admissions policies, ethos, and curriculums might be remarkably similar. Of course, the similarities between different Church schools might be explained by other factors, such as the presence of a national curriculum in England. Nevertheless, my thought is that it is not obvious that the participation of well-resourced religious institutions within the publicly funded school system improves, rather than impedes, the kind of diversity that fuels educational progress compared to a regime in which all schools are neutral with respect to religion.

Secondly, we need to identify what kind of diversity is valuable. It would be wrong straightforwardly to read off an education policy from a general account of the progressive properties of experimentation for society. Mill's appeal to a marketplace of ideas is nested within a utilitarian moral theory, which liberal anti-perfectionists reject. They reject it because what might be good for society as a whole may be disastrous for particular individuals. Anti-perfectionists tend to emphasize the "separateness of persons" and are concerned with the fate of each and every citizen rather than the aggregate good of society. In the case of schooling, the worry is that if an education experiment fails, particular individuals are harmed or wronged, perhaps seriously, by being denied an appropriate education. To be sure, diversity in schooling has its place and, no doubt, there are good arguments against uniform, data-driven approaches to education that have been favoured in education over the past few decades.[24] Nevertheless, anti-perfectionist ideals draw a limit to the extent of permissible diversity.

Lastly, it is important not to draw hasty conclusions about this debate. Some who make the argument from diversity point to the bland uniformity of non-religious schools *that exist here and now* and their inattention to spiritual, moral, and ethical questions. They point out that religious schools offer something genuinely distinctive. In reply, an anti-perfectionist critic of state-funded religious schools might observe that under *ideal* educational arrangements spiritual, ethical, and moral questions would be addressed more systematically than they are under current arrangements and, while directive religious instruction would not be part of that provision, there would be plenty of opportunity for schools to specialize in different kinds of education as their students develop. As I shall argue in Section 5, the argument for religious schools looks better when those schools are compared to non-religious schools as they operate here and now than when they are compared to religiously neutral schools as they might be. For now, it is enough to ask why the right kind of diversity in schooling is not possible within a school system that does not include directive religious schools.

I have reviewed some arguments that purport to give the right kind of justification of schools that aim to direct children towards belief in controversial conceptions of the good. My review is incomplete. Consequently, it might be possible for advocates of state-funded religious schools to offer other arguments that satisfy the demands of justificatory neutrality. As suggested above, I believe that child-centred arguments are more promising than those that appeal to the interests of parents. Nevertheless, there is a standing challenge to child-centred arguments for religious schools: they need to explain why the purported neutrally defined benefits of directive religious schooling cannot be delivered without religious direction. That's a difficult challenge to meet.

3.3 Citizen Educational Vouchers

Before addressing private religious schools, it is worth briefly considering a third kind of response to the simple argument, one which emphasizes the claims of *citizens*. Perhaps state-funded religious schools can be defended as part of a scheme that distributes educational vouchers to citizens who may use them to fund schools that promote the conceptions of the good they favour. School voucher schemes that exist today enable *parents* to fund schools they want their children to attend. If the arguments above are sound, then the case for giving parents the right to an allocation of public funds to maintain schools of their choice is unconvincing. Still, we can imagine a different kind of voucher scheme in which each citizen has the opportunity to allocate an equal share of public funds to pay for schools that direct children towards the conception of the good she favours. Under that scheme, there would be a range of different schools in society, some of which promote while others discourage religious observance.[25] Such a scheme would be consistent with the principle of neutrality, it seems, because the state would not be recognizing or promoting any particular conception of the good; it would be individual citizens who would be using their fair allocation of educational resources to promote their distinctive views concerning religion and human flourishing.

Notwithstanding its neutral credentials, the voucher scheme would, in all likelihood, have poor educational consequences. The scheme would allow childless citizens to fund schools that promote their favoured conception of the good, which may well be different to the kinds of school preferred by parents. To take an extreme case, imagine a society in which childless evangelical atheists account for half the citizenry but the overwhelming majority of parents are religious. In such a society, we might expect about half the state-funded schools to be ones that actively steer their students away from forming religious beliefs or goals. Many religious parents would face the prospect of having to send their child to schools that try to undermine the messages they promote at home. That is likely to generate various tensions between home and school to the detriment of the child's education and family life. A school system that is non-directive with respect to religion, which refused either to promote or discourage particular conceptions of the good, would, it seems, elicit greater cooperation and enthusiasm from parents with consequent educational benefits for children.

Even if practical concerns about the scheme can be resolved, however, we should reject citizen educational vouchers for violating children's political autonomy which, as established above, is an important justification of political neutrality. No doubt, the scheme would provide every citizen with an equal opportunity to promote her conception of the good by establishing schools that try to recruit the next generation to her particular view. But it remains problematic because it would force some students to attend schools that favour particular religions or conceptions of the good that they reject, if not now then in the future. Under the scheme, students might be forced to participate in religious rites that go against their emerging beliefs or be forced to study a curriculum that promotes a particular conception of the good they believe is unworthy of pursuit. Even if the students do not presently object to the schooling they receive, as I shall argue in the next section in connection with private religious schools, they might as adults retrospectively reject the religious ideals they were forced to follow and learn as a child. In that respect, for part of their lives, some individuals would be forced by others—in this case by citizens who fund schools in order to promote particular conceptions of the good—to follow conceptions of the good they believe are misguided or anathema to them. That would be a violation of the non-consequentialist ideal of political autonomy.

Discussing citizen educational vouchers enables us to see that there is more to anti-perfectionist liberalism than the principle of neutrality. Children have interests in being schooled in a way that develops their sense of justice and their capacity to fashion for themselves, on the basis of appropriate reflection, their own conception of the good. But they also have the right to political autonomy, to live under laws and policies justified by ideals they can accept whilst regarding themselves as free and equal citizens and in light of the distinctive conception of the good they go on to hold in their lives. Indeed, the argument from political autonomy is an argument against all religious schools, whether the school is funded by the political community or privately by religious organizations or parents. Since the argument from political autonomy is best illustrated by examining the moral principles that regulate parental conduct, I now turn to that issue and related questions concerning privately funded religious schools.

4. Against Private Religious Schools

In Section 3, I argued that if it is important that reasonable citizens accept the justification of the rules that govern them it is difficult to see how the public funding of schools that prioritize distinctive ethical or religious values can be justified. But that doesn't imply that all religious schools should be legally prohibited. A state that refused to recognize or promote a particular religion through the schools it funds with the use of public money might allow the existence of *privately funded* religious schools. In such a society one might expect to see a mixed educational regime. First, there would be a state sector in which schools and teachers educate in a neutral way, not taking a stand on the merits of different conceptions of religion, occupation, sexuality, or leisure pursuits and, instead, concentrating on enhancing pupils' capacities to develop and exercise a sense of justice and their own independent judgment about these further matters. Second, it's likely that there would be a range of private schools that cater for parents who want their children to be directed towards distinctive conceptions of the good.

However, as noted above, there is another dimension to the issue of anti-perfectionist liberalism and children, which challenges the mixed regime so described. In other work, I have suggested that the relationship between parents and children is similar to the state–citizen relationship in morally relevant ways and, because that's the case, parents are duty-bound to remain neutral when raising their children. If the extension of neutrality to regulate parental conduct is sound, then the justice of privately provided religious schools is also called into question.[26]

What is it about the state's relationship with its citizens that supports political neutrality? Rawls' argument rests on the observation that the relationship is non-voluntary, coercive, and profoundly affects the life chances and values of citizens.[27] First, it is non-voluntary because, putting aside complicating cases raised by migration, most citizens have no choice with respect to the political arrangements that govern their lives: they are born into them and escaping from them is often very difficult or costly. Second, the state exercises considerable power and coercion over the lives of citizens by enacting and enforcing laws. Finally, the laws of a society profoundly affect the life chances of different citizens and the values they come to hold. As reviewed above, Rawls' ideal of political autonomy demands that the state–citizen relationship be regulated by neutral principles of justice that can be endorsed by every reasonable citizen regardless of the distinctive conception of the good or religion she practises.

The argument for *parental* neutrality begins by noting that the three features Rawls believes justify the need for political autonomy and, therefore, neutrality, are also present in the relationship between parents and children. First, a child's membership of the family in which she is raised is non-voluntary—she is either born into it or allocated to it by prevailing adoption arrangements, and there are few opportunities to leave it in childhood. Second, parents exercise force and, sometimes, coercion over the child they raise. Although she often takes more control over her life as she develops into youth, the characteristics of a young child's life—the activities she engages in, the children she plays with, the books she reads, and so on—are largely chosen for her by her parents. Indeed, it is often necessary that parents make these coercive choices for the sake of the child's development. Furthermore, these decisions can significantly affect her life chances and her values. If Rawls is right that these features support the need for regulatory and foundational principles that can be endorsed by those they affect, then it seems that the principles that apply to parenting must similarly be ones that are acceptable to the children over whom parental power is exercised.

This argument faces the challenge that political autonomy is important to realize only for those who are capable of enjoying it. Because many children, particularly young children, lack well-formed beliefs and values, they are incapable of enjoying political autonomy in the sense of endorsing the coercive rules that constrain their lives in the light of their own well-formed conception of the good. For that reason, parents need not worry about constraining their conduct out of respect for the political autonomy of their children.[28]

This objection proceeds too quickly. Even though a young child is incapable of endorsing the principles that guide her parents' conduct, in the course of a human life that extends into adulthood she will be able later to review and endorse or reject the principles that governed her upbringing. Since that's the case, according to the ideal of political autonomy her parents must regulate their conduct as parents by principles that aren't *retrospectively* rejected by their child. It is morally important for us as adults to be able to look back and see that as children we were governed by ideals and principles that don't go against the religious or ethical views we hold now.

The retrospective application of political autonomy supports an extension of the principle of neutrality to parenting. Parents cannot know the particular religious doctrine or view of the good life around which their child will organize her life as an adult. It appears, then, that they are duty-bound to parent according to values and principles their child can retrospectively endorse regardless of the specific conception of the good she adopts later in life. In short, they must observe the principle of *parental neutrality*.[29]

What does parental neutrality demand? In the first instance, it is important to note how revolutionary the ideal is compared to current practice. The majority of parents throughout the world regard themselves as morally permitted to raise and educate their children so that they come to know the truth about religion and how to make a success of their lives. The principle of parental neutrality takes a different view. It claims that parents should disregard certain kinds of knowledge when it comes to raising their child. For the sake of her political autonomy, they must exclude from consideration even sound convictions about religion and raise their child according to reasons that she can later share regardless of the religious or ethical ideals that guide her life. So, parents must not baptize their children or educate them directively, that is, school them with the aim that they endorse and practise a particular faith. Similarly, atheists may not design an upbringing for their children that encourages them to reject theism or religion.

Notice, however, that parental neutrality is not the same as its political counterpart. In the family context, children have an interest in developing an intimate relationship with their parents.[30] For that reason, even though they do not aim to recruit their children to a particular view of religion, the role of parents is to care for children, to develop their sense of justice and to attend to their specific needs and interests. For the sake of a flourishing, intimate relationship between parent and child, which aids the development of the child into an independent and morally motivated individual, neutral parents should not display the same kind of impartiality and foresight as neutral judges or politicians do. Accordingly, if neutrality ought to regulate parental conduct, the ideal needs to be elaborated in a way that is tailored to the specific roles parents play in society.[31]

In addition, anti-perfectionists who advocate parental neutrality are also liberals who support arrangements that develop the child's civic and moral capacities and her personal autonomy. For that reason, parental neutralists would join with those who advocate that every child receives an upbringing that preserves for her an "open future" with respect to religious affiliation;[32] and they would also insist on the cultivation of a sense of morality and justice—the disposition to treat others with concern and respect.

One prominent argument against parental neutrality is that the kind of parent–child intimacy that is required for children to develop into just and independent adults permits or requires parents to induct their child into their own religious or irreligious conception of the good. We simply do not have familial intimacy of the right sort if parents are not morally permitted to enrol their child into the religion they practise or shape her views in accordance with that religion so that all family members can get to know each other well and jointly pursue shared goals and projects. Or so the argument goes.[33]

The appeal to familial intimacy doesn't give us reasons to exempt parents from the duty to raise their children neutrally. I don't deny that a child needs an intimate relationship with her parents in which they reveal their conception of the good to her and family members share some pursuits in common. However, intimacy is compatible with parental neutrality. Parents can reveal their religious commitments to their child without making her practise them and without intentionally encouraging her to share them. And there are plenty of activities and goals they can share with their child without making her pursue their religious commitments. The neutralist view includes many moral and political ideals that follow from concern and respect for everyone in society, which parents can pursue with their child. And, of course, as she develops, the child adopts many enthusiasms of her own; parents can help her to accomplish *her* goals and projects. So, parental neutrality is not inconsistent with the maintenance of intimate family relationships that are so important for children's development.

A different prominent objection claims that parental neutrality places unreasonable costs on parents. For example, religious parents who regard themselves as under a duty raise their children according to the beliefs and rites of their religion would be morally forbidden from doing so; they wouldn't be able to live according to the dictates of their conscience. This objection is reminiscent of the argument from the right to pursue one's conception of the good, and my reply is similar. The principle of parental neutrality doesn't require adults who are parents to give up the religious convictions that animate their lives. Every adult is permitted to adopt and pursue a particular religion. However, they aren't permitted to treat the character of someone else's life—their child's life—as if it's theirs to choose. The right to follow one's conscience is a profoundly important right, but it does not extend to permitting people with power and authority over others to impose their conscience on them.

Let us turn, finally, to the question of the justice of religious schools that are privately funded by parents or religious organizations. It is important to note that the argument for parental neutrality concerns how parents ought to treat their children. It has not yet said anything about legal issues and, in particular, about whether the law should allow private religious schools. For example, it might be that, although it is unjust for parents to enrol their children into the traditions and practices of a particular religion, they should be legally free to do so.

That position is certainly coherent, but is it plausible? Would it wrong parents or children if the community legally prohibited such schools? I have argued that children have a weighty moral claim against being enrolled into a controversial conception of the good and parents have no moral right to enrol them. If I am right, then the question is whether parents should enjoy a legal right to wrong their child. The argument for the legal permissibility of private schools would need to establish that, notwithstanding the moral wrongness of parents opting for schooling that directs their child towards a particular religion, it is unjust for the political community to interfere with such enrolling activity.

That argument can be successfully prosecuted in some related cases. The injustice of the religious enrolment of children does not give the political community a conclusive reason to set up video recorders in people's homes or in religious buildings to check that people are acting justly and to enforce compliance with parental neutrality. But here we are not discussing what goes on in the home, church, or mosque, but rather what goes on in schools. I take it for granted that privately funded schools, and indeed home education, fall within the regulatory gaze of the state, at least in reasonably just societies. The state is permitted to inspect and enforce standards with respect to how private schools are governed to ensure their policies concerning admissions, inclusion, discrimination, child protection, and so on, and the quality of their teaching, are appropriate. Given that it already has a duty to regulate such schools, it does not appear too intrusive for the state to enforce the child's claim not to be enrolled into a particular religion.[34]

I have offered arguments against both state- and privately funded religious schools. No doubt, my arguments are incomplete. My main aim has been to set out the nature and appeal of anti-perfectionist liberal political morality and to show how, in different ways, its principles require religiously neutral schools. My argument against private religious schools (and the citizen voucher scheme), which appeals to the child's moral claim to political autonomy, is more controversial than my arguments against state-funded religious schools. It is worth noting that if my child-centred case against religious enrolment succeeds, arguments against the public funding of religious schools, which appeal to the reasonable complaints of other citizens, are not needed. It is also important to note, however, that the case against state-funded religious schools does not rely on the argument for parental neutrality. One can maintain a hostile stance towards state-funded religious schools in ways that are compatible with the view that parents should enjoy the legal right to spend their own money on schooling that helps them to enrol their children into a particular religion.[35] Still, I offer both arguments here, not least because I believe both to be sound.

5. Arguments for Phased Abolition

For the reasons given, I believe an ideal political community would prohibit both state-funded and private religious schools. But it doesn't follow that societies should prohibit such schools here and now. When we consider principles that apply to the unjust world in which we live, we must take into account certain facts that wouldn't exist in an ideal world. Some of these facts, I argue, give us reason to be cautious about the abolition of religious schools. Consequently, although I believe that religious schools should eventually be prohibited, their disappearance should coincide with other developments in education, politics, and society that ensure that the positive features that religious schools bring to current societies are not lost. Here, I identify some of the valuable roles religious schools play in contemporary society to illustrate how the case for the prohibition of religious schools is more complicated than might be thought.

5.1 Resources

At the most mundane level, religious schools that currently exist contribute resources to the education system of a society. Other things being equal, their abolition would diminish, perhaps considerably, the level of funding devoted to the education of children. Many religious schools are privately funded. Other religious schools pay some, but not all, of the costs of their pupils' education. Either way, it is likely that, without putting in place compensatory measures, the prohibition of religious schools would involve fewer resources being devoted to children's schooling.

The expected loss of resources is explained by the fact that parents and religious institutions are prepared to invest more in schools that promote their religious viewpoint compared to schools that don't. That motive may not be a universal one. Some religious organizations are changing their attitude towards the schools they run. For example, Nigel Genders, the Church of England's Chief Education Officer has stated that "our schools are not faith schools for Christians, but Church schools for all".[36] The Church of England now sees itself as having a (religious) mission to educate the young and is, for example, gradually abandoning admissions policies that discriminate in favour of pupils whose parents are practising Christians. Although such schools don't exhibit religious neutrality in their curriculum, it might be that some can be persuaded to continue to fund schools that are genuinely neutral. Still, it's likely that many religious organizations would withdraw from the education sector if they weren't legally allowed to run schools that enrol pupils into their particular traditions, rites and beliefs.[37]

The loss of educational funding we can expect from prohibiting religious schools is not a serious objection to the case for their prohibition. Compare the campaign against exploitation in the workplace. Advocates of a minimum wage, for example, face the objection that if employers are required to pay a decent wage to their workers, they will employ fewer workers. One response to that possibility is for the larger community to ensure that no one has less than an adequate share of resources, whether they are in work or not. Similarly, in our case, the right response to religious organizations or parents who threaten to withdraw money from the education sector if they cannot use it to promote their particular religious view is for the political community to fund an appropriate neutral liberal education for every child.

The resource issue, then, can easily be resolved in theory. However, it is worth noting that in certain environments—I have in mind the recent politics of many countries that have pursued economic policies that significantly (and unjustly) decrease the level of public spending across the board—citizens are unwilling to fund education to the degree required by justice. One can imagine cases in which the level of funding provided by religious organizations is so high, and the appetite of citizens to fill the funding gap that would be left by these organizations' withdrawal from the sector so low, that the promotion of liberal ideals through education would be best served by working to regulate religious schools rather than by abolishing them. That would be acquiescence in the face of injustice, but acquiescence is sometimes rational.[38]

5.2 Inclusion in a Competitive Educational Environment

Religious schools can, and often do, act as a bulwark against unjust or indecent practices that are encouraged by educational markets. As the educational commentator Fiona Millar notes,

> if you put schools into a market and expect them to compete, you probably shouldn't be surprised if they use the tools of the market to succeed, even if this means weeding out what might be perceived as the weak raw material—otherwise known as real children—before prized exam results become public.[39]

The context of Millar's remarks is England's educational market where schools compete for students in a regime in which the test results of its pupils are published and routinely used as an important indicator of quality by the national inspection body. She documents the common practice of "off-rolling" whereby pupils who will not succeed to the standard that is beneficial for the school are removed from the school roll before the census date that is used to fix the school cohort whose performance is the "quality" indicator.

Off-rolling has, for some time, been widespread in English state-funded schools and in the US public school system;[40] it has been a characteristic of private schools for far longer. It is part of a wider set of tools school managers use to game the system for the benefit of the school (and themselves). Students who are difficult or costly to teach to the standard that reaps benefits for the school might not be admitted to a school, they might be excluded for bad behaviour, or their parents asked to withdraw their child because "she would be better off being educated elsewhere". And children who disrupt the learning of other pupils are often excluded to preserve the school's ability to achieve the relevant standards of academic success for the cohort overall. Schools respond to incentives to achieve good results by choosing students who are easier to educate rather than by treating their intake as given and seeking to do the best they can for the pupils they have.

These competitive practices are problematic in many respects. I mention two. In the first place, it means that the published academic results of schools—how many of their pupils achieve or exceed national standards, for example—cannot be taken to be an indicator of *educational* success, because we cannot tell whether the results are evidence of good or poor teaching or, rather, the schools' ability to cherry-pick students who are easy to teach or already well educated. Second, more importantly, the system exacerbates the injustices suffered by the disadvantaged. As Millar notes, excluded individuals or those who are refused admission in such a regime are "real children" and, indeed, often children who are disadvantaged by poverty or learning differences not of their choosing. A just society would prioritize rather than ignore the interests of disadvantaged children. But educational markets as they currently operate encourage schools to behave in ways that go against the demands of justice.[41]

Religious schools are often motivated by an ethos of service rather than narrowly interpreted economic gain or prestige. Of course, this is a generalization. No doubt, some, perhaps many, religious schools seek to game the system as much as non-religious schools, and many non-religious schools steadfastly refuse to play the results game.[42] Nevertheless, in general, one would expect religious schools, particularly those associated with religions that are inclusive, hospitable, egalitarian, or concerned with the fate of the disadvantaged, to be more likely to act as educational refuges for children excluded by self-serving schools because they are deemed disruptive or have educational needs that are costly to satisfy. There is some evidence to suggest that religious schools are, indeed, providing opportunities to pupils who would otherwise be casualties of the educational market, at least as it is practised in England.[43] If so, that's a significant positive outcome of having religious schools in our unjust world.

If religious schools are serving the interests of less advantaged children in the way described above, then the case for their prohibition must be conditional: religious schools should disappear when, but only when, provision is made to cater for the educational needs of all children, particularly the disadvantaged and those who are difficult or costly to teach.

We can think of various ways in which a fairer educational regime might be achieved. Some have suggested that educational markets are not, in themselves, problematic. They argue that they might be organized in ways that promote rather than impede the realization of educational justice. They point out that education policy might financially penalize schools who have particularly high levels of exclusion; or it might reward schools that admit pupils from disadvantaged backgrounds; and so on.[44]

A different kind of institutional solution would be to pursue a non-market-based approach to schooling. Perhaps justice is best served by an education policy that recruits and maintains well-educated, highly paid, and respected teachers for whom education is a vocation rather than simply a means of self-interested gain. Maintaining such a workforce and proceeding without league tables and parental choice between schools might satisfy the requirements of educational justice, or at least realize them better than current arrangements that create many perverse incentives.[45]

We need not pursue these matters here. My point is that we should remove religious schools only in sequence with other educational developments that ensure that the benefits that religious schools deliver to those excluded by current arrangements are not lost.

5.3 Self-Respect in the Face of Discrimination

Relatedly, some have argued that religious schools can be a safe haven for children who suffer religious or racial discrimination. For example, Michael Merry argues that, notwithstanding the risk of religious indoctrination they present, separate Muslim schools should be encouraged to avoid the harm of stigmatization that Muslim pupils would suffer if they were educated in religiously neutral common schools within existing societies in which discrimination against Muslim minorities is widespread. Muslim schools are safe havens, he claims, for several reasons: they provide environments that are free of discrimination, which, among other things, prevent Muslim pupils from internalizing the stigmatizing dominant culture; they are staffed by teachers who have "cultural competence", a better understanding of the challenges faced by Muslim pupils; and they provide environments in which pupils can reflect with others who face similar injustices and consider how to resist discrimination.[46]

Merry's argument should be taken seriously, because, as Rawls suggests, self-respect is perhaps the most important good a society should protect.[47] It is of the utmost value that individuals view themselves as having equal moral importance to others, that they have confidence in their ability to adopt and pursue a reasonable life-plan regardless of its content, and that they do not experience shame for having a particular ethnic heritage. If the maintenance of neutral common schools for the sake of individuals' political autonomy threatened the self-respect of stigmatized groups in societies, then that would be a serious objection to them. The prohibition of religious schools should, therefore, be conditional upon arrangements being in place that sustain the self-respect of groups that suffer discrimination in the wider society.

How serious a constraint on the campaign against religious schools is the duty to promote and maintain the self-respect of all pupils? It might be that the duty to promote self-respect speaks in favour of separate schooling for certain groups in certain unjust societies, but not for others in other non-ideal societies. It has been shown, for example, that the educational integration of pupils with different ethnic heritages can be helpful for encouraging trust and respect.[48] To the extent that the self-respect of minority groups is threatened by discrimination by the majority in society, which is, in turn, explained by fear, distrust, and misunderstanding, the existence of separate, segregated schools appears to be counterproductive. If so, then self-respect for all might be promoted, rather than impeded, by the abolition of religious schools. Still, critics of religious schools must be mindful of the important consideration of self-respect.

5.4 Moral and Political Education

Finally, a common argument for religious schools is that they provide better education with respect to civic and moral development compared to non-religious schools, at least those in many educational regimes here and now. A central feature of many religions is that they provide opportunities to reflect on, and codes that inform, how one ought to treat others. For example, many religions recommend or require individuals to be charitable and display concern and respect for others. This represents a directive education in which pupils are encouraged to embrace moral values that ask pupils to reign in the pursuit of their self-interest for the sake of others.

It is vital for the promotion and maintenance of a just society that schools provide directive moral education that is centred on the recognition that individuals have claims to freedom and equality. Citizens ought to vote for, and in other ways promote, arrangements in which everyone enjoys civic freedoms to reflect on and pursue their own distinctive conception of the good, the right to participate as an equal in society, and a fair share of resources. Now, as I have argued, directive religious schools are problematic in various ways, because they deny individuals' political autonomy: if they are state-funded, they force the non-religious to fund schooling that promotes metaphysical or ethical views they believe to be mistaken; and private religious schools impose on the child views that they might later reject as unworthy of pursuit. Indeed, although it is important for pupils to acquire a sense of morality and justice—a sense of their obligations and duties to others as well as of the rights they enjoy—this sense *can* be imparted without the controversial inflection that religions give morality. We do not have to believe in a god to be brought to the view that we ought to distribute resources fairly or to respect other people's choices in life. Rather, the neutralist liberal argument is that pupils can be taught to adopt the right moral norms without schools' taking a stand on further disputes concerning the existence of gods or their relevance for our moral duties.

The liberal view, then, is that, ideally, individuals should be taught to embrace liberal values in a religiously neutral way, in a way that does not tie those values to particular religious or ethical doctrines. But how should we proceed if the neutral schools that are available *here and now* are good at respecting religious neutrality but poor at encouraging pupils to develop concern and respect for others? In that scenario, we would face a hard choice between, on the one hand, maintaining religious schools that violate neutrality but do a good job of encouraging a sense of justice, and, on the other, neutral schools that are less good at developing their pupils' civic and moral capacities.

The hard choice is not merely hypothetical. There is sometimes reluctance on the part of many state-funded schools in various countries to engage in directive moral education. Many teachers in neutral schools that exist in various countries here and now worry about engaging in directive moral teaching. They say that there is a disagreement about whether everyone should have access to housing, health care, education, and so on, and that fact is a reason for them not to direct their pupils towards a particular view of justice. More worryingly, governments require state-employed teachers not to promote any particular conception of socio-economic justice.[49] That is a deeply unfortunate state of affairs, because living together in a just society depends on individuals' coming to embrace the moral norm that universal access to these and other goods is an enforceable entitlement, and directive moral education is essential for that outcome reliably to be achieved.

If we face a choice in schooling between maintaining religious neutrality and moral education that promotes and sustains a liberal society, it is likely that we should side with the latter. To be clear, the hard choice we face is avoidable and, indeed, many religiously neutral schools no doubt do a good job with respect to liberal moral education. However, where religious schools do better with respect to creating a liberal citizenry compared to neutral schools, we need to think twice before prohibiting them. This is another illustration of how the removal of religious schools needs to proceed in sequence with enhancements to the moral education offered by neutral schools so that the liberal project is not jeopardized.[50]

6. Conclusion

I have emphasized the ways in which critics of religious schools should be attentive to the valuable features of such schools in unjust circumstances. Religious schools should be phased out, I have argued, but that process should proceed in tandem with the introduction of arrangements in religiously neutral schools that match the positive roles played by religious schools in our world. Nevertheless, I have also argued that religious schools are fundamentally unjust, because their existence violates the political autonomy of many citizens and all children. Even if we should be reluctant to prohibit them in certain non-ideal circumstances, we should work to establish conditions under which they can be prohibited. After all, religious schools would not be allowed to exist in an ideal society.

How to Think about Religious Schools: Principles and Policies. Matthew Clayton, Andrew Mason, and Adam Swift, Oxford University Press. © Matthew Clayton, Andrew Mason, and Adam Swift 2024.
DOI: 10.1093/9780198924036.003.0004

5

Parents' Rights, Children's Schools

Adam Swift

When they are born, children have no religious views and they cannot identify as members of a religion. They become adherents of a religion—they
come to engage in certain practices or endorse certain beliefs—just as they
become atheists or agnostics: through a process of socialization, and
upbringing, and education. Religious freedom is hugely important; people
must be at liberty to act on their religious beliefs (or lack of them). But that
leaves a question about parents' rights to raise other people—their children—in ways that reflect their own beliefs.

Liberal political philosophy struggles with that question. Its core thought
is that individuals should exercise their own judgment about how they are
to live. One of the things that many choose to do with their lives, and one
that many regard as among their most important life projects, is to raise
children—and to exercise their own judgment about how to raise them. But
parental rights are rights over others, others who have no realistic exit
option and whose interest in making their own judgments about how they
are to live their lives is no less important than that of the adults raising them.

It is difficult to know how to strike the right balance between the interests
of parents and children, but that task is all the more challenging because
children's healthy development itself depends on their experiencing a very
special kind of relationship with their parents. I will argue that, to become
autonomous individuals, children need to grow up identifying with, and
developing strong attachments towards, those who exercise authority over
them. If that is right, then the kind of parent–child relationship that serves
children's interest in developing autonomy can itself pose a threat to that
interest. Any plausible theory of parents' rights must attend to the complex
ways in which the agency of parents and children, and their well-being, are
bound together.

This book is about religious schooling, and this chapter will indeed
deliver conclusions about that. But arguments about religious schools tend
to take for granted deep background assumptions that unduly constrain our

thinking and themselves require critical attention. To answer questions about when the state may step in to limit parents' authority over their children—for example, by regulating the kind of schooling children may receive—we need to understand why they should get to exercise *any* authority. Nobody thinks that it would be permissible for me to raise your child in my religion. Why should I get to do that to mine? *Should* I get to do that to mine?

I start from a basic commitment to liberal equality. The "liberal" element means that it is important that people are free to form, critically reflect on, and act in accordance with their own judgments about how to live.[1] They should be authors of their own lives, allowed and encouraged to develop the capacity for autonomy, without coercion or undue interference by others; it is part of the state's function to protect and nurture that capacity. As we suggested in Chapter 2, the case for autonomy is overdetermined. On the one hand, in consequentialist terms, autonomy contributes to people's well-being—whether instrumentally in helping them choose and live a life that goes well, or intrinsically in being itself part of a good life (or both). On the other hand, from a non-consequentialist perspective, people are morally entitled to develop and exercise their capacity to judge for themselves how they are to live their lives, whether or not their lives go better as a result. The "equality" element means that each person counts equally—nobody's freedom is more important than anybody else's and, from the state's point of view, each person's living the life of her choice matters equally.

This vision, originally developed to liberate citizens from an overbearing state founded on hierarchy, has been extended to the sphere formerly regarded as "private" with transformative implications for relations between men and women, but it has not yet had the same impact on relations between parents and children. Many children today are a bit like women were in the not-so-distant past, victims of an ideology that failed to recognize their claims to liberty and equality. We continue to grant parents extensive rights to control their children—including the right deliberately to inculcate the parents' own views in ways that inhibit the development of children's capacity to exercise or act on their own judgment about how they are to live their lives when they reach adulthood. And we fail to treat children as equal in importance with their parents: although we intervene to prevent abuse or neglect, we routinely allow children to be subordinated to their parents' projects, to be treated as vehicles through which parents may seek to realize their own ideas about how to live. Advocates of school choice, for example, typically invoke the importance of parents' getting to choose their children's schools as if what mattered was the satisfaction of parents' preferences rather than the interests of those subject to their choices.

Tackling questions about religious schooling forces us back to philosophical basics. To decide whether parents have the right to send their children to a religious school, or to one that teaches that all religion is a delusion, we need to know what rights they have with respect to their children's upbringing in general. We need to think about why parents should get to exercise *any* authority in that—and indeed in any other—domain.[2]

My answer will appeal to the goods—"familial relationship goods"—that can be realized in parent–child relationships.[3] These are not goods like cars or washing machines; they are goods simply in being good for people—aspects of people's lives that make those lives go well rather than badly. Only by understanding why it's valuable that children should have parents at all can we think seriously about what rights parents should have to do things to, with, and for their children. Only then can we assess claims about the extent of their right to influence their children's emerging values, and only with that assessment in place can we work through the implications for religious schooling.

To develop the very capacities that liberals value, children need an intimate-but-authoritative relationship with particular adults. So those committed to liberal equality do not deny that parents should have the right to exercise considerable control over their children's lives. Some discretionary authority—unmonitored by others, and to some extent unmonitored even by themselves—is essential if parents are to play their role in their children's healthy development. As standardly framed, the philosophical challenge is to identify the proper limits on parents' authority over their children; to strike the right balance between respecting parents' freedom to live their lives according to their own beliefs, which for many include beliefs about how their children should be raised, and children's interest in developing the capacity for autonomy. Focusing on familial relationship goods, and on the quality of the parent–child relationship, offers a distinctive way of approaching that challenge. In order to develop autonomy, and for many other reasons, children themselves need a close emotional bond which permits, and indeed requires, parents to be spontaneous and open in their relationships with their children. Making that kind of relationship central opens the door to more specific and difficult questions. How much, or what kinds of, authority must parents have for the relationship to work its magic? To what extent does the valuable intimacy between parent and child depend on parents' being free to share themselves—including their religious views—with their children? How, if at all, might the kind of parent–child relationship that is in children's interests depend on parents being free to influence the content of their children's schooling?

The view to be presented invokes claims with which many religious parents will disagree, as will some atheists. Those who regard their children's following the true path as more important than those children's capacity to judge for themselves whether the path in question is indeed true will reject the autonomy condition. So will those who care more that their children see the falsity of all religious doctrines than that they come to see it for themselves. Both will deny my more specific claim that one of the duties that parents owe their children is overseeing the development of their capacity to decide for themselves how they want to live their lives. Building the facilitation of children's autonomy into the parental role is, I believe, the right approach, and another way in which the familial relationship goods approach reconceives the more conventional opposition between parents' and children's interests. But it ups the stakes in the disagreement with the parent who simply denies that autonomy matters: on the view to be presented here, that parent has not only failed to recognize what she in fact owes her children, she has also not understood what it is that grounds her claim to be a parent in the first place.

Of course, parents' rights and children's interest in developing the capacity for autonomy are just two considerations relevant to the assessment of policy on religious schooling. The analytical framework set out in Chapter 2 emphasized that various different factors have to be taken into account, and my argument will indeed have implications for many of them. Correcting mistaken views about parents' rights is a crucial part of the overall picture because excessive deference to parents imposes a variety of costs on many others. Misjudging the proper extent of parents' rights to control their children's schooling affects *all* children, not only those having the control exercised over them. And it deprives them of more than the capacity of autonomy. That's partly because many of the outcomes we rely on schools to achieve depend—in part—on the kinds of children who go to them.[4] If parents are allowed to opt for segregated schools, then all children, not just their own, miss out on the educational benefits of mixed school composition. This applies most obviously to the other-regarding or "civic" educational goods, such as the capacity and disposition to treat others as moral equals. These too, like the capacity for autonomy, are important on both consequentialist and non-consequentialist grounds. If parents have the right to protect their children from knowledge of other religions, or to deny them the kind of school environment that is most likely to foster tolerant attitudes, then we may all be condemned to share a society, and a democracy, with intolerant others who know little about their fellow citizens.[5] And since spending time with others from different home cultures promotes critical reflection, and provides a sense of the different ways of living one's life, mixed schools are also conducive to personal autonomy. If members of a religious faith school their children in particular ways that exclude, or are simply not attractive to, others, all children are deprived of the educational benefits they would get from being schooled alongside such children.

Correctly identifying the scope and content of parents' rights with respect to children's religious schooling is important, then, not only for the sake of their children's autonomy—though that would be reason enough—but because it affects the education of other people's children, and indeed of all future citizens. By offering an alternative understanding of the nature and basis of parents' rights, my aim is primarily to discredit the prevalent view, thereby removing—at least at the level of theory—an obstacle to education policies that would both respect everyone's moral entitlements and achieve better, and fairer, outcomes for all our children.

Our society currently gets parents' rights not just marginally but massively wrong. We have, of course, moved well beyond the classical Roman view that a child was the father's property and could be killed at his behest, but much of our thinking remains "proprietarian". We accord parents rights over their children as if children are quasi-property—as if they *belong* to their parents in some sense. In many countries, parents who wish to raise their children in ways inimical to their developing the capacity for autonomy are free to "school" them at home, thereby avoiding almost all regulation, or to send them to private schools which, though regulated to some extent, can in practice reinforce the home culture so thoroughly that it becomes very hard for children to gain critical distance. But that is only the far end of the spectrum. Many readers who share the liberal commitment to autonomy and object to that kind of upbringing nonetheless see no problem with parents' subjecting their children to the parents' own views—religious or otherwise—in ways that exceed the proper limits of the parental role, as I understand it. Parents' rights require more than incremental revision; they need to be fundamentally reconceived.

The chapter proceeds in three sections. Section 1 presents the familial relationship goods account of parents' rights. Section 2 explores the implications of that account for questions about the right to raise one's child as a member of one's religion. Section 3 focuses on the issue of religious schooling.

1. Familial Relationship Goods and Parents' Rights

To understand what rights parents should have over the children they parent, we have to start with what may seem like an odd question: why should children be raised by parents at all? The biological sense of "parent"—parent as procreator—is so common that it is natural to hear that question as asking why biological parents should get to raise the children they have produced. That question is indeed unsettling, but I mean to address a more fundamental issue. Properly to address the question of parents' rights we need to take a step further back and consider the reasons for wanting children to be raised in families, by parents—whether biological *or* adoptive—in the first place. Children's upbringing could be handed over to state-run quasi-orphanages. Doubtless readers will baulk at that suggestion, but other forms of collective or communal child-raising, such as the kibbutz, are less dystopian. What, if anything, would be lost if we were to get rid of the family and go with these alternatives? Only with a clear view of what is so valuable about the family, and the parent–child relationship in particular, can we think systematically about what rights parents need to have for that value to be realized.

Parent–child relationships make possible distinctive and weighty goods in people's lives. I will argue that a very particular kind of relationship with one or more (but not too many) adults is valuable for children: it is essential both for their emotional, cognitive, and moral development and it contributes to their well-being during childhood itself. Since children are—at least initially—dependent, vulnerable, and involuntary participants in the process of being raised, and since childhood experiences have formative influence on our lives as a whole, children's interests matter most. So the case for the family depends primarily on parent–child relationships being good for children and the adults they become. But the well-being of adults is also affected in a different way by how children are raised, and many have an interest in getting to play the role of parent. In the world of state-run quasi-orphanages, children would lack the kind of relationships with particular adults that they need both to flourish as children and to develop into flourishing adults, while adults would be deprived of the special—distinctive and weighty—goods that many achieve through parenting a child.

Let me start with children. Children's interests—the things that make their lives go well—can be categorized in various ways. They have current interests, which contribute to their well-being during their childhoods, but they also have developmental interests—interests in developing the physical, cognitive, emotional, and moral capacities that will enable their lives to go well as adults. Raising children well is a matter of getting something like the right balance between these various considerations. Some of the things that children need could indeed be provided by impersonal state functionaries: healthy nutrition, adequate clothing, and protection from physical danger presumably fall into that category. But one does not have to be an expert in psychology or child development to know that healthy emotional development depends on children forming deep attachments to particular adults who are emotionally attuned to them, whom they experience as loving them, as having a special duty of care towards them, and with whom they can enjoy long-term intimate relationships. More interestingly, perhaps, children also need to experience their attentive carers as their central disciplinary models. To learn and internalize self-control, empathy, deferred gratification, and other modes of self-regulation, the child needs to see these traits modelled in people with whom she identifies; for children, identification comes through love and admiration, which are themselves responses to loving warmth in the carer.[6] Healthy emotional development, in other words, depends on children experiencing intimate-yet-authoritative relationships with particular adults. That is the core of the child-centred case for parents and the family as the best way of raising children.

It is important, further, that those adults with authority over the child are experienced by her as acting at least somewhat spontaneously, as expressing their own individuality and sharing themselves with their children, and as having the discretion to act on their own judgments. Someone who, when deciding what to cook for supper, or what stories to read at bedtime, robotically executes the detailed instructions contained in an official state-approved child-raising manual will hardly be providing the kind of emotional responsiveness that tends to induce loving identification with the authority figure, nor herself experiencing the parent–child relationship as a source of joy and satisfaction in the way most helpful to the child's emotional development. Some degree of external guidance will doubtless not spoil the relationship. Parents' administering medicines to their children according to doctors' instructions are likely to be experienced as acting on an entirely healthy loving motivation. And, for some parents, following a more extensive "instruction manual"—such as a religious text—may be precisely how they manifest and share their own sense of what matters with their children. In such cases, however, it is significant that the parent is acting on her own judgment rather than regarding the manual as an authoritative directive imposed by others.

But the importance of that kind of relationship goes far beyond the child's interest in emotional well-being. Emotional, cognitive, and moral development are so intertwined that parent–child relationships play a crucial role in these other dimensions too. According to developmental psychologists, even basic mental processes like representational thinking, which is the precursor for symbolization and conceptual thought, and the capacity to imagine, which allows one to take the other's point of view, depend on internalization of the caregiving relationship. As Anne C. Dailey puts it: "the capacity for reasoned thinking represents a developmental line, or maturational sequence, beginning in the earliest physical interactions with an emotionally responsive caregiver and ending in a mature complex capacity to lead an independent, autonomous, self-directed life".[7] The capacity for autonomy is complex partly in that it combines cognitive, emotional and moral aspects: the autonomous person can not only reflect on the options available to her, process information, and identify means to her ends; she can also trust and cooperate with others, defer gratification, and contain disruptive and destructive feelings. That complex capacity is best fostered when children are raised in intimate-yet-authoritative relationships with particular adults; that is, when they are raised in families, by parents.

What about adults? What ways of raising children would be best for them? That might seem like a trick question. After all, all adults started out as children, and the last two paragraphs were mainly about the kind of upbringing that would be good for children not in the sense of being good for them during their childhoods but in the developmental sense of being good for them as the adults they will become. One response to the question, then, not falling for the trick, would be: "Adults are just developed children; they are the same people! So the way of raising children that is best for adults must be the same as the way that best serves children's developmental interests." Which is what we have just been talking about.

That way of formulating the question is salutary. In highlighting the fundamental continuity between children and adults it reminds us that the issue of how children should be raised just is the question of how *people* should be raised and makes it less likely that we will misjudge the balance of interests between children and the adults who raise them. But that doesn't make it a trick question; there is indeed a residual issue about how different ways of organizing children's upbringing might be good or bad for people-as-adults. The kind of developmental interests appealed to in the previous paragraphs were quite general—and their very generality helps to explain their importance. But there remain questions about the specific ways in which childrearing arrangements might contribute to the well-being of adults, and whether that contribution might affect the overall judgment about how childrearing should be arranged. Suppose my story about why children need parents turns out to be false: robots can do the job just as well—maybe even a bit better—and it is proposed that we hand the task over to them. Parenting would be banned. Even though robot-raised people would suffer no other loss—and even if they enjoyed a gain in other ways— many would resist the proposal. Some might do so selfishly—just because it suited them to get to be a parent and the cost would be borne by others— but that need not be part of the argument. Looking at the issue impartially, one could reasonably think that parenting a child makes enough of a contribution to enough people's lives that our collectively retaining that option would be worth missing out on whatever other benefits were produced by the robot scenario.

Nearly everybody agrees that the adult interest in parenting is weighty enough to ground a right to be a parent, that we would be failing in our duties to one another if we denied people the opportunity to engage in that activity. And certainly many people make great efforts to become parents, regard raising a child as one of their most important life projects, and sacrifice lots of other valued opportunities in the process. But adults become parents for many different reasons and there is considerable dispute about how best to understand the value of parenting and the basis of the right to be a parent.[8] Some point to the significance of raising children as a way of extending or continuing oneself into the future, passing on some aspects of oneself to a child; those who take this kind of view can disagree about the specific nature of the extension or continuity that is valuable— perhaps it is one's genes, perhaps one's property, perhaps one's religious identity.[9] Others see raising a child primarily as a creative activity, or an opportunity for self-expression, a bit like an artist shaping a piece of marble into a sculpture.[10] These different grounds for holding that there is a right *to* parent (i.e. the right to become a parent) will suggest different views about the rights *of* parents (i.e. the rights that parents have over their children)—including views about parents' rights to influence their children's values and beliefs.

The common problem with such accounts is that they make children means to their parents' ends; the child is regarded, and treated, as a vehicle through which parents can achieve their own purposes. True, the child may not only be a means. If the interest in developing autonomy is satisfied, then a parent may plausibly claim that she has treated her child also as an end. Nonetheless, there is something inappropriately self-serving about this kind of attempt to justify the claim to parent a child. Of course, what we are looking for is precisely a way in which parenting contributes to the well-being of the adults doing it, so some element of adult self-interest is unavoidable. But the interest in question must be distinctive and weighty enough to provide a plausible answer to the question of why adults should get to parent children even if robots would do a better job. There are many ways in which people can extend or continue themselves into the future, or express themselves creatively, without claiming the right to control another human being. And there are different ways in which they can enjoy fulfilling and intimate relationships with others, so blanket appeals to the value of intimate affective relationships cannot succeed either.[11] In my view, what is special about parenting, and important enough to count for something in the balance when weighed against our other interests, is the parents' role as their children's fiduciary. The parent has a special duty to protect and promote the child's interests including the interest most children have in developing the capacity for autonomy and becoming someone who has no need of a parent's special duty of care. The idea that parents have fiduciary duties towards their children is familiar from Locke.[12] The additional claim here is that adults have a non-fiduciary interest in being able to play a fiduciary role; it is valuable for their children that they play it well, but it is also a distinctive source of their own flourishing that they play it.

Some elements in what is special about being a fiduciary for a child concern the fact that what we're talking about here is a *child*. Relevant here are the distinctive properties and moral standing of the person for whom one is acting as fiduciary: her possessing the capacity to develop into an autonomous adult, her degree of vulnerability to one's responses and judgments, her involuntary dependence on one, her natural tendency to develop a deep attachment to one. Failing adequately to discharge your fiduciary duties to a child would be different from failing to discharge those owed to a client or patient, or even to an ageing parent, even if what was involved in fulfilling the duties were the same. But of course they are not the same. Other elements concern *what* it is that children need from their fiduciaries. As we have seen, they need a special kind of *relationship*—a relationship in which the adult offers love and authority, a complex and emotionally challenging combination of openness and restraint, of spontaneity and self-monitoring, of sharing and withholding. It's that kind of relationship that many adults have an interest in too.

Imagine a world in which human children didn't need much more looking after than guinea pigs, or Tamagotchi toys. Imagine that they could fully develop into autonomous, emotionally adjusted adults, and enjoy the intrinsic goods of childhood, with that kind and level of input from adults. Even in that hypothetical world, there would be *some* value to being the person responsible for ensuring that children's interests were met. But what's really valuable in the case of parenting is not being the fiduciary per se but having the kind of relationship that is, in fact, the kind that children need to develop into healthy adults. It's that kind of relationship which presents a distinctive challenge, and distinctive sources of fulfilment, which together give adults unique opportunities for flourishing.

Parents' rights, on this account, are precisely the rights that parents need in order to have the kind of relationship that justifies children being raised by parents—rather than robots, state functionaries, or interchangeable members of a commune—in the first place. We can assess on a case by case basis whether an appeal to familial relationship goods justifies parents' claims to control—to exercise authority over—children by looking at the role those rights play in realizing familial relationship goods. Roughly, familial relationship goods give us strong reason to grant parents the rights they require to fulfil the fiduciary role, to create or sustain the kind of intimate-and-authoritative relationship that children need and that is also valuable to the parent. The relationship goods approach helps us work out what room is necessary for what Rawls calls the "free and flourishing internal life appropriate" to the family.[13] Parents have the right to engage in those activities and interactions with their children that facilitate the realization of the extremely valuable goods that justify the family in the first place.

Parental claims to the right to do things to, with and for their children that cannot be justified by appeal to those goods may perhaps be defended in other ways; parents are not *only* parents and they may have other interests or prerogatives that can properly influence their dealings with their children. But those other considerations will not ground parents' rights as that category is understood here; they will not be rights that they have in virtue of being parents. As we will see, the question of whether such non- or extra-parental considerations mean that parents have the right to act on their religious views when deciding matters for their children, and in what ways, will be important when thinking about religious schooling.

This account of the nature and basis of parents' rights is deliberately quite general. The next section will consider its implications for the issue of parents' rights to shape their children's emerging beliefs and values, and of religious beliefs and values in particular. Before moving on, however, it may be helpful to highlight a few features of the general approach proposed so far. In my view these are attractive, but readers may suspect some sleight of hand in the way the various elements of the picture fit together, so it is better to have them out in the open.

First, the thrust of the approach is to start from children's interests and identify what it is that children need from adults. That starting point does much to generate the conclusion that parents' rights are just those rights that it is in children's interests for parents to have, and some may regard it as biased or prejudicial. Certainly it has profound and transformative implications for the way we think about familial relationships. But children's vulnerability, their involuntary subject to control by another person, and the far-reaching implications of how they are raised for their lives as a whole suggest that any approach that gives greater weight to the interests of parents is indefensible. As Shelley Burtt puts it: "authority over other human beings should extend only so far as making up the deficits that legitimate their subordination…the way we think of children and their needs determines the sort of authority we think it is appropriate to exercise over them".[14]

Second, the claim that the special value of parenting, for adults, consists in playing the fiduciary role—providing the kind of relationship that children need—is certainly controversial. Its effect is to change the picture of the relationship between parents and children in a way that massively reduces the scope for genuine conflicts of interest—and of rights—between the two. That may seem too good to be true. Of course, adults may want to be parents for a variety of reasons, and some may regard the proposed view about the distinctive value of parenthood as misidentifying what is at stake. Those who see their mission as populating the world with followers of a particular religious faith, or who view their children as means for them to express and realize their powers of creative self-expression, will think I neglect their true interests qua *parents*, and will leave greater scope for genuine conflicts between their own and their children's interests. But such alternative specifications of the value of parenting do not provide plausible answers to the question of why people should have the right to parent children even when others—whether robots, state functionaries or simply other parents—would do a better job.

Third, the claim that parents' rights are derivative of children's interests means, in effect, that the adult interest in being a parent—the basis of the right *to* parent—plays no further role in the argument. We will need to consider how their *other* interests may properly influence parents' relationships with their children, but from here on the adult interest in parenting drops out of the picture. My defence of a particular specification of that interest is important to the position as a whole, of course, because it challenges competing views that grant parents more extensive rights to shape their children's values. But the effect of that defence was precisely to direct attention to what children need from their parents, and what rights parents must have in order to give them what they need. That is where our attention will indeed be directed from here on.

Fourth, autonomy plays a central role in the account. It is important that children develop the capacity for autonomy and parent–child relationships with a particular character are important for its development. As their fiduciaries, parents are charged with the task of facilitating the process whereby their children become capable of making independent and reflective decisions about how they are to live their lives. That process begins with a mixture of affective connection and clear and consistent regulation—the "downloading" from the parent of the capacity to contain and regulate her own desires and emotions—but as children begin to develop their own preferences and perspectives, it also requires parents to exercise the self-restraint that allows their children to begin to trust and act on their own judgments. That is challenging even for those parents who accept the importance of autonomy—it is hard to resist the temptation to use one's authoritative position paternalistically, to attempt to shape one's children's beliefs, values, and choices according to one's own judgments about what it is to live well. But many reject that element of the fiduciary picture and conceive their role precisely as deploying their parental authority to guide their children towards (their own views about) how best to live. Here, as I have said, we hit bedrock disagreement: those who deny the importance of autonomy will reject all liberal views, including standard approaches that treat the facilitation of children's autonomy as an external constraint on parents. For them, my account—on which facilitating autonomy is internal to the parental role and helps to explain why there is a right to parent, even when others would do a better job—will only make matters worse.

2. Parents' Rights, Children's Religion

We can now explore what this view about the basis and nature of parents' rights means for their right to raise their children as members of a particular religion. Where other theorists see those rights as part of parents' own expressive liberty,[15] or as an implication of their own religious freedom as individuals,[16] or as deriving from their own interest in a relationship with their children based on shared identity,[17] the approach proposed here frames the issue very differently. Suppose that an intimate-but-authoritative relationship is indeed important for children's development, including the development of their autonomy, and that parents' rights should be derived entirely from the fiduciary aspect of the relationship. What are the implications for rights to control, or even to influence, the development of their children's religious beliefs and identity?

Before addressing that question, we should be clear that, on the liberal picture, there is a big difference between people's views about how they should live their own lives and their views about how others should be treated. The values that children need to acquire as part of their moral development—the liberal virtues such as tolerance, respect for others, and what Rawls calls "a sense of justice"[18]—have a different status from the kind that individuals may choose to endorse as a matter of private conscience, such as those attaching to full-blown religious systems or ethical doctrines. To put it crudely, it is much more important that people get to form and act on their own views about the former than about the latter: the fact that we owe duties to others—that we are morally *required* to treat them in certain ways—means that people's views about how to treat others do not demand the same kind of respect as their judgments about how to live their own lives more generally. This gives parents a very different role in the formation of their children's moral views from that which is appropriate in the case of their religious beliefs. I said earlier that the parent–child relationship itself is justified partly because of the role that parents play in children's moral development; the important point here is that some deliberate shaping of their children's emerging values is itself part of that job. There will be other influences, of course, but instilling in children the virtue of honesty, the ability to distinguish right from wrong, and the sense that others are moral equals irrespective of their skin colour, religion, or gender, is a task primarily charged to parents and part of their fiduciary duty to their children (as well as being in the interest of third parties).

Returning to the particular issue of religion, parents' role is to serve as loving authorities—to exercise the kind of discretion and induce the kind of identification that children need for their own development, including their moral development—while helping their children acquire the capacity to judge religious matters for themselves. That is a challenging job description, especially for parents with deep religious convictions (including atheism). To develop the kind of attachment that children need, they must gradually get to know their parents—who they are, what they care about—and parents must be free to be spontaneous, and to share themselves with their children. To conceal their religious views, or not to allow those views in any way to inform their exercise of parental authority, would require a kind of withholding, and a degree of self-monitoring, that is inimical to an intimate loving relationship. Parents whose religious convictions require them to say prayers before eating, for example, or prescribe and proscribe particular kinds of food, must have some discretion to act on those beliefs in the way they conduct family life. Apart from anything else, loving parents are naturally motivated to benefit their children, and religious views affect what is regarded as "benefit". A parent who believes that her child will be condemned to eternal damnation unless she comes to endorse a particular doctrine cannot entirely bracket that belief in her relationship with the child without depriving the child of at least some of those very expressions of parental love that the child needs. But precisely because, when all goes well, children love and identify with their parents—want to please them, want to be like them—that same relationship inevitably threatens the autonomy that it is also the parent's task to develop. So not only must children be exposed to other beliefs at appropriate ages, and in such a way that other ways of life become genuine options for them, but also those very processes of attachment and identification with the parent that are needed on developmental grounds have to be carefully managed so that those alternatives are not unthinkable, or adoptable only at excessive emotional cost.

On the proposed account of parents' rights, then, parents must have the right to act in ways that will tend to influence their children's religious views. In a healthy parent–child relationship, a parent's religious views are bound to shape those of her children. Some influence will arise simply as a result of parents being themselves in their relationships with their children, and exercising in a more or less unreflective and personal way their sphere of discretion over the particular ways in which they interact with them. Some will arise from parents' acting on their natural motivation to help their children's lives go better. A loving parent who thinks that her child will benefit if she loves God is bound to find herself nudging her in that direction simply because of her automatic and natural tendency to relate to her child in ways that she thinks will be good for her. The same applies to the loving parent who decries belief in God as the opiate of the masses, or regards it as an irrational projection of human psychological needs. Parents will naturally tend to denigrate, and unthinkingly steer their children away from, what they take to be bad influences. The idea that parents should constantly monitor themselves in order to screen out anything that might influence their children's views about religion would risk distancing them, creating artifice in the relationship, and depriving their children of the possibility of the warm, spontaneous, genuine relationship that they need. Most of us cannot simultaneously shield our children from those values and commitments that are central to our identities and spontaneously share ourselves with them in the way that the healthy parent–child relationship demands.

I have emphasized the significance of unmonitored discretion and spontaneity, but what does the account imply for parents' right deliberately to act in ways likely to influence to their children's religious beliefs? To answer that we must distinguish two things that might be going on under that description. On the one hand, a parent might be deliberately directing her child towards a particular faith—or towards a rejection of any—in the sense that she intends that the child come to endorse her own view. That, of course, is a right that parents conventionally claim—and that they are everywhere granted. On the other hand, the parent may simply be trying to give her child the right kind of relationship. Even if she does not herself consciously frame things in such terms, her aim, in this second case, is to provide her child with the "familial relationship goods" that, if I am right, explain why she has any rights at all over the child. Here the influencing of her children's religious views, though deliberate, is ultimately motivated by a concern that her relationship with the child should go well.

Parents who see themselves as justified in deliberately guiding their children towards their own religious views, in the first sense, have misunderstood their role and the moral character of the parent–child relationship. If the relationship goods approach is right, children are of course helping parents to realize familial relationship goods in their lives, and their parents may have chosen to be parents for that very reason. Still, that approach gives parents no permission to treat their children as means by which they may permissibly seek to realize their own values in other ways, or to pursue their own, controversial, conception of how one should live. Asked "Why should adults get to exercise authority over children?", we are not tempted to answer: "So that they can direct children towards their preferred religious doctrine". Typically, then, when parents deliberately direct their children on religious matters, they are deploying their power improperly. This is certainly true of those parents who try to direct their children's religious views without regard to the development of their children's autonomy (i.e. their capacity to judge such matters for themselves). But it can be true also of parents who do take their children's moral separateness seriously in that way. In assuming the authority to direct and control their children's lives in ways that exceed the proper scope and basis of their rights as parents, they too are failing to give due weight to a relevant non-consequentialist consideration: their children's right not to be subject to illegitimate authority. Recall Burtt's nice articulation of the principle at stake: "authority over other human beings should extend only so far as making up the deficits that legitimate their subordination". Even where their concern to guide their children towards the true path is motivated entirely by a loving concern for their children's well-being, it is not their proper role, as parents, to exercise parental authority in that way. This is consistent with the view that parents may be distinctively well placed to discern their children's particular developing talents and emerging interests, and on that basis may legitimately exercise their authority in ways conducive to their well-being.[19]

But parents may deliberately introduce their children to their religious views, or their views about religion, in ways that can be understood as part of the sharing with, or revealing to, the child that is itself conducive to the kind of relationship I have described. Here there need be no intention that the child should come to endorse the views in question. I have emphasized the extent to which parents' revealing and sharing their religious commitments would naturally result from the spontaneous, unmonitored, quality of the relationship, but a parent may be right to think that the relationship will go better if she also acts in a considered way to show her child who she is and what she cares about. When a Christian parent takes his daughter to church, that is not usually an unthinking and automatic sharing of self between parent and child. It is more likely a deliberate decision to introduce the child to a world of belief and practice that the parent judges valuable. To be sure, that introduction is typically motivated by the desire that the child will come to share that judgment, but it need not be. The same applies to deliberate decisions to say prayers at certain times, such as before meals. The parent might require her child to engage in such practices as a way of introducing the child to the parent's religious views, believing that her relationship with the child will be closer—the child will know her parent better—if the child experiences those practices for herself.

This justification extends to deliberate and considered parental exercises of authority the same claim that underpinned the case for spontaneous, unmonitored interactions between parent and child. The thought is that, for the relationship properly to serve children, there needs to be a kind of emotional bond and mutual identification that is incompatible with the requirement that parents withhold and conceal their own views on religious matters. To confine parents to the spontaneous expression of those views—to deny them the freedom deliberately to reveal their views to their children, including by means that involve controlling their children's behaviour, such as taking them to church—would be to do children a disservice.

Perhaps paradoxically, the possibility of children's rejecting their parents' religious commitments is another reason why exposure—including deliberate exposure—to those commitments can be in children's interests. Everything in the last few paragraphs has assumed that, whatever else they are doing to and with their children, parents are not obstructing the development of their children's autonomy.

Autonomous individuals can make up their own minds about what to believe, and they may well end up believing different things from their parents. If we think not only about the developmental benefits of parent–child relationships but also about their value when people reach adulthood, it seems that, where the child *does* break from the parents' values, the parent–child relationship will probably be sustained in a more meaningful way, and has a better chance of being sustained, if child and parent are in a position at least to appreciate the other's point of view, to understand where the other is coming from. In the child's case, that can only happen if the parent has indeed made sure that the child has a real appreciation of how she lives her life and how she sees the world.[20]

This view about the permissibility of parents' deliberately introducing their children to their religious views when it is important for their relationship raises a number of complexities. One concerns how much of an "introduction" is really needed for the child to relate to her parent in the way that the account requires. One visit to a church, temple, mosque, or synagogue is hardly going to do the job, but it is implausible to regard this justification as permitting parents to require weekly visits for many years, or to demand that their children acquire a level of familiarity with the doctrine in the way that might justify requiring a high level of religious instruction. The thought is that children should have a sense of who their parents are, and what matters to them, not that they should develop an advanced understanding of the views to which their parents subscribe. The same applies to practices like praying. Even if it is permissible for parents to introduce their children to such a practice, that will not justify its becoming part of their daily routine, or at least not for long.

The example of praying raises a distinctive concern about the permissibility of requiring children themselves to engage in particular practices rather than merely observing their parents, and other adults, do so. One can imagine a parent maintaining that it is only by, say, actually praying to a divine being that one understands what it means to pray to that divine being, or to any divine being, and that without that experience a child will not really have been "introduced" to those things that matter to the parent. To lessen the oddity of that claim, consider that a parent who worships Beethoven is presumably permitted to take her child to a concert, and make her listen to the music, not just to observe others doing so. Of course, praying to a divine being seems to presuppose beliefs—such as that the divine being exists—of a kind that some regard as distinctively objectionable but the familial relationship goods account nonetheless has scope for that level and kind of deliberate introduction.

Third, a parent who exercises parental authority in a way that is likely to influence her child's religious views, albeit without any intention of doing so and motivated only by relationship considerations, may nonetheless *hope* that the exposure will result in the child's coming to endorse the parent's own views. It is demanding enough to expect a parent committed to particular religious views to respect her child's moral separateness not only by facilitating the development of her autonomy but also by abjuring any action intended to guide her towards those views. It would be psychologically impossible for such a parent not even to wish that the child will autonomously come to share them. Indeed, a parent who did not even want her child to choose what, *ex hypothesi*, she regards as the best way to live would surely be failing to provide the kind of loving relationship the child needs.

We will soon move on from this general discussion of parents' rights to raise their children as members of a religion to the issue of schooling in particular. To lay the ground, a few more features of the proposed approach are worth bringing out. Most important is the point that parents constitute a standing threat to their children's independence, understood as their capacity to choose their own lives. Close, intimate-but-authoritative, relationships between parents and children are vital, but such relationships can easily be *too* close. Even those influences that arise spontaneously in a loving parent–child relationship can threaten autonomy; that threat is all the greater where influence arises as a result of the parent's deliberate decision to share herself with her child. In all cases, parents mindful of their duties to their children will take care not to engage in the kinds of revealing and sharing that will impede the development of the child's capacity to make her own judgments about whatever is being shared and revealed. What kinds will in fact do that partly depends, of course, on the child's age or stage of development. For young children, the emphasis can be on fostering the processes of identification and attachment. As they mature and become able to question their parents' views, the balance needs to shift toward facilitating the process of separation and individuation.

So far I have talked about "religious views" in the abstract, paying no attention to their content or the differences between them. But different religious doctrines can have very different implications for children's developing autonomy, and the extent to which parents may share their religious views with their children will vary accordingly. In a healthy parent–child relationship, children are naturally inclined to identify with their parents, and to seek their parents' approval. So it makes a difference what it is that parents do and do not approve. Other things being equal, children whose parents reveal their belief that all who do not subscribe to their own religion are wicked, or condemned to eternal damnation, are likely to find it harder to break with their parents' religious views than those whose parents hold more moderate views. Given the variety in people's constitutions and characters, children who know that their parents regard homosexuality as wicked, or girls who learn that their parents see motherhood and homemaking as divinely ordained for women, may find it harder to live a life that is right for them than those whose parents take a more tolerant line. On the other hand, where a religious doctrine itself puts great weight on the importance of people critically judging its validity for themselves and living according to their consciences, or simply regards what is at stake in such judgments as less weighty, there will be fewer obstacles to children developing their own views on religious matters; it may even be positively encouraged.

My view about parental rights, then, is not "neutral" between different religious views. Indeed, those who reject the claim that parents are under a fiduciary duty to facilitate their children's autonomy will already have found that conception of the parental role to be biased against religious doctrines that deny the importance of autonomy. So it is no surprise that the view permits parents whose religious views themselves endorse liberal values to share their views with their children in ways that may be impermissible for those who do not. This is not an embarrassment—but it does point to a paradox. On my account, it is parents whose religious convictions do not put much, or any, weight on autonomy who must be most careful about sharing those convictions with children—for the sake of their children's autonomy. While the argument is indeed unlikely to have much motivational traction with such parents—since they will simply reject the initial account of their parental duties—that is no objection. Nor is the fact that my view yields differential implications for believers in different religions. Both simply show how much rests on the validity of that account.

But what about parents whose religious convictions are such that it is simply psychologically impossible for them to have the kind of relationship their children need without exceeding the constraints on the exercise of parental authority that I have argued for? Consider someone who is convinced that her child will suffer eternal damnation, or merely that he will live a worthless life, unless he comes to endorse her own doctrine. Her spontaneous sharing and revealing of herself is bound to exert a level of emotional pressure that is inimical to the child's enjoying a genuinely "open future". And there may be no way for her to refrain from deliberately guiding him towards a doctrine the endorsement of which will have (she believes) such a huge impact on his well-being: there may be no gap, for her, between acting in ways that the child needs her to act if he is to feel loved, on the one hand, and at least nudging him towards a flourishing life, on the other. Here, it seems, there is no morally costless resolution to the conflict. Such a parent is unable to provide her child with the kind of loving relationship that the child needs without simultaneously threatening her autonomy and exceeding the proper limits on her parental authority in the process.

To be sure, in such cases we might *excuse* the parent's wrongful treatment of her children. To find oneself unable to give one's child the love he needs without failing fully to acknowledge his independent moral status is very different from simply treating him as a means to a greater good or as a vehicle for the pursuit of one's own preferences. To see this, and to differentiate between different kinds of failure, imagine the child of four kinds of religious parents. First, one whose parents, entirely unconcerned for his well-being or agency, see him only as a means for increasing the number of true believers in the world; second, one whose parents love him and care for his well-being, but, confident in their belief that they know what is best for him, show no concern at all for his autonomy; third, one whose parents, though mindful of their duty not to hamper his capacity for autonomy, have strong religious convictions of such a kind that, despite their best efforts, spontaneous family life makes it hard for him to develop and exercise it; fourth, one whose parents, while careful to ensure that he does develop the capacity for autonomy, find that their love for him sometimes takes the form of deliberately guiding him towards their own religious views.

Although, if my account is right, all four exceed the proper limits of the parental role, it seems clear that they do so to different, and decreasing, degrees. All these children have a complaint against their parents, but those complaints become progressively less severe. In the first case, there is a complete absence of concern for the child; in the second, a failure to recognize the importance of the child's being able to form and act on her own religious views. The third and fourth cases have a more subtle relation to my proposed account. In both, the parents are well motivated and are providing their child with the right kind of relationship—the problem is that, given their religious views, the only way they can do that either impedes the child's autonomy (third case) or involves a regrettable compromise between different aspects of the parental role (fourth case). In these two cases we can readily imagine the child forgiving or excusing his parents—after all, they were doing their best for him, given their convictions—and their misjudgments about their proper role were less serious.[21]

I want to end this section by considering two objections to the proposed view of the rights that parents have to influence their children's religious views. Both worry that I go too far in prioritizing children's interests and do not give enough weight to parents', and both will be relevant to the question of religious schooling. First, imagine a critic who says: "I'm willing to grant not only your suggestion that parents' rights are those that are needed to fulfil the parental role but also your account of what the parental role *is*. I'll even accept your view about what that means for parents' rights with respect to their children's religious upbringing. But parents are not *only* parents. As you said at the beginning, they are individuals with their own lives to lead. Surely there must be some scope for them to lead those lives in ways that suit them, and for those ways to affect their interactions with their children, even if they are not thereby serving their children's interests." The suggestion here is that a full account of how parents may treat their children must take account of *non*-parental rights, rather than relying entirely on an account of rights defined in terms of the parental role and its fiduciary responsibilities. Alternatively, suppose someone says: "I agree with you that parents' dealings with their children must be constrained by the duty to facilitate their children's autonomy and in other ways to provide children with the kind of relationship that serves their interests. But, as long as they meet those demanding conditions, I don't see why their rights with respect to their treatment of their children shouldn't *also* reflect their own views about what matters in life. Rather than merely 'hoping' that her child will come to endorse her own views, surely a parent should be permitted deliberately to guide him towards them." The issue here is whether we should adopt a "strict" or "lax" interpretation of parents' rights. On the strict view, parents are limited to those exercises of authority that are demanded by children's interest in familial relationship goods; on the lax view, they have more discretion.

Although analytically distinct—one appeals to non-parental rights, the other adopts a lax interpretation of parents' rights themselves—these two objections make a similar point. Both deny that parents should be limited in their dealings with their children to those interactions that they need to engage in to fulfil the parental role and provide the requisite relationship goods; both hold that there is some space for them to act on their own preferences where doing so is *not* justified by their children's interests—as long as they do not thereby fail to deliver what their children need from the relationship. Although more sympathetic to the former way of formulating the point—which leaves the proposed analysis of parents' rights intact—I will treat them together.

The general objection gets something right: parents' interactions with their children may permissibly sometimes reflect their own preferences. Not only in the spontaneous, unmonitored way discussed above, but also as a result of deliberate considered decision. Parents are people too and it is reasonable for the shared life of the family to reflect their own enthusiasms and interests to some extent. This is partly because it is in *children's* interests that their parents are experienced as people with lives of their own. The familial relationship goods account itself emphasizes the value, to children, of parents' sharing themselves—who they are and what matters to them— with their children. But, even where these distinctively familial relationships are not at stake (i.e. where a parent *cannot* claim that a particular choice about how to exercise authority is serving her children's interests), she should be able to continue, at least to some extent, her own, independent, life, by, for example, taking her children with her on holiday to places she wants to see, or to visit friends of hers. This is so even though doing that kind of thing tends to influence, as it surely will, the values and beliefs her children will come to hold. It is in children's interests that their parents take them on holiday; at that level of description the exercise of authority does indeed comply with Burtt's claim that "authority over other human beings should extend only so far as making up the deficits that legitimate their subordination". But that principle is too strict if it is taken also to apply to the particular choice of destination, which—precisely because parents are adults with their own lives to lead—may properly reflect the parent's own interests and enthusiasms.

None of this, however, justifies the use of parental authority *deliberately* to guide or direct children towards particular religious views. They are, obviously, free to explain the merits of their preferred doctrines to other adults; in this and other ways they can live their religious lives as they see fit when it comes to those over whom they do not exercise authority and who are not captive audiences. But their authority over their children derives from children's interests in a relationship of a certain sort, not from their own interest in pursuing and promoting their own religious convictions. If they want to visit a holy place and their children's interests are served by turning the trip into a family outing, then they may take their children with them. In doing so, they are not exercising a distinctively parental right; they are pursuing their non-parental interests in a way that permissibly affects their children. And since those children had no say in the matter of who their parents are, and have no escape from subjection to parental authority, those non-parental interests may permissibly be pursued only where doing so is compatible with discharging their fiduciary duties.

3. Religious Schools

Religious schools come in many shapes and sizes. I have already emphasized that the content of different religious views itself varies in ways that are significant for the issue of parents' rights but when it comes to schools we are dealing with various new kinds of variation. Schools cater to children of different ages. Some are funded by the public purse, some rely on private resources. Some accept only children raised in a particular faith, others offer them preferential access, still others take no account of the religious background of their would-be students when choosing whom to educate. They vary also in their purposes: some seek to direct their students towards a particular religious view; others offer a non-directive and autonomy-promoting education that is nonetheless intended for those raised in a particular religious tradition and suffused by its ethos; still others aim to educate all children, without regard to their religious origins or destinations, albeit in a way that is somehow informed by a particular religious standpoint. These cross-cutting differences generate many distinct types of religious school. Even if we completely ignore potentially relevant differences in the content of religious views, and simplify the age issue by imagining children as attending only primary and secondary schools, the various differences listed above would generate a matrix with 36 cells! In one corner is a publically funded primary school that, while mildly religious in its ethos, is equally available to all and makes no attempt to guide its students towards any particular faith; in the opposite corner is a privately funded secondary school that admits only those who identify as members of a particular religion and teaches that doctrine as truth. My account of parents' rights might mean that we are morally required to respect their freedom to choose of some of these types but not others.

In general terms, the implications of that account for issues concerning religious schooling are rather straightforward. Most obviously, the duty to ensure that their children develop the capacity for autonomy precludes forms of education—whether at school or in the home—that deny children the knowledge, skills, attitudes, and dispositions needed for them to make and act on their own judgments about the variety of ways in which they might choose to live their lives. Children are wronged if they do not learn about a range of different views on religious matters. And they are wronged if, though informed about that range, alternative views are presented in ways that preclude their coming to see them as real, rather than merely hypothetical, options—whether because the alternatives are presented as unworthy in themselves or because of the excessive emotional and psychological cost of choosing them. This implication—which applies to private or independent schools just as much as to those funded by citizens collectively, and to schools propounding atheism just as much as to those promoting other religious views—is already enough to impugn a great deal of the schooling that is tolerated throughout the world.

Though widely rejected in practice, the state's duty to protect children's autonomy is fairly uncontroversial among liberal political philosophers. True, by focusing on the fiduciary nature of the parental role—which includes the duty to help their children to become autonomous—and on the interest in playing that role as the basis of the right to be a parent in the first place, my view offers a distinctive frame. Where most theorists would see the state as restricting parents' rights for the sake of children's interests, I suggest a more integrated, less conflictual, way of conceptualizing the issues. But the implications of the familial relationship goods approach for religious schooling go beyond providing a new frame for a familiar conclusion. If I am right, parents do not have the right to send their children to schools that will direct them towards a particular religion, or away from all religions, even where those schools also succeed in providing the kind of autonomy-facilitating education that is demanded by the more conventional liberal position. The fact that one is a child's parent does not give one the authority deliberately to guide her towards one's own religious views even in the conduct of family life at home. It certainly doesn't justify sending her to a school for that purpose.

Might the familial relationship goods account of parents' rights offer alternative justifications for parents' decisions to educate their children in religious schools? In the previous section, I noted the difference between the spontaneous and deliberate mechanisms by which parents might influence their children's religious views. Clearly sending one's child to a particular kind of school cannot be regarded as the kind of unplanned, un-self-monitored, interaction that parents need to be free to engage in for family life to go well. Just as choosing elite private schooling differs from spontaneous helping with homework,[22] so the proper concern to protect valuable familial interactions from counterproductive regulation or self-monitoring yields no support for religious schooling. I also suggested that, since parents are not only parents, it is permissible for them to pursue their own independent interests, at least to some extent, in ways that could be expected to exert that kind of effect. While it's true that participation in a school's activities, and other forms of association with co-believers facilitated by a shared school, might serve parents' own interest in pursuing their religious life, directing their children to attend such a school is different from, for example, taking them on holiday to visit a site of religious significance. In the latter, the parent is pursuing her own interests only in choosing a particular instantiation of a type of activity—taking her child on holiday—that is itself beneficial, in terms of familial relationship goods, for the child. The former has no equivalent justification.

But I also considered various ways in which the proposed account might regard *deliberate* decisions likely to influence their children's religious views as legitimate exercises of parental authority, so there remains a question about whether any of those apply to religious schooling. Before getting on to those, let me bring out one more general point about the relation between family and school. Where many see the school as an extension of the home, with parental authority naturally extending from home to school, the account I have proposed instead regards the school as a corrective to the home, a crucial safeguard against the risks that inevitably confront those engaging in the challenging task of parenting. The former view has no problem with, and may even prize, continuity between family and school; the latter sees discontinuity as valuable in assisting parents to discharge their fiduciary duties to their children.

Raising children to become autonomous adults is challenging, especially for parents with strong religious convictions. For their healthy emotional, moral, and cognitive development, young children need to feel securely attached to, and to identify with, their parents. Yet attachment and identification themselves can easily hamper the development of children's capacity to make and act on their own judgments about who they are, what matters to them, and how they want to live their lives. Although the familial relationship goods account insists that parents should be mindful of the ways in which the conduct of family life may pose dangers to that development, it leaves room for spontaneous, un-self-monitored, familial interactions that have the potential to obstruct it even though they fall within the scope of parents' discretionary authority. And quite apart from these psychological developmental factors, even well-intentioned parents may simply be badly placed to provide their children with the requisite knowledge, skills, attitudes, and dispositions. Schools exist partly because parents cannot be expected to educate their children properly on their own—think about science, mathematics, humanities. The same applies to autonomy. It is through schooling that the state is most easily able to supply the raw materials needed for autonomy: through the curriculum children can experience intellectual and emotional encounters with ideas, values, and traditions that are different from, and sometimes conflict with, those they are raised with in the home. Perhaps more importantly, in a socially and culturally diverse school they can become acquainted with different ideas, values, and traditions through the friendships they make and through intimate interactions with their friends' families. A culturally diverse teaching force can provide children with a range of adult role models who are unlike them and whom they can come to admire. A robust and well-designed extra-curriculum can lead them to discover enthusiasms and interests that would never have been stimulated by their home culture. Discontinuity is educationally valuable.[23]

Somewhat simplistically, then, the more that schools take on the task of promoting children's autonomy, the less parents need to worry about the autonomy-inhibiting effects of the ways in which, on my account, they may permissibly interact with their children. We might think of this as a division of labour between family/home and school. The former meets children's affective, emotional, and psychological developmental needs through intimate-but-authoritative relationships with particular adults. The latter supplements and complements that familial contribution by widening children's horizons, by introducing them to perspectives different from those they are exposed to at home, and by teaching them to reflect critically on the choices available to them concerning how they are to live their lives.

The division of labour cannot be complete. However well they play their part, schools have only limited potential to counteract the threat that parents pose to their children's autonomy, so we should not think that an appropriately constituted school system could leave parents free to conduct family life along religious lines.[24] Parents can adopt strategies to immunize their children from the autonomy-facilitating lessons and experiences that the school provides. Those strategies may sometimes fail, but they will succeed often enough for parents' choices about how to respond to schools' attempts to promote critical reflection on the values they themselves hold to remain important. Even where parents make no deliberate attempts at immunization, the emotional pull of their parents' enthusiasms will be enough to prevent many children from responding to the schools' messages. This is especially likely if parents take the awareness that another institution is taking care of autonomy as giving them the freedom to be completely uninhibited in their promotion of—or even the non-directive revealing and sharing of—their own values. And because it is important that schools not damage healthy familial relationships, the autonomy-promoting role of schools itself places limits on what parents may teach children at home. Consider parents who, thinking themselves freed from the responsibility for promoting their child's autonomy by the presence of an autonomy-facilitating school, teach her that homosexuality, or apostasy, are sins punishable by eternal damnation. One can easily imagine that what the school would have to do to facilitate that child's autonomy would interfere with the familial relationship. The same applies to parents who are deeply hostile to anything other than atheism. We cannot relieve parents of the duty to participate conscientiously in developing their child's autonomy.

On the question of whether deliberate choices for religious schools might be justified by appeal to familial relationship goods, there are a number of different scenarios to consider. I argued, first, that a parent might be justified in sharing himself with, or revealing himself to, his child in ways that go beyond spontaneous informal interactions. He might permissibly take his child to his place of worship, for example, and he might even require her to experience—and not merely observe—some aspects of his religious practice. As far as schooling is concerned, this suggests a right at most to a school that will teach the child *about* her parents' religion. Whether that implies a school with a distinct religious ethos is far from clear: one could imagine a secular school system teaching children enough about their parents' various religious views that no supplementation was required. In some contexts, perhaps, this rationale might extend to sending one's child to Sunday school, or its equivalent in other faiths, but only for a limited period and again, and crucially, only where the faith is presented in non-directive terms. The point is to inform and educate the child about the parents' views—*ex hypothesi* in ways that the parent cannot do at home—not to guide her towards their endorsement. Where parents do indeed need to draw on this kind of ancillary provision, they should bear the cost privately, just as non-religious parents are expected to use their own resources when sharing their sporting or cultural enthusiasms with their children.

What are the schooling implications of cases where parents' religious views are such that they can only give their children the loving relationship they need if they are deliberately directing those children towards (their view of) the truth on religious matters? These are those parents for whom sharing, revealing, and hoping are not enough. I suggested that they should be regarded as wronging their children—even if excusably so, and even if their children might reasonably forgive them—with the degree of wrong varying across different specifications of the case. The state cannot police familial interactions within the home without denying parents the discretion they need to discharge their relationship duties—so it has to permit parents the space to misuse their authority in that context—but, at least in principle, it can identify schools that are complicit in those wrongs. To ban religious schooling that guides children towards a particular religious view is to protect children from the illegitimate exercise of parental authority. This is so even where that schooling also provides them with the capacity for autonomy.

Readers may wonder whether my claim about the value of discontinuity applies to children at all ages. Given my focus on the developmental significance of parent–child relationships and the obvious point that healthy development involves children's relationships with their parents changing over time, it may seem strange that I have felt able to ignore the difference between pre-school children and those at primary school, or between primary and secondary education. Even those who agree that a concern for autonomy rules out religious schooling at the secondary stage may think that it is permissible that children attend primary schools that immerse them in a particular religious tradition and teach them to reason in accordance with the ethical framework that it provides. One reason offered for that view is precisely that it is important, for the development of autonomy itself, that a young child's school experience be consonant with the primary culture that she receives at home. If they are to develop the kind of secure and stable identity that is a precondition of autonomy, young children need their schooling to reinforce the messages they get from their parents, not to undermine them.[25]

Suppose this claim is right. It leaves the issue of primary schooling hostage to the way that parents choose to conduct life within the home. Parents can indeed instil in their young children such firm religious beliefs, and beliefs about issues of such high stakes (such as a fear of eternal damnation), that those children may suffer if they are informed about, never mind encouraged to consider the merits of, alternative views. The same can apply in the case of more moderate doctrines, if family life is so suffused with religious practice and observance that children experience the world entirely in its terms. Some of the harm may be specifically to the stability of their identity, and affect the development of autonomy that way, some may be to the familial relationship more generally. What this shows is the extent of the power that parents have over their children—which is why it matters so much that they not exceed its proper exercise. The familial relationship goods account of parents' rights permits parents to share and reveal their religious views but not deliberately, let alone systematically, to direct children towards those views. We cannot—should not—police what goes on within the home, so public policy with respect to religious schooling will doubtless have a remedial aspect, adjusting itself to parents' illegitimate choices and doing the best for children in the circumstances. But if parents observe the proposed constraints, children will not need to be protected from different perspectives, even at the primary stage of education.

This last point takes us into questions about non-ideal circumstances. Chapter 7 will present some policy proposals that are consciously tailored to various feasibility constraints, but my argument has been pitched at a purely philosophical level. The aim has been to bracket many real-world considerations and enquire into the nature of parents' rights over their children's religious upbringing in a rather abstract and idealized manner. The focus has been almost entirely on what freedoms the state must, in principle, grant in that domain and on how parents may permissibly exercise those freedoms if granted. This question about how policy should respond to parents' exceeding their legitimate authority in their home is just one of many issues that demand attention once we factor in the various different ways that parents, or policies, may fall short of the prescribed ideals. For example, most of my arguments apply both to private schools and to those that are publicly funded. Because it results in a substantial narrowing of the scope of the proper exercise of parental authority, my attempt to go back to basics means denying the public/private distinction its conventional status as an organizing principle to guide policy. But it remains an interesting and important question how the state sector should respond if, as is in fact the case—and as many believe it should be—the regulation of independent religious schools, or of homeschooling, is less strict than that of schools funded at taxpayers' expense. Just as parents' acting beyond the proper scope of their authority may warrant remedial special measures when it comes to primary schooling, so policies for the public sector may justifiably be affected by the other options that are available. It could be appropriate to adjust the regulation of state schools so as to accommodate parental preferences and thereby reduce parental exit into even less regulated private alternatives. Another example concerns the situation where one particular religion, such as the Church of England, is granted privileged status within the state system. It may be wrong that Anglican parents can send their children to schools that endorse their preferred religion, but it may also be unfair that they can do so while members of other faiths cannot. This comparative worry concerns those elements of our analytical framework concerned with distributive principles. Is it right, all things considered, to extend equally to all parents the option of misusing their parental authority, or is that a kind of "levelling down" that unjustifiably imposes a wrong on all children, rather than just on some of them, in the name of fairness?

I don't have space here to discuss such matters but one general point is too important to pass by. When I claim, for example, that parents have no right to send their children to a directive religious school, I mean specific-ally that the state would not be wronging parents if it prevented them from doing so: a policy banning all such schools would not violate parents' rights. I do *not* mean that, where such schools are in fact permitted, a parent would never be justified in sending her child to such a school: the options she faces may be such that she not only has the right to choose such a school but even that she has the duty to do so.[26] Schools vary in many different ways, and conscientious parents will take into account the full range of their obligations to their children. Sometimes parents might choose a religious school not for its religion but for its other properties.

Suppose, for example, that, of the options available to her, only a religious school is "good enough". In terms of the three distributive principles identified in Chapter 2, this would constitute an adequacy view, albeit applied at the individual rather than the societal level. Suppose, that is, that all the available non-religious schools are inadequate, in the sense that, in one way or another, parents who chose such a school would be failing to discharge their fiduciary duties to their children. Perhaps the other schools are dangerous, or rife with religious harassment, or perhaps the educational standards are so low that, given her other circumstances, the child does not have a realistic prospect of achieving self-respect or avoiding a life of poverty.[27] Perhaps, indeed, the alternative schools are less likely to facilitate children's autonomy than the religious option. After all, nothing in my argument has ruled out the possibility that even a directive religious school may be more conducive to the development of children's autonomy than the available non-religious alternatives. That will depend, in part, on the content of the religious views to which the child is being directed and the continuity, if any, between those views and the parents' own.

Many parents believe that they have a right to choose the best available school for their children; some think that they have a duty to do so. If an option is legally available, they are justified in taking it. That is not my claim. Nor, in my view, is their choice justified simply because they *believe* it is the only one that is "good enough". Many parents have implausible moral views about what counts as "good enough" and many have false beliefs about what the schools available to them are actually like. My point is simply that we should distinguish the question of whether the state would wrong parents if religious schools were banned, which is what I have been discussing here, from that of whether and when parents may be justified in using such a school where it is available. That is by no means to condone all those parents—whether religious or otherwise—who choose a religious school because they think it better than the alternatives.

4. Conclusion

By getting clear on what parents are for, and why it is so valuable for many people that they get to be one, we put ourselves in a position to think coherently about the proper scope of parents' rights. If the familial relationship goods account presented here is correct, then there are many ways in which our current practice is too deferential to parents. Allowing them to raise their children as adherents of their own religion is one such way. Where that is done at the expense of children's developing the various capacities needed to make and live by their own judgments on religious matters, the wrong—and often harm—we thereby permit parents to inflict on their children is grave indeed. But even where autonomy is not impeded, parents nonetheless exceed the proper limits of their authority, and thereby fail to respect an important non-consequentialist consideration, if they use their power over their children deliberately to guide their children in their preferred direction. Children's interest in a particular kind of relationship with their parents means that we must leave plenty of room for interactions by which parents will, in fact, tend to influence their children's views about religious matters. The relationship itself, and the discretion it affords to parents, pose a standing threat to children's developing the requisite independence. By following the misguided view that policy must respect parents' preferences for their children's schooling, and so allowing schools to reinforce the religious messages they get from home, we are depriving those children of their key protection against that threat.

But it is not only their children who suffer from excessive deference to parents. As I suggested at the beginning, that deference also obstructs the legitimate pursuit of the civic and moral educational goods outlined in Chapter 2. My argument has focused entirely on parents' rights over, and duties to, their own children, but many similar policy conclusions would follow simply from giving proper weight to the interests of their fellow citizens. We all have a legitimate interest in how other people's children are raised; that interest extends beyond the concern that they be trustworthy, capable of trusting others, and able to limit their pursuit of self-interest for the sake of mutually beneficial cooperation. It matters also that they are equipped to play their role as democratic citizens in a liberal state, which requires a range of deliberative and moral capacities that are best developed through contact with, and understanding of, others raised in different religious traditions, and none. Schools are the obvious place for that contact and understanding to be accomplished.

One might reject my restrictive view of parents' rights, and grant parents more extensive authority over their children's religious education, while recognizing that parents, qua citizens, also have civic duties that properly inform policy with respect to religious schooling. As far as that issue is concerned, my main aim has been to propose a different way of thinking about the relation between parenthood and citizenship. Just as my approach offers an unusually integrated account of parents' and children's rights, so too it reduces the conflict between people's roles as parents and citizens. Rather than balancing parents' right to send their children to a religious school against the legitimate pursuit of civic goals, we should deny that they have that right in the first place.

How to Think about Religious Schools: Principles and Policies. Matthew Clayton, Andrew Mason, and Adam Swift, Oxford University Press. © Matthew Clayton, Andrew Mason, and Adam Swift 2024.
DOI: 10.1093/9780198924036.003.0005

PART III

FROM PRINCIPLES
TO POLICIES

6
Being Realistic

In Chapter 2 we set out a normative analytical framework that provides a helpful way of understanding what is at stake, morally speaking, in the various political controversies surrounding religious schools. We also defended a view about which of its elements should be the most important drivers of education policy; namely, cultivating children's autonomy and their disposition to treat others as equals. That was all common ground. In Chapters 3, 4, and 5, on the other hand, we went our separate ways. Each of us offered his own perspective on the philosophical issues, coming at them from his own angle, and reaching somewhat different conclusions. To be sure, the conclusions we reached individually were not *that* different. We all share some basic liberal assumptions, such as the importance of personal autonomy. Doubtless some readers will be more struck by what our supposedly diverging arguments have in common than by the sometimes subtle differences between them. Sometimes, indeed, we argue for the same conclusions by different routes. That said, we trust that it is illuminating to compare and contrast our individual approaches—our distinctive starting-points, and our detailed views about how to interpret, weigh, and combine the various normative considerations that constitute the framework.

Part III of the book is again jointly authored. This is the part where we move from principles to policies, and we can write with one voice partly because we agree about how to do that. Indeed, we agree about three different things. First, as we have explained, we share some judgments about which normative considerations are particularly important. Second, we share a view about how to make the transition from abstract, "in principle", philosophical discussion to concrete policy recommendations for a particular time and place. That view, about method in applied political philosophy, is the topic of this chapter. And third, we agree in a proposal for a regulatory framework that should apply to religious schools in England here and now. Applying the suggested method, we reach the same substantive conclusions about how religious schools should be regulated in this particular time and place. The next chapter presents those conclusions.

We emphasize these points about coincidence and divergence in our views because they show something about the relation between philosophical positions and policy recommendations. Simply put, there is no one-to-one correspondence between the two. People who agree entirely at the level of values may disagree about what policies it makes sense to endorse here and now. Perhaps, for example, they hold different empirical beliefs about the likely consequences of the different policies. Some may think that a particular policy will cultivate a strong disposition to treat others as equals while others, no less supportive of that goal, think that the policy will have the opposite effect. And, conversely, people who disagree philosophically about values may nonetheless agree, at the level of political action, about what governments should do—about what rules they should enforce—in current circumstances. That's what happens in this book. Our philosophical differences—for example concerning parent's rights to raise their children as members of a particular religion—count for nothing when it comes to our proposal for how religious schools in England should be regulated in England.

That may seem strange. Worse, it may suggest that our disagreements are "academic", in the pejorative use of that word which equates it with "irrelevant" or "a waste of time". Why bother engaging with all that philosophical complexity if there is no practical pay-off? One answer is that one can't know in advance what one's philosophical conclusions will be. So one can't know in advance whether they will or won't have practical implications. It's only after getting at least reasonably clear on one's views at the philosophical level that one can go on to work out what they mean for policy questions here and now. There is no way to shortcut that process. Another answer is that, when it comes to political decisions, people typically want to know not only the *what* but also the *why*.

Suppose that, without engaging with the philosophical issues that lie beneath, you were nonetheless completely confident about which policies for regulating religious schools are the right ones. Surely you'd want to know *why* they are the right ones? You might want to know so that you could explain and justify your reasons to others. After all, if you don't understand your reasons for favouring a particular policy, you're not well placed to respond to others' objections. You haven't even thought about whether those objections might be valid. But even if you're not interested in explaining and justifying to others—imagine that you're the education minister in a dictatorship with absolute power to choose the rules however you want—still you ought to care about whether you can justify your policy preferences to yourself, and in a way that does not appeal merely to your own interests, or the interests of your family or class. The alternative is arbitrariness, irresponsibility, or injustice—and potentially all three. Our individual chapters are simply our attempts to present in more detail our views about the normative considerations that are most relevant when assessing policies to regulate religious schools. There we reach conclusions that we believe to be justifiable to others as well as ourselves—despite failing to persuade each other of the merits of our own particular nuanced way of interpreting and balancing the normative factors that we agree are important!

Why do our diverging philosophical views converge on the same policies? Part of the answer is that we all think that the development of children's capacities for personal autonomy and civic and political understanding should be the primary drivers of education policy. Another part is that we want our policy proposals to be realistic and feasible, and we want their adoption to make things better. Much political philosophy operates at the level of "ideal theory", or "theory of ideals".[1] The aim is to identify the general principles that would apply in the ideal society, or perhaps, a bit more modestly, to establish what some of its specific institutions would look like: the ideal taxation policy, the ideal health care system, the ideal education system, and so on. Unlike some of its more trenchant critics, we have no objection to that kind of work. Indeed, some parts of our individual chapters can be thought of as engaging in exactly that exercise. Imagine a society where political and social arrangements are exactly as they should be. As far as education is concerned, the right mixture of educational goods is being produced and distributed just as it should be, everybody is respecting their duties to others, everybody is getting exactly what they have a right to. It's a perfectly sensible and interesting question to ask what rules would apply to religious schools in that ideal scenario. Or, putting it another way, to ask what the rules would need to be in order to produce those outcomes, ensure compliance with those duties, and respect those rights.

Those are excellent questions, and the kind of thinking that is needed to answer them clearly feeds into judgments about which policies would best be pursued here and now. Indeed, our normative framework is intended to help at that more "ideal" level just as much as at the level of concrete policy suggestions. We think of it as identifying the various "ideals" that should be factored in, and weighed against each other, at *all* levels. But the rules that would apply in the ideal society may not be realistic or feasible here and now. There may be aspects of the real world that make it impossible, or at least very unlikely, that they will be put into operation by those who get to decide these matters. And there may be real-world considerations that mean that, if they were put into operation, they would not produce the same results as they would in the ideal scenario. In effect, then, the real world— with all its non-ideal circumstances—acts as a kind of constraint or filter through which proposals that may be normatively desirable "in principle" have to pass in order to be effective and justified "in practice".

In different ways, our individual chapters have already touched on various "non-ideal" considerations. Andrew Mason notes that, when evaluating schools that are homogenous in terms of students' religious background, we must compare them not to the rarely instantiated ideal of a religiously diverse and well-integrated school but to the available, or at least feasible, alternatives. In the real world, for example, even religiously diverse schools can be rife with religiously motivated bullying, often against victimized minorities. Without addressing these wider social problems, rules prohibiting religiously homogenous schools might be better in principle but worse in practice. Matthew Clayton observes that, when compared to the status quo, religious schools offer a range of benefits: resources, inclusion in a competitive educational environment, self-respect in the face of discrimination, and the development of children's concern and respect for others. These complicate his "in principle" argument for their abolition and suggest that abolition may only make sense, all things considered, if accompanied by other reforms. Adam Swift suggests that the rules applying to state schools should take into account parents' legal right to opt for a private, and less regulated, alternative. In his view, that legal right is misconceived and private schools should be more heavily regulated. But since that right exists, it's likely that restricting parents' options with regard to state schools will drive many of them out of the state system and into private religious schools. That would be even worse for their children, and their fellow citizens, so introducing restrictions in the state system alone would be counterproductive.

In all these cases, empirical factors prevent a smooth and direct inference from judgments about normative considerations to concrete policy recommendations, even when we are clear about exactly how they should be interpreted and what weight they should each be given. Facts need to be taken into account too. Expectations about what non-religious schools will actually be like, for example, or about how parents might react to a particular reform, make a difference. They make a difference to whether a particular proposal will, in fact, bring about an improvement, normatively speaking. Perhaps, in practice, a well-intentioned and, in principle, normatively well-justified reform would make things worse. Our discussion of the analytical framework we presented in Chapter 2 already recognized this implicitly. Our emphasis on the need to make trade-offs between different educational goods, for example, in effect reflected the recognition that it was not possible to have it all. That's partly for empirical reasons. An obvious one is that resources are not infinite, so one has to prioritize some goals over others. And it's partly because the most effective means to produce some goods will not be the most effective way to produce others. Now that we are moving from philosophy to policy, the significance of empirical considerations becomes more explicit. We are still in the business of balancing different normative considerations—both consequentialist and non-consequentialist. But when it comes to concrete recommendations about the rules that should apply to religious schools, what's needed is a balancing of those considerations applied to our best guesses as to the scenarios realistically available to us here and now. When we do that, our views converge.

1. A Simple Method

Our method for getting from philosophy to policy is actually rather simple. It's simple in the sense that it is fairly easy to understand what needs to be done. That doesn't mean that it's easy to *do*. It involves combining normative judgments with interpretations of social-scientific evidence about the real world. Both elements are challenging. We've already seen, on the normative side, that various different considerations have to be balanced against each other. And interpreting the relevant empirical evidence, or even deciding which evidence is relevant, is by no means straightforward. In terms of academic disciplines, these are two different skill sets. Philosophy trains people to do the former; social science—sociology, economics, political science, psychology—trains them to do the latter. So combining the two, as our method proposes, requires one to be both a philosopher and a social scientist. That may seem unrealistically demanding. If so, the good news is that you're almost certainly already doing it. Anybody who has a view about policy on a matter of moral significance is in effect holding a mixture of moral and empirical judgments. They must be thinking something normative: what should we want to happen here? And they must be thinking something empirical: what's the best way to make that happen? So we're not really proposing a new method at all. We're just making explicit the kind of process people are going through, perhaps implicitly or unconsciously, anyway.

Policy proposals have to meet different standards from purely philosophical work. They must be sensitive to a variety of empirical factors that constrain the outcomes that are actually available in the particular context for which they are proposed. Policy should aim to achieve the best outcome that is realistically available in the circumstances. ("Best outcome" here stands for the outcome that best combines the salient consequentialist and non-consequentialist consideration.) So one needs to work out what outcomes are realistically available and which of them is best. It's that simple. The first component is empirical. It involves looking at the world, understanding how things are now, identifying the available options for reform, and assessing what would happen if we took them. The second component is normative. It involves thinking about the different values and principles at stake and judging which of the available outcomes best promotes and respects them. We are looking for the policies that will realize the best overall balance or combination of values and principles that is available to us, given where we are now and where we can realistically get to from here.

Although we presented these two components—empirical and normative—as "first" and "second", they do not form a sequence. They are analytically distinct and it's important to keep them separate in that sense. It's not a good idea to let one's normative judgments influence one's views about what is and isn't realistic; that amounts to wishful thinking and leads to bad policy. And, conversely, one shouldn't let one's views about what outcomes are realistic affect one's values; that leads to a version of adaptive preferences whereby, like the fox with the grapes in Aesop's fable, one gives up one's belief that something is valuable just because one thinks one can't have it. But a useful method for getting from philosophy to policy will have to involve both components simultaneously. The logical distinction does not imply a chronological one. There's no point working out which *bad* outcomes are realistically available, so normative judgments will naturally be factored in to the empirical process of assessing where we can realistically get to from here. And, from a policy perspective, it serves no purpose to identify the best conceivable outcome if it's obvious that it cannot be achieved.

If anything, it's the values and principles that come first, since those are what motivate policy proposals. People propose changes to policies—like the ones in the next chapter—because they judge that current policies are failing to achieve some valuable outcomes, or to respect some important principles. It's the normative considerations that provide the impetus for change, not the simple empirical recognition that change is possible. In that sense, though we agree entirely that policy should be "evidence-based", we insist that it must nonetheless be "values-driven".[2]

How, then, does one go about judging which of the available outcomes is best? Indeed, how does one judge whether an outcome is better or worse than another? Our normative framework in Chapter 2 emphasized the multiplicity of considerations at stake, both consequentialist and non-consequentialist. On the consequentialist side, there is a range of educational goods and a plurality of distributive considerations. On the non-consequentialist side, there are various rights or entitlements that people may have as parents, children, or citizens. We've said that our simple method involves looking for the best overall balance or combination of the values and principles at stake, but telling you what to look for may seem inadequate. What's needed, you may reasonably demand, is a method for finding it!

That method is what moral and political philosophers call "reflective equilibrium".[3] The "equilibrium" bit sounds like the "balancing" or "weighing" of different considerations that we have talked about. The idea is that we try to combine our various judgments and principles, any of which, taken on their own, might pull us in a different direction, into a coherent, stable overall view. The "reflective" bit means that we do that in a serious, thoughtful way (which you might think should go without saying). To explain, consider an educational issue that has nothing to do with religion. Suppose you have a clear conviction that expensive private schools should not be allowed. Reflecting on why you hold that view suggests that it comes from your endorsing a principle of equality of opportunity. You think that, as a general principle, it's wrong that children have unequal prospects in life just because they happen to be raised in different families. So far so good: judgment and principle fit together. But then you realize that you don't feel the same about parents' reading bedtime stories to their children. You're aware of the evidence showing that allowing parents to read bedtimes stories also gives some children better prospects than others, since not all children are lucky enough to have parents who read to them. But you're not inclined to ban bedtime stories. What to do? Either you have to revise your principle or you have to abandon your opposition to expensive private schools. This leads you to reflect on the differences between bedtime stories and expensive schools, and you come to think that banning the former would be much more damaging, in terms of the effects on family life, than banning the latter. So you revise your principle. It no longer condemns all inequalities between children that result from parental influence, only those that are not inevitably produced by valuable family relationships. Now you are back in reflective equilibrium. You are balancing the different considerations in a way that forms a coherent whole.[4]

Of course this is a hugely simplified micro-example of reflective equilibrium in action. In reality, the process of reflection is likely to reveal that you make many different judgments, and endorse many different principles, and that the complete set contains many inconsistencies. Getting them to fit together into a coherent overall picture is challenging. What about parents' right to spend their money as they wish? What about parents' duty to do the best they can for their children? What about parents' responsibilities to protect their children from harm? These considerations too, and many others, will probably have to be factored in to your holistic normative picture. Perhaps, when they are, you will indeed end up revising your initial judgment and come to the conclusion that expensive private schools should be permitted after all. Or perhaps you'll come to a complicated view whereby it's wrong that expensive private schools exist but not always wrong for parents to send their children to them if they do exist.[5]

In essence, then, the normative component of our method requires individuals to judge what balance of values and principles makes most sense to them overall, having taken into account the full range of relevant considerations and organized them into a coherent whole. In Chapter 2 we identified the different elements that we think should be considered in making that judgment. In Chapters 3–5 we offered our own views about how they should be combined—our own recipes, if you like, for combining the various ingredients into the best overall cake. Each of us had his own views about what that cake should be; the process of achieving reflective equilibrium led each of us to somewhat different conclusions. But there was enough common ground for us to come together when engaging with the empirical component. Indeed, our individual—"reflectively equilibrated"—overall views about the relevant normative criteria are similar enough to yield the same conclusions when it comes to evaluating policy proposals.

Whereas achieving reflective equilibrium involves balancing different normative considerations to yield the "all things considered" criteria by which to assess policy proposals as better or worse, the actual evaluation of those proposals involves combining those criteria with empirical factors. Empirical factors need to be taken into account in two different ways.

Sometimes a policy proposal is flawed because its advocates haven't thought hard enough about what would happen if it were put into practice. It might look as if it will have the desired effect but actually the evidence suggests that it will make things worse, or it will make things better in some ways but worse in others. When put into practice, policies can have unintended consequences. But sometimes the proposed policy is a complete non-starter because there is no way of putting it into practice in the first place. When operating at the level of ideal theory, or theory of ideals, we may well suggest reforms that are unrealistic in this second sense: they don't take seriously the limited range of policy options that are genuinely available.

Both of these can be expressed as points about what is feasible, rather than merely desirable. In both, the concern is that we take feasibility constraints into account. But we're talking about the feasibility of different things. In the former, what's at stake is the feasibility of the policy's desired outcome. To use one of the examples that comes up in our individual chapters, imagine that someone proposed abolishing religious schools because they wanted children from different religious backgrounds to mix and develop harmonious relationships. The problem with that proposal, taken on its own, is that it's far from clear that the policy would achieve the goal. Given the evidence on residential segregation, or the way students segregate within schools, and on the prevalence of hostility between groups even within religiously diverse schools, one might conclude that the policy is unfeasible in that its goal is beyond its reach. Its consequences will not be those that were intended by its advocates.

But one might also think that the policy is unfeasible in the other way too. It's the policy itself, not only its outcomes, that are unfeasible. It's not a sensible proposal because, even if the evidence suggested that it *would* achieve its goal, there are other reasons—legal and political reasons—why it's not going to be implemented in the first place. Legally, a government that tried to abolish all religious schools would probably be found by the courts to be violating parents' human rights. Politically, abolishing parents' freedom to choose a religious school would be so unpopular—or at least controversial—that no party would propose it. Both kinds of feasibility constraint are frustrating, but they're frustrating in different ways. It's frustrating to discover that a policy that looks good at first sight is unlikely actually to achieve its purpose. But in some ways it's even more frustrating to discover that a policy that *would* achieve its purpose stands little or no chance of being adopted.

Judgments about what is feasible tend to be probabilistic rather than certain or determinate. The available social-scientific evidence can tell us only what is likely to happen, not what will definitely happen. That's true even if the evidence is as good as it gets. In some natural sciences, like physics, experiments can be conducted under laboratory conditions, in others—like medicine—researchers can use randomized control trials to try to identify what exactly is causing what, and hence to predict the likely effects of any intervention. Things are more tricky in the social sciences, where it is harder to infer judgments about what is likely to happen in one time and place from evidence gathered in another.[6] So when we say, in summarizing our simple method, that "one needs to work out what outcomes are realistically available and which of them is best", that's a simplification. It really involves combining (i) judgments about the probability of various outcomes coming about, based on relevant available empirical evidence with (ii) an all things considered evaluation of those outcomes, based on the relevant normative considerations.

Imagine, for example, a policy that might achieve results that score very highly from a normative perspective. It promises to improve children's capacity for autonomy, and their civic and moral capacities, without doing any harm to their test scores. More than that, if successful, it would distribute this improved mixture of educational goods rather better than any of those goods is distributed at present. The least advantaged children will get an adequate level where currently they fall well below that acceptable minimum. And it would do all this whilst honouring both parents' and children's rights. Parents will still be free to exercise legitimate authority over their children, while children's moral status as independent people will be properly respected. That sounds wonderful. But suppose further that that there is only a small chance that the policy will in fact achieve these highly desirable outcomes. The evidence suggests that there's a good chance that it will make no difference whatsoever, and it may even backfire, leaving things worse than they were before. That should all be taken into account when evaluating the policy and comparing it to others.

It might seem that this point about feasibility judgments being probabilistic applies only to the first kind, concerning unintended consequences and the outcomes that would actually come about if a policy were put into practice. We used that kind of example to explain and illustrate the point, but in fact the same thought applies to the second kind of feasibility too. Sometimes, perhaps, we can be confident that a particular policy proposal has absolutely no chance of being adopted, but often the issue is less clear-cut. This is particularly relevant in the case of political feasibility. Considering whether a policy is politically feasible involves thinking about whether it might be adopted by the relevant decision-making actors. Who those are depends, of course, on the kind of policy that we're talking about. Sometimes they will be head teachers, or school governors, or members of religious organizations. But in the case of a national-level proposal for regulation of the kind we're interested in, we're talking about elected politicians who are somewhat responsive to citizen's views as expressed through the ballot box. Opinion polling is a sophisticated enterprise, but even so one can't always be certain, in advance, what will and will not garner popular support at any given time. And one certainly can't be sure that it will or won't succeed in doing that in the future. Proposals that were yesterday's electoral suicide become today's common sense. Once we build in a temporal perspective, and think about the likelihood of a policy being adopted not tomorrow but in 10 or 20 years' time, then we're definitely in the realm of probabilistic judgments. The same is true in the case of legal feasibility, although here the mechanisms are somewhat different. Human rights law may, at a particular time, definitely rule out a proposal like the complete abolition of religious schools, but even human rights law is not set in stone. It is perfectly coherent to consider the likelihood of its changing in a particular way over a particular time frame.

2. Feasibility Constraints

The next chapter offers our proposal for a regulatory framework to apply to religious schools in England. That is what results from our application of our "simple method". None of us regards it as ideal or perfect. In different ways, we each hope that one day circumstances will change so that an even better way of addressing the issues becomes available. But, given the current context, we suggest that our proposal would be a very substantial improvement.

Before spelling out the details in the next chapter, it will be helpful to identify clearly how we have factored in the various real-world feasibility constraints with which we take ourselves to be operating. We identified three different kinds of factor that need to be taken into account: unintended consequences, legal constraints, and political constraints in the form of public opinion. Let us address each of these in turn.

2.1 Unintended Consequences

The point here is that different regulatory regimes create different incentive structures, so good policies anticipate, and take into account, their likely effects on affected parties. A regulatory framework that would achieve its aims if agents subject to the regulation responded with one kind of choice might be counterproductive if they responded differently. For example, tighter regulation of maintained faith schools, perhaps motivated by a concern for children's autonomy, might cause parents to exit from the state sector into less regulated areas. In the absence of increased regulation of private and home education, that might jeopardize still further the autonomy of those children most at risk of failing to develop that capacity. There is a similar concern about how religious organizations that provide faith schools would respond to any regulatory changes. If unwilling to comply with policies enforced in the state sector, they might withdraw into the private sector. This would be problematic not only for the children attending them but also, in the case of the Church of England and the Catholic Church, from a resource perspective as it would leave a massive hole in funding that the public purse is ill equipped to fill.

There is some evidence that government policy has been motivated in part by a willingness to secure the inclusion, within the state system, of religious parents and organizations, most recently the debate around the 50 per cent cap on religious selection. While the principled nature of our approach means that we will sometimes push back against some of the more unreasonable demands and expectations of stakeholders, we acknowledge the importance of taking their reactions seriously. One important implication is that we explicitly offer our proposals as a package, not as suggestions to be considered on their individual merits. To accept some of our proposals but not others would be to increase the risk of counterproductive unintended consequences.

2.2 Legal Constraints

While policymakers have some power to alter the law, they are obliged to take decisions within pre-established legal frameworks. There is no point proposing a regulatory framework, however normatively compelling, that would be challenged and found to be illegal. While philosophically we might disagree with its content, our proposals must abide by existing human rights law, which grants parents significant rights to control their children's education, especially with regard to religion. This is particularly relevant to the regulation of the private sector, and especially those ways of educating children—including home education—that make no claims on the public purse. While governments need not help parents realize their preference to educate their children as members of a particular religion, or as atheists, human rights law means that they may not prevent them from doing so privately.

It is worth emphasizing how legal constraints and unintended consequences interact in limiting the outcomes available to us, however normatively desirable those outcomes might be. A sensible policy proposal will take into account parents' likely responses, given the options available to them. It is partly because human rights law says that parents must be free to send their children to religious schools, albeit privately funded ones, or to home educate, that policymakers need to take seriously the possibility of flight from the state sector and into the private sector and home education. For some of us, this affects the rules that we propose regarding schools' having a religious ethos, with knock-on implications for their admissions policies. If it were legally possible to ban religious schools altogether, then the policymaker would not need to anticipate that scenario.

2.3 Political Constraints and Public Opinion

It is important that our proposals are capable of securing popular support. Policy suggestions that ignore the significance of democratic approval are both normatively problematic and doomed to irrelevance. We believe that the values and principles—and judgments about how to combine them—that inform our proposals are valid whether or not our fellow citizens happen to agree with them. Indeed, we hope to persuade those who disagree with us that we're right and they're wrong. But we recognize, of course, that at least some degree of popular acceptance is a condition both of our proposals becoming legitimate policies and of their having any chance of being adopted in the real world.

That last sentence contains two importantly different thoughts. It's worth pausing to unpack them. On the one hand, we want our policy proposals to be legitimate. Here the challenge is normative. Legitimacy is a moral consideration, about what justifies a policy being imposed on those who have to follow it. On the other hand, we want our policies to have a realistic chance of being adopted. Here the challenge is practical. The issue simply concerns what policies we can and cannot get put into practice. Public opinion comes into both but it does so in very different ways.

To worry about whether a policy would be legitimate is to worry about its moral status. To see how public opinion is relevant, imagine again that you're the dictatorial education minister with the power to decide unilaterally how religious schools should be regulated. That seems wrong, and it seems wrong whatever regulations you decide to impose. What's objectionable is that you don't have the moral right to decide that question. You may have the power to decide it, but even if you make great decisions, your decisions will lack legitimacy. They will lack legitimacy because they don't stand in the right relation to the views of those who are subject to them. Political philosophers have offered many different theories about exactly what would count as the right relation, most of which appeal to the ideal of democracy. What's wrong with the education dictator is what's wrong with all dictators. The laws they impose lack legitimacy because they are not the outcome of a properly democratic process, one in which the rules are made collectively, and equally, by those who are subject to them, that is, by democratic citizens.

This is not the place to explore the niceties of democratic theory and the nature of political authority.[7] The important thing is to see how this reason for caring that a proposal can win the approval of public opinion differs from the second, straightforwardly strategic concern. Here the point is simply that, as a matter of empirical fact, we live in a system where laws are made, directly, by politicians and hence, indirectly, by the citizens who vote for them. Even if we rejected the democratic legitimacy case for taking account of public opinion, we'd still need to take that opinion into account as a feasibility constraint. To be clear, none of us regrets that fact. Though we all think there are big problems with the ways that our political decision-making processes currently operate in practice, none of us regards democratic procedures as regrettable impediments to our secret desire to impose our views on our fellow citizens. What we do regret is the content of public opinion. That's what we are trying to change in writing this book.

We take public opinion seriously, for both reasons just discussed. But that doesn't mean that we feel ourselves constrained to work within the bounds set by public opinion here and now. Indeed, we are confident that many—perhaps the majority—of our fellow citizens will object to our proposals and judge them prejudiced against parents and communities who wish to continue not only to raise but also to school their children as members of particular faiths. We do not expect any political party immediately to endorse our views and incorporate them into their next manifesto. What matters, for us, is that there is a plausible causal story whereby public debate about the issues leads to a gradual shift of opinion in our direction. Sometimes, as in the case of homosexuality and abortion, legislative change can itself help to foster such a shift. We believe that the considerations that motivate our views—the importance of treating children as morally independent of their parents, and of fostering tolerant and informed civic and moral attitudes—are persuasive enough that, given a fair and considered hearing, regulations that currently seem obvious and natural to many will in fact be amenable to quite radical revision. Here, we hope without grandiosity, we might cite John Stuart Mill's *The Subjection of Women* as a precedent.

3. Conclusion

This chapter has set out a method for moving from philosophy to policy. In one sense, that method is simple. It's quite easy to understand how, in our view, one should combine normative and empirical considerations to work out the best policy for our current circumstances. We want the set of policies that has the best outcome; that is, the outcome that best combines the salient consequentialist and non-consequentialist considerations. In another way, putting it into practice, it's very challenging. Some of our thinking has to be philosophical. How should we interpret the various different elements in our normative periodic table and how important are they? How should we weigh them against each other when they conflict and we have to make trade-offs? Some of it has to be social-scientific: What does the evidence show about the feasibility of any proposed reform? Will it have unintended consequences? Is it legally and politically realistic?

Part II of the book was devoted to our individual views on the deeper philosophical issues. There we have different interpretations of some of the normative considerations, like parents' and children's rights. But we come together when it comes to proposing policies to regulate religious schools in England. Our judgments about feasibility constraints help to explain that convergence. In effect, then, our empirical views—about what is realistically achievable—filter out the more fundamental, extreme, and diverging elements of our individual positions.

The regulatory framework we propose in the next chapter tries to steer a middle course between wishful thinking and pragmatic acquiescence.

Taking seriously the normative considerations we have identified, and getting the right balance between them, demands substantial changes to the way our society supports religious education, and to the kinds of schooling that parents are permitted to impose on their children. But we are not demanding the impossible. We are proposing neither the abolition of religious schools, nor even that they be ineligible for public funding. Rather, we make the case for their more extensive regulation. There is nothing in our recommendations that falls foul of current human rights law, we are hopeful that the responses of parents and religious organizations will not make the suggested changes counterproductive, and there is no reason to regard our proposals as beyond the pale in terms of public opinion and democratic approval.

How to Think about Religious Schools: Principles and Policies. Matthew Clayton, Andrew Mason, and Adam Swift, Oxford University Press. © Matthew Clayton, Andrew Mason, and Adam Swift 2024.
DOI: 10.1093/9780198924036.003.0006

7

A Regulatory Framework for England

We conclude with a series of proposals for the regulation of religious schools in England. Chapter 2 set out a framework for analysing the normative considerations at stake and identified the key normative views that we share. Chapters 3–5 offered our own individual perspectives on some of the key philosophical issues. Chapter 6 explained our method for combining normative views with empirical judgments about what outcomes are feasible in the circumstances. In this final chapter we present the implications. What kinds of religious school should the state support or permit? In what ways may its religious identity legitimately influence what happens in a school and who goes to it?

We start with and focus on publicly funded schools, which educate the great majority of children and where the case for regulation is strongest. But our holistic approach requires us to take a broad view of the likely effects that a regulatory regime will have across the board. We need to keep in mind the possibility that more extensive regulation of state schools will precipitate an increase in children being taken out of that sector, and we are in any case concerned to respect the interests of children who are already educated privately or at home. We thus conclude with suggestions for the rules that should apply in those domains too.

1. Religious Instruction and Formation

Our first proposal for the reform of state-funded faith schools is that religious instruction, by which we mean directive teaching towards (or against) religious commitment, ought to be prohibited. Directive teaching consists in teachers aiming to impart beliefs or commitments to their pupils. It is contrasted with non-directive teaching in which the teacher aims to introduce pupils to a debate or range of answers to a controversial topic without trying to get them to endorse a particular answer. In more commonsensical language, the difference is between teaching *a* religion and teaching *about* religion. Where religious instruction guides students towards particular views, the latter—which we will discuss below under its familiar label of Religious Education—comes from a more neutral perspective.

Directive teaching is rightly practised across a broad range of the curriculum. It is important for children to come to understand and embrace the truths of mathematics and to hold helpful scientific beliefs. They should also be encouraged to develop a commitment to certain moral and political views, such as the importance of toleration and respect and concern for others. Teaching religious propositions as true, however, should not be permitted, even in religious schools. There should be no classes that encourage children to believe that Jesus is the son of God whose crucifixion and resurrection redeemed humankind, that Allah is the one true God and only He is worthy of worship, or that there is no God and human beings can find ethical and spiritual fulfilment without belief in a divinity.

The proposal is motivated by the concern for personal autonomy that we outlined when presenting our normative framework. It is important for individuals to have the opportunity to decide for themselves what kind of life to live and to reflect and act upon those decisions in a well-informed manner. Some regard personal autonomy as a constitutive feature of how one ought to live: to live well an individual must endorse the goals she pursues on the basis of serious reflection about their merits. For others, it has instrumental value: if individuals enjoy opportunities to form beliefs about the values and goals around which they orientate their lives, rather than take them on trust from others, it is more likely that the values and goals they adopt will be good for them. There are many different kinds of good lives and people's talents and temperaments are suited to different lifestyles. Giving individuals the space to explore and come to their own view about what kind of life would be good for them is the best way of ensuring that they lead flourishing lives.[1] Still others see personal autonomy in non-consequentialist terms: in virtue of their moral status as separate individuals, people are entitled to be the authors of their own lives whether or not that will be good for them.[2]

We need not decide between these different defences of personal autonomy because they converge on broadly the same conclusion, namely, that it is important for individuals to be in a position to decide for themselves how they live their lives. The place of religion within an individual's life, if it has one, should be something that an individual is capable of deciding for herself through reflection on the merits of different religious and non-religious conceptions of what we ought to believe about the origins of the universe and what makes one's life go well. Of course, to be able to engage with religious questions autonomously, individuals need to be educated about religion. But that curriculum should not include directive religious teaching because it jeopardizes children's personal autonomy by posing a danger of closing their minds to other religious and non-religious ways of living.

Some offer a more straightforward objection to religious instruction. According to this view, since education is centrally concerned with the transmission of knowledge, it is morally permissible for teachers to try to get children to believe propositions only if those propositions are justified beyond reasonable doubt. Because religious propositions lack that status—there are plausible arguments both for and against many religious claims—religious instruction is morally impermissible.[3] Our proposal involves no such claims about religion's lack of epistemic warrant. It is quite compatible with our argument to hold that some or all religious commitments, or atheism, are, beyond reasonable doubt, valuable or right. We simply rely on the thought that religious instruction can threaten the child's development and exercise of the capacity for personal autonomy so that she is in a position to decide for herself the values and commitments around which she builds her life.

Our central concern about religious instruction in faith schools is that it would allow many children's imaginative horizons to be saturated by one particular world view and in doing so either deprive them of the capacity seriously to consider other world views, or make it very difficult or costly for them to do so; for example, by inducing shame at the prospect of abandoning that world view or by triggering an identity crisis at the mere questioning of its value. This is what we mean when we say that it risks closing the minds of children to other religious and nonreligious ways of living. Although not all children who attend such schools have parents who practise the religion of the school in question, very many of them do. If religious instruction is permitted, the messages those children receive at home about what to believe, what relationships and goals are worth pursuing, and more generally the virtues one's life should embody, are reinforced by a further set of authoritative figures, their teachers. This is problematic, because it matters that children develop the skills to understand, and have meaningful opportunities to reflect on, different conceptions about how lives should be lived.

We do not claim that religious instruction poses a serious risk to the autonomy of all children. One can imagine many cases in which a child receives religious instruction without having her imaginative horizons closed, especially where life outside school exposes her to alternative world views, prompting meaningful and unmanipulated deliberation and an acknowledgement of the need to decide for herself what path to follow. Our concern is simply to ensure that children's imaginations are not over-whelmed by a single world view, which is a clear danger if the values, vir-tues, and beliefs children are directed towards in school mirror those they receive from their parents and others in their social milieu. It is primarily for the sake of these "at risk" children that we propose a blanket prohibition on religious instruction in state schools. Even where schools aim to foster the capacity for critical reflection and independent judgment alongside their attempt to guide children in the direction of particular views, directive religious teaching—whether "instruction" or "formation"[4]—cannot help but reinforce, both cognitively and emotionally, the religious perspective that children will often be receiving from their parents.[5]

Our proposed prohibition applies not only to formal instruction, where the aim is to impart knowledge or understanding, but also to some reli-giously informed rituals and customs, particularly acts of collective wor-ship. Religion is not only a cognitive matter; it extends beyond beliefs and doctrines to include affective relations to practices. Even where a school's curriculum is not explicitly guiding children to regard particular beliefs as true, its ways of doing things become habitual for them. Its practices are "formative" in the sense that they form children's developing identities and create deep attachments. Where they coincide with those fostered in chil-dren outside the school, those too can sometimes obstruct children's auton-omy, by significantly increasing the emotional cost of choosing a different way of being or even by making different ways seem alien and impossible. Moreover, those practices themselves tend to presume—and to foster the presumption—that certain religious claims are true. The risks here are par-ticularly high where schools regularly assemble children to pray to a God, for children are likely to receive an emotionally powerful message that the God in question exists—even if no such view is imparted in classroom lessons. Both the curriculum and the practices of faith schools can be dir-ective, then, in a way that bears a high risk of obstructing some children's development of personal autonomy. This risk exists even where a school denies that it is engaging in directive religious education, even where it is making efforts to develop its pupils' capacity for critical reflection, and even where the direction in question comes in the form of acts of collective wor-ship rather than conventional teaching.

We do not expect school inspectors to check for autonomy itself, or to take into account what may be happening in children's lives beyond the school gates in assessing individual schools. That would be unrealistically demanding on them and costly to the state. Rather, our proposal requires school inspectors to monitor all the various ways in which schools may engage in directive activities that, in combination with children's life outside school, put autonomy at risk. Currently, religious teaching in faith schools is inspected by representatives of the faith group in question.[6] On our understanding of the purpose of regulation, that arrangement is inappropriate and the job should be done in the normal way by Ofsted Inspectors.

Before moving on to our positive proposals for the religious education curriculum it is worth commenting on a particular objection to our proposal that religious instruction should be prohibited. This objection highlights a different element identified in our normative framework—personal fulfilment. Some claim that that good is threatened if children are not both initiated into a particular belief system, such as a religious doctrine, and protected from exposure to others, particularly where personal fulfilment is understood in terms of a having a sense of spirituality. The argument is that to encourage children to become fully initiated in the rites, practices, and beliefs of a religious view that will give them a proper appreciation of the spiritual dimension to human lives, it is necessary to shield them from the allure of other secular perspectives, for example those valuing the pursuit of wealth and material consumption. On this argument, we have to choose between personal fulfilment, especially if that is understood in spiritual terms, and autonomy. The claim is that these two considerations conflict; we have to choose between them, and we should prefer the former, with clear implications for children's religious upbringing, including their schooling.

We disagree with this analysis for three reasons. First, we reject the claim that personal fulfilment—even spiritual fulfilment—requires the pursuit of a religious life: there are countless ways, some of which do not require belief in a god, of engaging in goals and relationships that develop and exercise not only one's physical, aesthetic, and intellectual but also one's spiritual faculties. Second, autonomy is not a hindrance to one's adopting and pursuing religious beliefs: the many individuals who don't receive a religious upbringing and go on to embrace religious lifestyles show that autonomy is compatible with religious belief. And, third, as we explain below, we share the concern that many modern schooling systems in advanced industrial societies devote insufficient time to questions about how to live well, the nature of personal well-being, and our place in the universe. Our proposals for the regulation of religious schools, and indeed non-religious schools, are informed by that concern. Enabling children to become autonomous is a demanding educational aim that requires school students to engage seriously with competing views about religion, ethics, and different conceptions of fulfilment and spirituality. So we are no supporters of "secularism" if that is understood as a "utilitarian and materialist approach to education".[7] Rather, we have a less restrictive view about what constitutes personal fulfilment and a different understanding of how it relates to personal autonomy.

2. Religious Education

If directive religious instruction or formation are not a part of state-funded religious schools, what is the place of religion in the school curriculum? It matters, of course, that children learn *about* religion. This is partly because an understanding of the differing religious traditions—including different non-religious conceptions such as humanism—contributes to personal autonomy simply by informing children about the range of ways of living their lives available to them. And it is partly because, whatever judgments they may end up making about such matters, they will inevitably find themselves sharing social and political institutions with others who see the world very differently. The capacity to regard others as having equal moral status and to treat them accordingly, respecting and tolerating differences is best fostered by schooling that teaches children about a range of religious and non-religious world views. That said, the development of civic and moral capacities involves a lot more than knowledge about religious traditions and we see no reason to give religion any special status in the curriculum. We therefore join others who have made related suggestions[8] and call for a national entitlement to a curriculum in civic, religious, ethical and moral values (CREaM) that would subsume the current subject of Religious Education and incorporate both relevant aspects of what is currently taught as Citizenship Education and the issues covered under the ill-conceived label of "British Values".

Because it is important that every child develops the knowledge, skills, and dispositions the group of topics is designed to foster, we propose that CREaM education be common to all state schools, whether religious or not. Since the 1944 Education Act, the religious education syllabus has been determined locally, with each local authority having its own Standing

Advisory Council for Religious *Education* (SACRE). We see the case for religious organizations being involved in devising the syllabus at national level, alongside those with academic expertise in the study of religion, but their involvement in local bodies should be confined to matters of implementation.[9] Moreover, religious perspectives should be supplemented with representatives from the humanist tradition and others, such as philosophy societies, concerned more specifically with civic and moral values. Furthermore, owing to its non-directive nature with respect to questions of faith, parents should no longer be granted the right to withdraw their children from these lessons.[10]

The proposed CREaM syllabus would explicitly place religion alongside a broader education in citizenship, ethics, and morality. Religions provide answers to several different kinds of question: metaphysical, such as "does a deity, or do deities, exist?" and "why and how did the universe begin?"; ethical, such as, "what is the meaning of life?" and "what does living well consist in?"; and moral, such as "how should we treat each other?" or "what do we owe to each other?". Since 1944, religion, particularly Christianity, has been given a privileged place within the English school system and, accordingly, children have been encouraged to focus primarily on religious answers to these questions. This convention overlooks the answers offered by many non-religious approaches developed by philosophers, both ancient and modern. If we care about personal autonomy then the curriculum must get children to understand and engage critically with non-religious views on these important matters.[11]

CREaM education must combine directive and non-directive aims. Its non-directive purpose is to equip children with the understanding and capacity to decide for themselves what gods (if any) there are, and what goals and relationships are worth pursuing. The CREaM syllabus is also the place to teach children about how their social and political institutions work, so that they can take their place as competent, effective members of a democratic society.

For reasons discussed in the previous section, they should not be guided towards particular views on questions such as whether there is a god, what a good life consists in, or what kinds of life projects are valuable. But fostering civic and moral capacities in children requires directive education— education in how we ought to live with and treat others in society. The directive (broadly liberal) education we have in mind aims to impart to children the ability and motivation to regard and treat each other as equals, to promote and comply with democratic institutions, and to trust and respect others regardless of race, ethnicity, gender, sexuality, religion, or class. Direction is justified here because the considerations at stake are moral rather than ethical: they concern not what it means for an individual to live well but what she owes to others. Religions tend to have views on both sets of questions, but, philosophically speaking, they are very different. We explained above why education on ethical matters should be non-directive: direction threatens personal autonomy, which is a good for, or entitlement of, the person who has it. It is a good either because those who make their own judgments about how to live are most likely to choose well (instrumental) or because an individual's living well itself requires that she has made her own judgments (intrinsic). It is an entitlement because morally independent individuals are entitled to authorship of their own lives. But, as we see most clearly in the case of enforceable duties, moral issues are different: when it comes to doing right by others—treating them morally, or justly, or with respect—forming and acting on one's own judgment is simply less important. Of course, in proposing directive moral and civic education with a particular, liberal democratic content we are endorsing a political morality that puts citizens' equality, especially their equal claims to autonomy and well-being, centre stage. In a sense then, autonomy explains both why teaching on religious matters should be non-directive and why the state may legitimately require all children to receive the CREaM curriculum that directs them towards liberal democratic values.

We conclude by stressing that our proposals should not be interpreted as a downgrading of the importance of religious education within schools, religious or otherwise. On the contrary, we join many religious organizations in lamenting the lack of serious reflection about religion, ethics, and morality in society. Indeed, our proposal would give those topics a more prominent place in the curriculum than they have recently had, particularly since the 1988 Education Reform Act.

3. Direction towards Liberal Democratic Values

We'll not go into detail about the content of the directive liberal democratic education we have in mind, but it is worth highlighting a few central ideas and the shared reasons that guide us.[12]

Although liberal democratic society is marked by disagreement about what law and policy should be, we have already said that a concern for autonomy doesn't justify a right to a non-directive education in all moral and political matters. Children have no right to form their own views free of direction by others, as they have with religious views. That's because we all have an obligation to treat each other as equal citizens who have an interest in pursuing their personal ambitions autonomously. Many further directive educational aims follow from that obligation.

Some of these are moral in nature. We owe it to each other not to discriminate on grounds of gender, sexuality, race, ethnicity, social class, and disability, and to understand the history and historical legacy of demeaning discrimination, persecution, and oppression. But an education in equality demands more than cultivating norms of anti-discrimination. Some are lucky in their health prospects or the economic and social background into which they are born. Others are unlucky. Living in a liberal democratic society involves citizens' sharing good and bad luck, at least to some extent. Thus, the directive moral education we have in mind involves encouraging children to look out for each other: not to take advantage of another's vulnerability for their own personal gain and to help others in need or distress. This kind of moral education is routinely practised by schools and we see every reason for it to continue.

These moral norms extend to political education. If we have duties to look out for each other, schools should be encouraging children, in age-appropriate ways, to think about social policies concerned with education, health, housing, income, and employment by reference to our status as equal citizens. Of course, people have different views about the demands of equal citizenship, but it is hard to believe that a society is acceptable if it fails to provide every citizen with adequate opportunity to access these goods. Schools in Britain should be extolling the moral principles that underpin the National Health Service, health care available to all on the basis of clinical need rather than ability to pay, for example.[13] We also agree that providing everyone with adequate social and economic opportunity extends internationally and intergenerationally, giving teachers reasons to explain to their students that we all have duties to work for global institutions and climate policies that respect everyone's right not to suffer severe poverty regardless of place or time. Modest though they are, these ideas are controversial. Still, our concern for everybody's personal autonomy commits us to this kind of directive political education.

That concern also supports schools' cultivating in children a commitment to support and protect the set of civil rights with which we are familiar: freedom of religion and conscience, the right to privacy, freedom of expression, freedom of association and occupational choice. There are some interesting debates about these rights to which school students should be introduced as they mature, such as what kinds of speech may be criminalized, whether rights of abortion or to assisted dying are supported by freedom of religion or privacy, how freedom of association may be restricted to protect freedom from discrimination, and so on. Putting such complexities aside, however, there are various core elements of the civil liberties that children should be taught to value, both as school students and in their wider lives as citizens of society.[14]

Finally, schools have an important role to play in preparing their students to be democratic citizens. Part of the direction here is to encourage fidelity to democratically chosen laws, at least when they are not too unjust. Fidelity can be expressed in multiple ways: supporting democratic institutions, acknowledging a standing obligation to obey the law, while also understanding that citizens have a right to engage in civil disobedience.[15] Democratic education is also about encouraging students to reflect on the processes by which laws are made—to what extent do those processes really realize democratic values?—and quite generally equipping them with the skills to engage with each other in debates about the important moral and political issues we face. Alongside direction towards various democratic moral norms, this capacity-building aspect of political education gives children the wherewithal to realize their interests as moral agents and democratic citizens.

4. Direction in Science

What about science education? Given that we propose non-directive religious education to promote children's capacity for personal autonomy, it might seem that the same thought applies here: children should be taught to understand the disagreements between evolutionary biologists, creationists, and defenders of intelligent design, for example, but not directed to any particular view. But that's not our position. We accept the need for the broad-based education in the scientific method, and instruction in the findings of the different sciences, that characterize most systems of public education.

What explains the asymmetry in the way schools ought to approach disagreements about science, on the one hand, and religion on the other? One defence seeks to draw the distinction on the basis of the different epistemic status of science compared to religion. Recall the "epistemic criterion" for deciding whether to educate directively (for belief) or non-directly (for understanding a debate). Roughly speaking, that criterion says that direct-ive education is appropriate where we have knowledge or a robust justifica-tion of the matter at hand, but non-directive education is appropriate where we lack such knowledge or justification. Some who hold this view argue that, whereas we don't know whether most religious doctrines are true or false, we have robust justifications of countless scientific claims. Because of their respective epistemic status, teachers ought to teach science directively (albeit acknowledging the limits of our knowledge) but take a non-directive stance towards religion.[16]

We don't follow this argument for asymmetry because, as indicated earl-ier, our approach to religious schools is built on claims about the importance of personal autonomy, and of developing and exercising a sense of justice, not on an argument about whether religious views can be demonstrated to be true or false. So, we need to look elsewhere.

Science education in schools needs to be directive, we argue, because understanding the scientific method and having a knowledge of the main findings of biology, physics, chemistry, psychology, economics, and other social sciences is tremendously helpful for living just and autonomous lives. It's hard to see how, as voters, people can effectively discharge their duty to treat each other justly if they lack a decent understanding of the sciences. When faced with the prospect of a COVID-19-like pandemic, our exercis-ing a sense of justice is enhanced if we know about contagious diseases and how to read public health statistics. Citizens need to know about contagious viruses, how they can be transmitted between people, how they mutate, and their effects on people's health. Without that knowledge we cannot discharge our duty to take steps to minimize the risks our actions pose to others. That understanding is bound up with an understanding of the truths of biology, including some appreciation of genetics. Similarly, in the face of the climate crisis, we need to understand enough science fully to appreciate the impact of the choices we make on future generations to whom we have various duties.

Just as exercising our sense of justice is facilitated by our having a scien-tific understanding, so too is our opportunity to live autonomously. Even if science can't tell us what final ends we ought to adopt with respect to spirit-ual matters, occupation, cultural pursuits, sexuality, and so on, an under-standing of various sciences can help us pursue those ends. Among other things, living an autonomous life involves being able to identify effective means to achieve our ends, what activities are helpful to engage in if we are successfully to realize our personal ambitions. Some understanding of how society works—given by sociology, economics, social psychology, political science, and the law—helps us to orientate ourselves in a world of multiple agents. Reflection on the science of biases, rational choice, and failures of rationality also helps us to make informed decisions about the feasibility of different courses of action. In many ways, then, some understanding of various natural and social sciences is important for personal autonomy.[17]

5. Faith Ethos

We have argued that state schools should not be permitted to educate children in ways that direct them towards particular religious views. That prohibition applies whether the education is described as instruction or formation, and it applies to acts of collective worship given the high risks they pose to the development of children's autonomy. We recognize, however, that parents have the legal right to send their children to schools that reflect their religious views and may opt for the independent sector, or educate their children at home, if the state does nothing to accommodate their preference for such a school. In our view, moreover, there are various ways in which a school can be animated or shaped by a commitment to religious beliefs without guiding its students in their direction to such an extent that it threatens their autonomy, especially if it is delivering the CREaM syllabus just discussed. Applying the method set out in the previous chapter—balancing the different normative considerations at stake and taking feasibility constraints seriously—leads us to propose that the state should support schools that have a "faith ethos".

That label exists in the current English regulatory framework to describe a school that is run by a religious organization and, though not enjoying the extensive freedoms enjoyed by a school with a designated religious character, may nonetheless use a religious requirement in selecting all governors and senior staff and may put a religious slant on some aspects of the curriculum, such as sex and relationships education. We disagree with some details of the current arrangements.[18] But we accept that a school's mission statement, and some of its curriculum, extra-curricular activities, and rules and policies might all legitimately be influenced by religious commitments (including atheism) without losing its claim to public support—as long as students are not guided towards those commitments in a way that unduly risks their autonomy.

Here are our proposals for various ways in which a school might manifest its faith ethos:

5.1 Curriculum

- A school with a faith ethos might devote more of its curriculum than other schools to the study of the religion that shapes it. For example, in History lessons more time might be spent educating students in what is known about how the religion emerged and gained adherents, what obstacles it has faced in attracting followers, and how states have treated it.
- The selection of some of the subjects it offers as part of its curriculum might be influenced by its religious commitments. For example, an Islamic ethos school might offer Classical Arabic, or a Jewish ethos school Biblical Hebrew, to aid students' study of their sacred texts.
- It may emphasize the reasons offered by its own particular faith for endorsing the civic and democratic values that are directively taught in the CREaM curriculum. The leading religious traditions converge in affirming civic and moral values, like toleration and respect for civil liberties, but they reach that common ground in different ways. As long as it delivers the CREaM curriculum in such a way that students learn that others reach the same conclusion in different ways, a faith ethos school may give special place to its own reasons for subscribing to liberal democratic ideals.
- Faith ethos schools may require attendance at assemblies that have a spiritual dimension even though these must not take the form of collective worship. They may give a prominent role to ideas and values drawn from the faith to which the school is committed, provided that they also give adequate attention to ideas and values drawn from other faiths. Indeed, assemblies provide a valuable means for delivering the CREaM curriculum, introducing a diverse set of religious and humanistic ideas in a fair-minded way, so that students acquire a richer understanding of the variety of faith and non-faith ways of living that are available to them and endorsed by their fellow citizens.

5.2 Policies

- The values of the religion might inform the school's rules and its expectations governing appropriate behaviour. It might, for example, emphasize the religious origins of its policies on personal conduct (e.g. "Particular focus will be given to the attributes of character taught within the bible of love and care for other people")[19] although, again, students should be aware of other reasons for them.

- It might have a school uniform policy that reflects its religious values. For example, an Islamic faith ethos secondary school might encourage students to dress modestly and offer headscarves as an example of how to do that. It may not, however, impose any requirement to that effect or impose any sanctions on those who choose to observe the requirement in different ways, for justifying a more restrictive policy would require appealing to religious doctrines in a way that has the potential to threaten personal autonomy.
- It might have a school lunch menu that reflects its religious values, but only where this does not impose a special burden on those from other faith traditions. Because no religion requires the eating of meat or fish, a Hindu school might thus serve an exclusively vegetarian lunch, as long as it allowed those who want to eat meat or fish to bring in packed lunches. But a school may not serve only pork: parents should not have to provide their children with a packed lunch in order for them to comply with the relevant religious demands.

5.3 Extra-Curricular Activities

- A faith ethos school might provide various extra-curricular activities that reflect its religious values. For example, it might engage in fundraising to support projects that are designed to alleviate world poverty, justified by reference to its distinctive religious reasons for being committed to humanitarian charity, or it might focus its fundraising activities on alleviating the poverty of co-religionists in other countries.[20]
- We explained above why schools should not be permitted to hold acts of collective worship as part of their official business. As long as there is no pressure from the school for children to attend, faith ethos schools may, however, express that ethos by holding acts of collective worship out of school hours. They may similarly use school premises for a variety of extra-curricular activities that reflect their religious commitments, such as preparation for religious sacraments, carol services, and charity fundraisers.

This is a rather heterogeneous list, ranging as it does from what schools may teach and what activities can take place on their premises out of school hours to what food they may serve and how they may encourage their students to dress. That heterogeneity reflects the variety of ways in which religious world views suffuse people's lives, and so the variety of things that religious parents might want to find in their children's school.

Given the unusual structure of our book, and shape of our argument, it's worth highlighting that parents' preferences play into these "faith ethos" proposals in two different ways. Indeed, careful readers of Chapters 3–5 may have noticed that we arrive at them via different routes. Early in Chapter 1 we said that we would show how, by applying our method for moving from philosophy to policy, even those who have different views about how to interpret or weight different normative considerations may end up endorsing the same proposals. This is the main place where that happens. For Andrew Mason, parents have a legitimate interest in sending their children to a school with a religious ethos and it is proper for the state to use public money to support such schools for that reason. Those schools would exist even in ideal circumstances and can be defended without appealing to feasibility concerns. For Matthew Clayton and Adam Swift, on the other hand, albeit for somewhat different reasons, arguments for the public funding of religious schools that appeal to parents' claims are not plausible, even when those schools do not engage in religious instruction but are merely characterized by a faith ethos. Parents' preferences matter, on their view, only because, in the non-ideal circumstances that actually pertain, parents have the legal right to "exit" the state system and use independent schools, or educate at home. Schools with a faith ethos should be permitted because not permitting them would have the unintended consequence of driving religious parents out of the publically funded system altogether, and into schools, or home education, where they may receive autonomy-threatening religious instruction.

6. Admissions and Selection

So far, we have talked about what happens in faith schools. But it matters also who goes to them. Sociologists of education are familiar with "composition effects"—the way in which the composition of a school influences its ability to produce educational goods. Such effects are usually discussed in relation to the more familiar goods indicated by test scores and exam results, but they are perhaps even more relevant to the capacity for personal autonomy, and the civic and moral capacities, that are particularly salient in the case of religious schooling. Our proposal concerning the regulation of admissions to faith schools is that they should be permitted to select no more than 50 per cent of their pupils on the basis of faith. It is informed by sociological and psychological literature suggesting that excessive homogeneity in a school, and the segregation that that implies, are inimical to children's development of these important educational goods, particularly deterring harmonious relations between different religious and ethnic groups. Moreover, using religious criteria to select up to half its student body is, in our view, sufficient for a school to maintain a distinctive faith ethos of the kind discussed in the previous section.

Unlike the proposals discussed so far, and as we saw in Chapter 1, religious selection has been the focus of recent public debate. The current situation is that, when oversubscribed, established schools with a designated religious character can use religious criteria to select all their pupils, while new Academies (also known as Free Schools) may prioritize only 50 per cent of their pupils on faith grounds. The 50 per cent cap on new schools has, however, made some religious organizations, most notably the Catholic Church,[21] unwilling to open new schools and, citing evidence that the cap was failing in its objective to promote integration, the Conservative government's manifesto for the 2017 election announced its intention to remove it.[22] The government subsequently reneged on that commitment but offered more funding for local authorities to open voluntary-aided faith schools that may admit without a cap.[23] Two such schools were eventually approved, one Catholic, one Church of England.

That was a step in the wrong direction. Not only should there be no increase in the number of children educated in religiously homogenous schools, but the 50 per cent cap should apply to all faith schools in the state sector. Schools with a very high proportion of children from one faith background are poorly placed to produce some of the capacities we have identified. Some of these capacities, particularly the capacity to regard others as having equal moral status and to treat them accordingly, depend for their production on who children go to school with no less than on what they are taught in classrooms or assembly halls. For example, higher levels of contact between members of different religious and ethnic groups have been shown to reduce prejudice and foster positive attitudes and behaviours towards outgroups.[24] Such capacities play an important role in creating tolerant citizens and a cohesive society.

Unduly homogenous schools also threaten the production of personal autonomy, especially where they are continuous with similar homogeneity in children's lives outside school. Being educated in such a school may not rule out the possibility of a child's developing the capacity to make her own judgment about how she will live her life—especially if the school is regulated in the ways we have proposed above—but it exposes that development to unnecessary risk. The risk is unnecessary in the sense that there are no countervailing normative considerations, such as parents' rights to send their child to such a school, or religious organizations' rights to open one, that justify state support. Children are more likely to be in a position to make informed decisions about the kind of life they want to lead if they have meaningful opportunities to interact with those from other backgrounds. This applies just as much to those raised in secular or humanist homes as those whose home life is informed by a particular religious tradition.

We believe that a 50 per cent cap on religious selection meets the case of those who argue that the maintenance of a school's distinctive faith ethos depends on its reserving a proportion of places for children of co-religionists. Indeed, where this question has explicitly been considered, some propose the "critical mass" should be closer to 30 per cent or even as low as 10 per cent.[25] Furthermore, some religious organizations come close to suggesting that their purposes in providing schools can be fulfilled without the need for religious selection at all. The Church of England now actively endorses the position that the schools it runs are "not faith schools for the faithful", but "church schools for the community", and so should largely be open to all.[26] Although critics suggest that what happens on the ground does not match up to public pronouncements,[27] this official attitude shows that our insistence on a 50 per cent cap, and even on its extension to existing faith schools, is less outlandish than it might seem. That said, some organizations may continue to see their primary purpose as service to a particular religious community, rather than the provision of a religiously inflected education to all children. If our proposals were accepted, they might choose to withdraw from the maintained sector altogether and limit their provision to independent schools. We will present our proposals for the regulation of the independent sector—and of home education—shortly.

Admissions policies, as we are presenting them, are tools for influencing school compositions, which are themselves causal factors in the production of the capacities we are interested in. But admissions policies are very clumsy tools, as school compositions depend on many other things, most obviously residential patterns and parental choices. A school could be composed entirely of children whose parents endorse a particular faith without using religion as a criterion of selection, and it could be very mixed while giving preference to all co-religionists who apply. As well as extending the 50 per cent cap on religious selection to all faith schools, we therefore propose that the government should actively encourage religiously hetero-geneous school intakes by introducing a system of incentives—a kind of diversity and integration premium—to acknowledge and reward good practice with respect to inclusive admissions policies. Local demographics make mixed compositions harder to achieve in some places than others, and the premium we propose should recognize that, partly by incorporating data on interaction between pupils at different schools that may themselves be internally homogenous, perhaps through twinning arrangements. Similarly, while a diverse school composition will increase the likelihood that children from different backgrounds will interact meaningfully with one another, it is no guarantee. We therefore propose that the premium should take into account the practical steps a school has taken to encourage the kinds of interaction most conducive to producing citizens who respect, cooperate with, and value one another irrespective of faith and other differences.[28]

7. The Independent Sector and Home Education

Our proposals so far have concerned schools in receipt of public funding. But our emphasis on children's autonomy and civic educational goals, and our view that parents' preferences have less normative standing than they are typically given, reduce the significance of the distinction between state schools, on the one hand, and private schools or home education, on the other. There is a legitimate public interest in how children are educated, wherever that education takes place and whoever pays for it. That said, vari-ous considerations lead us to propose that religious independent schools, and religious parents who educate their children at home, should be subject to different regulation from maintained schools.

First, there is no point our proposing changes that would simply be judged illegal by relevant authorities and, rightly or wrongly, human rights law in this area is very deferential to parents.[29] After asserting that all chil-dren are entitled to a free education, Article 26 of the *Universal Declaration of Human Rights* (1948) states that "Parents have a prior right to choose the kind of education that shall be given to their children", and this was consoli-dated and extended in *European Convention on Human Rights*, which holds that "The state shall respect the right of parents to ensure such education and teaching in conformity with their own religious and philosophical convictions."[30] This would make it difficult lawfully to deny parents the freedom to choose a directive religious education for their children, and presumably one attended only by children of co-religionists, especially if the state need play no role in providing it. Second, we have to be realistic about the ways in which home education may feasibly be regulated. Existing legislation and practice in this area seem to us woefully inadequate. Not all parents are required to register their children as home educated. Local authorities simply fail to act on their statutory duty to ensure that those children who are registered are receiving an appropriate education and to take the steps necessary to ensure that all children who are required to be registered are registered. So we do in fact propose an increase in regulation here too.[31] But, given that parents are free to raise their children in accordance with their own religious views, we accept that it is unrealistic to expect and enforce those who choose to educate their children at home to comply with the same standards as schools.

The UK has about 2,400 independent schools.[32] About half of them are registered as charities,[33] which gives them various tax concessions that can be regarded as public subsidies. To qualify for charitable status, schools must provide "public benefit": such schools are expected to offer free or subsidized places to those unable to afford the fees or, increasingly, to "make provision for the poor" in other ways—through sponsoring academies or setting up a free school. The "public benefit" criterion, and political debate about the independent sector generally, is thus interpreted entirely in distributive terms. We propose that, when it comes to faith schools, the "public benefit" issue should be understood differently. Where such schools lead to religious segregation, the problem is not that they are contributing to an unfair distribution of educational goods; it is, rather, that they are making it harder to produce those goods in the first place. We have argued that religious instruction in schools composed exclusively—or even predominantly—of children from the same faith background hampers the development of tolerant attitudes towards members of other religions. Such schools do not serve the public good, however many children they may admit from deprived backgrounds. They also threaten children's right to autonomy in a way that makes them inappropriate recipients of public subsidy. To qualify for the financial advantages of charitable status, independent religious schools should conform to the same rules as those we have proposed for maintained schools.

Independent schools that do not seek charitable status must be free to provide a directive religious education, and to select all their students on the basis of religion. But they should be subject to an inspection regime that focuses on their potential to threaten children's autonomy and deny them the capacity for critical reflection. Independent schools are already required actively to promote values—which we regard as civic or liberal democratic rather than British—such as "democracy, the rule of law, individual liberty, and mutual respect and tolerance of those with different faiths and beliefs" and the other values we described in Section 3 of this chapter. Parents do not have the right to choose schools that neglect those values, or to remove their children from the relevant lessons or assemblies. We propose that those values should be taught primarily through the same CREaM curriculum delivered in maintained schools and, like maintained schools with a faith ethos, independent religious schools should be permitted to emphasize the way in which their own particular religion supports such values. But they should also be required to meet children of other faiths in some institutional setting, for example through twinning arrangements that would involve visits to and from children at schools with a different religious affiliation.[34] Additionally, mindful of the risk of closing minds posed by religious instruction continuous with children's home culture, inspectors should pay particular attention to the fostering of children's capacity critically to reflect both on the religion in which they are being instructed and on the alternative religious—and non-religious—beliefs to which they are already expected to show mutual respect and tolerance.

There are no precise statistics for how many children are home educated, but an estimate for 2023 put the figure at 86,200, with numbers increasing in recent years.[35] Unlike other jurisdictions, such as Germany, where home education is banned in almost all cases, in England the legal permission to educate at home is here to stay for the foreseeable future. If we accept that as given, it is imperative that home education is regulated appropriately. Parents who choose to educate their children at home should be required to register them and local authorities should be funded and required to monitor their development.

As things stand, the legal position in England, as stated in Section 7 of the 1996 Education Act, obliges parents to ensure that their child receives an "efficient education suitable (a) to his age, ability and aptitude, and (b) to any special educational needs...". In its 2019 guidance for local authorities on elective home education, the government explains how "suitable" is currently understood.[36] It makes some reference to autonomy—home education should "not foreclose the child's options in later life" and must facilitate the capacity to live "on an autonomous basis". It also places the requirement on parents to ensure that, even if it doesn't promote Fundamental British Values, the education they offer is not inconsistent with those values.

In our view, this guidance is a step in the right direction, because it incorporates a concern for personal autonomy and civic and moral capacities. That said, the resources devoted to helping local authorities ensure that home education is suitable needs increasing considerably. And the government's understanding of suitability must also be strengthened and given greater clarity.[37] To retain their legal right to educate a child at home, we propose that parents must attend to the development of the full range of educational goods that we have set out. There should be no requirement that they teach any particular syllabus, and they may emphasize religious grounds for endorsing civic values. But they should also be required to deliver the CREaM curriculum and ensure that the education they provide gives their children both a rich sense of the alternative lifestyles that are available and the resources critically to reflect on their merits. The right to educate one's children at home—and to provide a directive religious education—does not include the right to raise them in ignorance of other ways of living, or to demand exclusive control over their education in ways that are inimical to their developing tolerant and respectful attitudes to others.

We believe that these proposals are adequately sensitive to concerns about parents' likely responses to the different rules proposed for different kinds of schooling: maintained, independent charitable, independent non-charitable, and home.[38] We interpret governmental support for religious schooling as partly an attempt to bring into the maintained sector children who would otherwise "exit" into private or home schooling. Stricter regulation of state schools of the kind we propose risks encouraging such tendencies. Our strategy has been to increase the regulation of all kinds of schooling—to the extent we judge compatible with human rights law and realism about the monitoring of home education—so that overly permissive options are no longer available to parents. Since all children would receive the CREaM curriculum and have their capacity for critical reflection monitored, our proposals would also reduce the differences between different types of schooling in a way that, we believe, would reduce the incentive to exit from the maintained sector to private or home education.

It is a further question how religious organizations would respond to our proposed regulatory regime. Perhaps some would be so keen to engage in directive education, and to admit entirely on the basis of religious affiliation, that they would forsake the maintained sector, and eschew claims to charitable status, in order to pursue those goals. We are optimistic that, perhaps after a period of serious public debate about the merits and demerits of such schools, religious groups would be content for their distinctive educational aims to be expressed through the kind of "faith ethos" that we have advocated.

8. Conclusion

Supporters of faith schools typically appeal to one or both of the following claims. On the one hand, parents have the right to decide how—and with whom—their children are educated. On the other hand, schools with a religious character tend to be good schools. Roughly speaking, the first explains why the state must allow religious schooling; the second justifies public support for it. We have argued that parents' rights over their children's education do not include the right to send them to a school so continuous with the culture at home that it risks depriving them of the capacity for autonomy. Nor do they forbid the state's acting to develop the civic and moral capacities required for a healthy, tolerant, liberal democracy. And the suggestion that faith schools are better than their non-faith counterparts involves, at best, a limited view about the capacities that we properly look to schools to produce. Human rights law means that parents must indeed be free to decide their children's education in the light of their own religious and philosophical commitments. But that does not imply that the state should support religious schooling that risks children's autonomy and it does not prevent the state's requiring children to learn about alternative ways of life, and about their own and others' moral and civic status as free and equal persons, even where doing so runs counter to parents' preferences.

Our proposals imply a radical departure from current practice and they run directly counter to the current direction of travel. Some readers may regard them as unrealistic. If that turns out to be true, we think that will be because children's education is at the mercy of vested interests—whether parents' or religious organizations'—that resist the compelling case for reforms along the lines we have suggested. In setting out, as clearly as we can, the core normative considerations at stake in debates about religious schooling, we aim at least to flush out the moral views that underpin and motivate existing policy, at best to reveal their inadequacy.

How to Think about Religious Schools: Principles and Policies. Matthew Clayton, Andrew Mason, and Adam Swift, Oxford University Press. © Matthew Clayton, Andrew Mason, and Adam Swift 2024.
DOI: 10.1093/9780198924036.003.0007

Notes

Notes to Chapter 1

1. Protocol 1 to the European Convention for the Protection of Human Rights and Fundamental Freedoms, Council of Europe, 20 March 1952, last amendment 2021, https://www.echr.coe.int/documents/d/echr/convention_ENG (accessed 13 November 2023).
2. UK Department for Education, 'Schools, Pupils and their Characteristics', January 2023, https://explore-education-statistics.service.gov.uk/find-statistics/school-pupils-and-their-characteristics (accessed 13 November 2023).
3. See Government of the Netherlands, 'Public Authority and Private Schools', https://www.government.nl/topics/freedom-of-education/public-authority-and-private-schools.
4. See R. Dericquebourg, 'Religious Education in France', in D. H. Davis and E. Miroshnikova (eds), *The Routledge International Handbook of Religious Education* (Abingdon: Routledge, 2013), 113–21.
5. Religious schools in the USA can, however, receive state support in the form of vouchers. In fact, the Supreme Court recently ruled that the state has to fund access to private religious schools if it funds other kinds of private education. See 'U.S. Supreme Court Backs Public Money for Religious Schools', *Reuters*, 21 June 2022, https://www.reuters.com/legal/government/us-supreme-court-backs-public-money-religious-schools-maine-case-2022-06-21/ (accessed 13 November 2023).
6. K. Williams, 'Republic of Ireland', in L. Philip Barnes (ed.), *Debates in Religious Education* (London: Routledge, 2012), 45–51, at 44.
7. J. Holmwood and T. O'Toole, *Countering Extremism in British Schools? The Truth about the Birmingham Trojan Horse Affair* (Bristol: Policy Press, 2017); C. Diamond, *The Birmingham Book: Lessons in Urban Educational Leadership and Policy from the Trojan Horse Affair* (Carmarthen: Crown House Publishing, 2022).
8. See D. Cameron, 'Prime Minister's Speech at Munich Security Conference', 5 February 2011, https://www.gov.uk/government/speeches/pms-speech-at-munich-security-conference (accessed 13 November 2023).
9. T. May, 'Britain, the Great Meritocracy: Prime Minister's Speech', 9 November 2016, https://www.gov.uk/government/speeches/britain-the-great-meritocracy-prime-ministers-speech (accessed 13 November 2023).
10. UK Home Office, *Community Cohesion: A Report of the Independent Review Team Chaired by Ted Cantle* (2001), https://tedcantle.co.uk/pdf/communitycohesion%20cantlereport.pdf (accessed 13 November 2023), referred to as the Cantle Report.
11. '"Socially Selective" Faith Schools Must Introduce Fairer Admissions to Increase Poorer Students, Charity Says', *Independent*, 25 March 2019, https://www.independent.co.uk/news/education/education-news/faith-schools-sutton-trust-admissions-secondary-places-poorer-students-social-mobility-a8839236.html (accessed 13 November 2023).
12. *Faith School Menace?*, written and presented by Richard Dawkins, directed by Molly Milton, released 18 August 2010, https://documentaryheaven.com/richard-dawkins-faith-school-menace/ (accessed 13 November 2023).
13. Humanists UK, 'Private Faith Schools', https://humanists.uk/campaigns/schools-and-education/faith-schools/private-faith-schools (accessed 13 November 2023). For relevant discussion, see also R. Wareham, 'The Problem with Faith-Based Carve-Outs: RSE Policy, Religion and Educational Goods', *Journal of Philosophy of Education* 56 (2022): 707–26.

14. '"We Can't Give In": The Birmingham School on the Frontline of Anti-LGBT Protests', *The Guardian*, 26 May 2019, https://www.theguardian.com/uk-news/2019/may/26/birmingham-anderton-park-primary-muslim-protests-lgbt-teaching-rights (accessed 13 November 2023).

15. P. Chadwick, *Shifting Alliances: Church and State in English Education* (London: Cassell, 1997), cited in R. Pring, *The Future of Publicly Funded Faith Schools: A Critical Perspective* (London: Routledge, 2018), 69.

16. B. Watson, 'Why Religious Education Matters', in L. Philip Barnes (ed.), *Debates in Religious Education* (London: Routledge, 2012), 13–21, at 17–18.

17. A. Swift, *How Not to Be a Hypocrite: School Choice for the Morally Perplexed Parent* (London: Routledge, 2003).

18. For some of our views on how to think about the distinction between "ideal and non-ideal theory", see Z. Stemplowska and A. Swift, 'Ideal and Nonideal Theory', in D. Estlund (ed.), *The Oxford Handbook of Political Philosophy* (New York: Oxford University Press, 2012), 373–90; and A. Mason, 'Justice, Feasibility, and Ideal Theory: A Pluralist Approach', *Social Philosophy and Policy* 33 (2016): 32–54.

19. J. Feinberg, 'The Child's Right to an Open Future', in *Freedom and Fulfillment* (Princeton, NJ: Princeton University Press, 1992).

20. We talk about "home education", rather than "home schooling", to respect those home educators who object to the latter phrase.

21. See D. Cameron, 'British Values Aren't Optional, They're Vital. That's Why I Will Promote Them in EVERY School', *Daily Mail*, 15 June 2014, http://www.dailymail.co.uk/debate/article-2658171/DAVID-CAMERON-British-values-arent-optional-theyre-vital-Thats-I-promote-EVERY-school-As-row-rages-Trojan-Horse-takeover-classrooms-Prime-Minister-delivers-uncompromising-pledge.html (accessed 13 November 2023). For relevant discussion, see A. Mason, 'The Critique of Multiculturalism in Britain: Integration, Separation, and Shared Identification', *Critical Review of International Social and Political Philosophy* 21 (2018): 22–45, especially 34–5.

22. See, for example, K. Greenawalt, *Does God Belong in Public Schools?* (Princeton, NJ: Princeton University Press, 2005); B. Justice and C. Macleod, *Have a Little Faith: Religion, Democracy and the Public School* (Chicago, IL: Chicago University Press, 2016); R. Pring, *The Future of Publicly Funded Faith Schools: A Critical Perspective* (London: Routledge, 2018), 2.

23. R. Dworkin, *Religion without God* (Cambridge, MA: Harvard University Press, 2013).

24. W. L. Craig, 'Five Reasons God Exists', in W. L. Craig and W. Sinnott-Armstrong, *God? A Debate between a Christian and an Atheist* (New York: Oxford University Press, 2004), 17–21.

Notes to Chapter 2

1. e.g. During his inaugural education questions session in Parliament, the then Minister for Education Damian Hinds claimed that "Church and Faith Schools…are consistently…high-performing and popular schools." See House of Commons, UK Parliament, 'Topical Questions. Volume 635: debated on Monday 29 January 2018', https://hansard.parliament.uk/Commons/2018-01-29/debates/4F2A0469-2F29-4E94-8337-474108AD25AA/TopicalQuestions (accessed 13 November 2023).

2. Workable, 'What Are Soft Skills?', https://resources.workable.com/hr-terms/what-are-soft-skills (accessed 13 November 2023).

3. H. Brighouse, H. F. Ladd, S. Loeb, and A. Swift, 'Educational Goods and Values: A Framework for Decision-Makers', *Theory and Research in Education* 14 (2016): 3–25; and *Educational Goods: Values, Evidence and Decision Making* (Chicago, IL: University of Chicago Press, 2018).

4. R. Allen and A. West, 'Religious Schools in London: School Admissions, Religious Composition and Selectivity', *Oxford Review of Education* 35 (2009): 471–94; and 'Why Do Faith Secondary Schools Have Advantaged Intakes? The Relative Importance of Neighbourhood Characteristics, Social Background and Religious Identification Amongst

Parents', *British Educational Research Journal* 37 (2011): 691–712; J. Andrews and R. Johnes, *Faith Schools, Pupil Performance and Social Selection* (London: Education Policy Institute, 2016); G. Dreissen, A. Orhan, and M. S. Merry, 'The Gross and Net Effects of Primary School Denomination on Pupil Performance', *Educational Review* 68 (2016): 466–80 (although they note that Islamic schools are an exception to this rule). Sullivan et al. suggest that it was children's religious background, not the religious character of their schools, that explains those schools' superior performance: see A. Sullivan, S. Parsons, F. Green, R. D. Wiggins, G. Ploubidis, and T. Huynh, 'Educational Attainment in the Short and Long Term: Was There an Advantage to Attending Faith, Private and Selective Schools for Pupils in the 1980s?', *Oxford Review of Education* 44 (2018): 806–22.

5. M. Hewstone, A. Al Ramiah, K. Schmid, C. Floe, M. van Zalk, R. Wölfer, and R. New, 'Influence of Segregation versus Mixing: Intergroup Contact and Attitudes among White-British and Asian-British Students in High Schools in Oldham, England', *Theory and Research in Education* 16 (2018): 179–203.

6. For philosophical discussions of childhood goods, see C. Macleod, 'Primary Goods, Capabilities and Children', in H. Brighouse and I. Robeyns (eds), *Measuring Justice: Primary Goods and Capabilities* (Cambridge: Cambridge University Press, 2010); S. Brennan, 'The Goods of Childhood and Children's Rights', in F. Baylis and C. Mcleod (eds), *Family-Making: Contemporary Ethical Challenges* (Oxford: Oxford University Press, 2014); A. Gheaus, 'The "Intrinsic Goods of Childhood" and the Just Society', in A. Bagattini and C. Macleod (eds), *The Nature of Children's Well-Being* (Dordrecht: Springer, 2015); P. Tomlin, 'The Value of Childhood', in A. Gheaus, G. Calder, and J. Wispelaere (eds), *The Routledge Handbook of the Philosophy of Childhood and Children* (London: Routledge, 2019); and A. Cormier and M. Rossi, 'Is Children's Wellbeing Different from Adults' Wellbeing?', *Canadian Journal of Philosophy* 49 (2019): 1146–68.

7. C. Jencks, 'Whom Must We Treat Equally for Educational Opportunity to be Equal?', *Ethics* 98 (1988): 518–33; A. Mason, *Levelling the Playing Field: The Idea of Equal Opportunity and Its Place in Egalitarian Thought* (Oxford: Oxford University Press 2006); H. Brighouse and A. Swift, 'The Place of Educational Equality in Educational Justice', in K. Meyer (ed.), *Education, Justice and the Human Good* (Abingdon: Routledge, 2014), 14–33.

8. D. Satz, 'Equality, Adequacy, and Education for Citizenship', *Ethics* 117 (2007): 623–48; H. Brighouse and A. Swift, 'Educational Adequacy versus Educational Equality', *Journal of Applied Philosophy* 26 (2009): 117–28.

9. Brighouse and Swift, 'The Place of Educational Equality in Educational Justice'; Brighouse et al., *Educational Goods*; M. Clayton, 'Education', in S. Olsaretti (ed.), *The Oxford Handbook of Distributive Justice* (Oxford: Oxford University Press, 2018).

10. Other versions are possible. For example, it might be that children have a claim to have their views about their schooling listened to or, sometimes, to have their views determine how they are educated. For views of this kind, see A. Mullin, 'Children, Paternalism and the Development of Autonomy', *Ethical Theory and Moral Practice* 17 (2014): 413–26; P. Bou-Habib and S. Olsaretti, 'Autonomy and Children's Well-Being', in A. Baggatini and C. Macleod (eds), *The Nature of Children's Well-Being: Theory and Practice* (Dordrecht: Springer, 2015), 15–33.

11. V. Tadros, 'Wrongful Intentions without Closeness', *Philosophy and Public Affairs* 43 (2015): 52–74.

12. M. Clayton, *Justice and Legitimacy in Upbringing* (Oxford: Oxford University, 2006); and *Independence for Children* (Oxford: Oxford University Press, forthcoming).

13. M. Moschella, *To Whom Do Children Belong? Parental Rights, Civic Education and Children's Autonomy* (Cambridge: Cambridge University Press, 2016).

14. T. Fowler, *Liberalism, Childhood and Justice* (Bristol: Bristol University Press, 2020), 81–4; C. Easton, 'LGBT-Inclusive Education in Liberal Pluralist Societies', *Journal of Applied Philosophy* 40 (2023): 550–68.

15. J. Raz, *The Morality of Freedom* (Oxford: Oxford University Press, 1986); S. Wall, *Liberalism, Perfectionism and Restraint* (Cambridge: Cambridge University Press, 1998); M. Kramer, *Liberalism with Excellence* (Oxford: Oxford University Press, 2017).

16. J. Rawls, *Political Liberalism* (1993); R. Dworkin, *Religion without God* (Cambridge, MA: Harvard University Press, 2013), ch. 3; J. Quong, *Liberalism without Perfection* (Oxford: Oxford University Press, 2011).
17. I. MacMullen, *Faith in Schools: Autonomy, Citizenship, and Religious Education in the Liberal State* (Princeton, NJ: Princeton University Press, 2007).

Notes to Chapter 3

1. I shall use the expressions "religious schools" and "schools with a religious character" to mean the same thing, despite some differences in their ordinary uses and wider resonances.
2. I shall not say anything more about the moral issues that arise when teachers and other employees are selected in a way that gives priority to applicants who share the religious affiliation of the school since much of what I have to say about selecting students on religious grounds also applies in this context.
3. Indoctrination can be defined in different ways. Eamonn Callan, for example, defines it in a way that departs from my characterization. He seems to suppose that indoctrination occurs whenever a belief is inculcated without due regard for relevant evidence and argument: see E. Callan, *Creating Citizens: Political Education and Liberal Democracy* (Oxford: Oxford University Press, 1997), 115. Michael Hand also maintains that indoctrination would "be involved in any attempt to make children believe that there are good reasons for subscribing to a moral code when in fact there are not" (M. Hand, 'Towards a Theory of Moral Education', *Journal of Philosophy of Education* 48 (2014): 519–32, at 526). What matters for my purposes is that the distinction is drawn in a morally relevant way, and there may be more than one approach to doing that. I try to show that my way of drawing it is morally relevant in the discussion that follows.
4. For relevant discussion, see B. Colburn, *Autonomy and Liberalism* (London: Routledge, 2013); G. Dworkin, *The Theory and Practice of Autonomy* (Cambridge: Cambridge University Press, 1988); A. Mason, 'Autonomy, Liberalism, and State Neutrality', *The Philosophical Quarterly* 40 (1990): 433–52; J. Raz, *The Morality of Freedom* (Oxford: Oxford University Press, 1986), chs 14–15.
5. Joseph Raz defends a variant of this claim in relation to what he calls "autonomy-supporting cultures": see Raz, *The Morality of Freedom*, 391.
6. See W. Kymlicka, *Contemporary Political Philosophy: An Introduction*, second edition (Oxford: Oxford University Press, 2002), 216. Cf. R. Dworkin, *Sovereign Virtue* (Cambridge, MA: Harvard University Press, 2000), 217–18.
7. Callan, *Creating Citizens*, 68, 151.
8. H. Brighouse, *School Choice and Social Justice* (Oxford: Oxford University Press, 2002), 68–73; I. MacMullen, *Faith in Schools? Autonomy, Citizenship, and Religious Education in the Liberal State* (Princeton, NJ: Princeton University Press, 2007), 96–103.
9. J. S. Mill, 'On Liberty', in M. Warnock (ed.), *Utilitarianism* (London: Collins, 1962), 197.
10. See H. Brighouse and A. Swift, *Family Values: The Ethics of Parent-Child Relationships* (Princeton, NJ: Princeton University Press, 2014), 167.
11. For a powerful elaboration of this argument, see M. Clayton, *Justice and Legitimacy in Upbringing* (Oxford: Oxford University Press, 2006), 103–5.
12. Clayton, *Justice and Legitimacy in Upbringing*, 88–92, 102–5.
13. Is it an implication of such a view that there is no wrong involved in intentionally shaping the values of an adult who loses her capacity for critical reflection, perhaps as a result of suffering from dementia? The fact that she once had a capacity to form and revise a conception of the good makes a moral difference here, and affects what it is to respect her. Even if she no longer has the potential to develop a capacity for critical reflection, the fact that she once had such a capacity makes a difference to how we are morally permitted to treat her.
14. And there are more examples. Joseph Raz maintains that autonomy has non-instrumental value but only when it is exercised in pursuit of the good: see Raz, *The Morality of Freedom*, 381. Equality might be regarded as non-instrumentally valuable but only when it is not created by levelling down: see A. Mason, 'Egalitarianism and the Levelling Down Objection', *Analysis* 61 (2001): 246–54.

15. A number of arguments are presented in the literature for why weight should sometimes be given to parents' desires for a particular kind of education for their child. See Callan, *Creating Citizens*, 142–5; C. Fried, *Right and Wrong* (Cambridge, MA: Harvard University Press, 1976), 152; W. Galston, *Liberal Pluralism: The Implications of Value Pluralism for Political Theory and Practice* (Cambridge: Cambridge University Press, 2002), 102; MacMullen, *Faith in Schools?*, 119–24; R. Nozick, *The Examined Life: Philosophical Meditations* (New York: Simon and Schuster, 1989), 28. In this paragraph, I merely endorse the general view that the burdens that may be placed on parents by their inability to send their children to a school with a religious character may sometimes give a legitimate reason for permitting such schools to exist and to provide them with public funding.

16. See Brighouse and Swift, *Family Values*, ch. 6, especially 153–61.

17. See Clayton, *Justice and Legitimacy in Upbringing*, 117–18.

18. See MacMullen, *Faith in Schools?*, 186.

19. For relevant evidence and discussion, see D. Moulin, 'Religious Identity Choices in English Secondary Schools', *British Educational Research Journal* 41 (2015): 489–504.

20. See M. Merry, 'Indoctrination, Islamic Schools, and the Broader Scope of Harm', *Theory and Research in Education* 16 (2018): 162–78.

21. See W. P. Vogt, *Tolerance and Education: Learning to Live with Diversity and Difference* (Thousand Oaks, CA: Sage, 1997), 177. What evidence exists suggests that, in a US context at least, civic education has little impact on political attitudes. See, for example, L. H. Ehman, 'The American School in the Political Socialization Process', *Review of Educational Research* 50 (1980): 99–119. However, there was an experiment conducted in Minnesota involving 300 ninth grade students, which aimed to cultivate tolerance through a four-week period of instruction. Although it did not have uniformly positive results, on average students' tolerance scores went up by two points on a 30-point scale. See P. Avery, D. Hoffman, J. L. Sullivan, and K. Thalhammer, 'Exploring Political Toleration with Adolescents', *Theory and Research in Social Education* 20 (1992): 386–20; Vogt, *Tolerance and Education*, 192–5.

22. J. Rawls, *Political Liberalism*, paperback edition (New York: Columbia University Press, 1996), 56–7.

23. Callan, *Creating Citizens*, 34–6.

24. Some faith traditions may reject even the endorsement thesis, for they may hold that whether a person flourishes or not depends solely on whether she lives in accordance with its doctrines, irrespective of whether or not she affirms those doctrines.

25. Cf. MacMullen, *Faith in Schools?*, 50–1.

26. See A. Mason, *Levelling the Playing Field: The Idea of Equal Opportunity and Its Place in Egalitarian Thought* (Oxford: Oxford University Press, 2006), chs 4–6.

27. MacMullen, *Faith in Schools?*, 19–20, 31–2.

28. G. W. Allport, *The Nature of Prejudice* (Cambridge, MA: Addison Wesley, 1954); T. Pettigrew and L. Tropp, 'A Meta-Analytic Test of Intergroup Contact Theory', *Journal of Personality and Social Psychology* 90 (2006): 751–83; N. Tausch and M. Hewstone, 'Intergroup Contact', in J. F. Dividio, M. Hewstone, P. Glick, and V. M. Esses (eds), *The Sage Handbook of Prejudice, Stereotyping and Discrimination* (London: Sage, 2010), 544–60. The hypothesis has become more nuanced over time, with a better appreciation of what kind of factors might inhibit the reduction of prejudice, and of the kind of mechanisms involved: see Tausch and Hewstone, 'Intergroup Contact'.

29. See H. Brighouse, 'Faith Schools, Personal Autonomy and Democratic Competence', in G. Haydon (ed.), *Faith in Education: A Tribute to Terence McLaughlin* (London: Institute of Education, 2009), 78–93, at 85.

30. For a more wide-ranging discussion of these issues, see A. Mason, 'Religious Schools and the Cultivation of Tolerance', *Theory and Research in Education* 16 (2018): 204–25.

31. See B. Cooper, 'Schools with a Religious Character and Social Cohesion: A Study of Faith Based Approaches to Educational Environments and Aims' (PhD thesis, University of Southampton, 2015), 43; G. Short, 'Religious Schools and Social Cohesion: Opening up the Debate', *British Journal of Religious Education* 25 (2003): 129–41, at 132. Turner et al. argue that children's attitudes towards those from other religious groups can be affected by the knowledge that some of their friends with the same religious affiliation have friends

from these other groups: see R. Turner, T. Tam, M. Hewstone, J. Kenworthy, and E. Cairns, 'Contact between Catholic and Protestant Schoolchildren in Northern Ireland', *Journal of Applied Social Psychology* 43 (2013): E216–E228, especially E217–E218, E225.

32. See Short, 'Religious Schools and Social Cohesion', 134.
33. E. M. Uslaner, *Segregation and Mistrust: Diversity, Isolation and Social Cohesion* (Cambridge: Cambridge University Press, 2012), 40; Allport, *The Nature of Prejudice*, 260.
34. See M. Merry, *Equality, Citizenship, and Segregation: A Defense of Separation* (Basingstoke: Palgrave Macmillan, 2013), especially ch. 2; Merry, 'Indoctrination, Islamic Schools, and the Broader Scope of Harm'.
35. See T. F. Pettigrew and L. R. Tropp, 'Allport's Intergroup Contact Hypothesis: Its History and Influence', in J. F. Dividio, P. Glick, and L. A. Rudman (eds), *On the Nature of Prejudice: Fifty Years after Allport* (Oxford: Blackwell, 2005), 271. Whether contact is beneficial in terms of reducing prejudice and promoting mutual respect may depend in part on a person's background "social world view beliefs" and their deeper values and motivational goals. Evidence suggests that those with a "social dominance orientation" regard the world as "a ruthlessly competitive jungle" as opposed to "a place of cooperative harmony", and that this social world view belief makes salient "the value or motivational goals of power, dominance, and superiority over others" (J. Duckett and C. Sibley, 'A Dual-Process Motivational Model of Ideology, Politics and Prejudice', *Psychological Inquiry* 20 (2009): 98–109, at 102). People with this orientation are likely to feel threatened by contact with others when it challenges their power over them, and it might be thought that such contact is likely to provoke hostility, and to reinforce rather than erode prejudices. See also L. Thomsen, E. Green, and J. Sidanius, 'We Will Hunt Them Down: How Social Dominance Orientation and Right-Wing Authoritarianism Fuel Ethnic Persecution of Immigrants in Fundamentally Different Ways', *Journal of Experimental Social Psychology* 44 (2008): 1455–64. The idea that when contact occurs between those with a social dominance orientation and groups that threaten their power, then this will reinforce their prejudices, is questioned by K. Dhont, A. Van Hiel, and M. Hewstone in 'Changing the Ideological Roots of Prejudice: Longitudinal Effects of Ethnic Intergroup Contact on Social Dominance Orientation', *Group Processes & Intergroup Relations* 17 (2014): 27–44.
36. Note, however, that even if sustaining the school's ethos should be given some weight, it's not clear that this requires religious selection as opposed to selection on the basis of values. Of course, this would be even more open to abuse. How do we ascertain the values of families? What if parents attend church regularly but in their lives act against the values endorsed there; for example, commit adultery or live together when unmarried?
37. The Cantle Report into the disturbances (as they were called) in various northern towns in the late spring and early summer of 2001 argued that religious schools should offer 25% of their places to other faiths or denominations (UK Home Office, *Community Cohesion: A Report of the Independent Review Team Chaired by Ted Cantle* (2001), https://tedcantle. co.uk/pdf/communitycohesion%20cantlereport.pdf (accessed 13 November 2023), 37). After vigorous opposition from the Catholic Church and the Board of Deputies of British Jews, that proposal was not adopted, but when the system of Free Schools and Academies was introduced in 2010 those with a religious character were required to cap the proportion of places that they filled by using faith-based criteria at 50%. Harry Brighouse argues that 70% of places at a religious school should be allocated by a lottery that gives no preference to those who come from families that share the faith of the school: see Brighouse, 'Faith Schools, Personal Autonomy and Democratic Competence', 89–90.

Notes to Chapter 4

1. A prominent defender of this view is Michael Hand. See his 'What Should We Teach as Controversial: A Defense of the Epistemic Criterion', *Educational Theory* 58 (2008): 213–28.
2. For this view, albeit without the Rawlsian explanation on which I rely, see M. Hollis, 'The Pen and the Purse', *Journal of Philosophy of Education* 5 (1971): 153–69.
3. J. Dwyer, 'Regulating Child Rearing in a Culturally Diverse Society', in E. Brake and L. Ferguson (eds), *Philosophical Foundations of Children's and Family Law* (Oxford: Oxford University Press, 2018).

4. Notice that this society is different from ours because, as Dwyer notes, in our society maintaining parents' rights over children involves the state exercising coercion over every other citizen. In our society, then, even allowing parents to spend their own resources on private education for their child involves an exercise of coercive force over every citizen. I consider an imaginary case that doesn't have this feature, because it helps us to see that children are often directly coerced by their parents.

5. Here I follow Jonathan Quong's view that anti-perfectionism applies to citizens. See his 'The Scope of Public Reason', *Political Studies* 52 (2004): 233–50.

6. J. Rawls, *Political Liberalism*, paperback edition (New York: Columbia University Press, 1996), 173–95; R. Dworkin, *A Matter of Principle* (Oxford: Oxford University Press, 1985), ch. 8; and *Justice for Hedgehogs* (Cambridge, MA: Harvard University Press, 2011), 364–78.

7. This idea of neutrality is criticized by Joseph Raz in *The Morality of Freedom* (Oxford: Clarendon Press, 1986), ch. 5.

8. W. Kymlicka, 'Liberal Individualism and Liberal Neutrality', *Ethics* 99 (1989): 883–905; Rawls, *Political Liberalism*, 190–4; R. Dworkin, *Sovereign Virtue: The Theory and Practice of Equality* (Cambridge, MA: Harvard University Press, 2000), 153–5, 281–2; and *Religion without God* (Cambridge, MA: Harvard University Press, 2013), 129–37.

9. For the general idea of exclusionary reasons, see J. Raz, *Practical Reason and Norms*, second edition (Princeton, NJ: Princeton University Press, 1990), 182–6.

10. B. Ackerman, *Social Justice and the Liberal State* (New Haven, CT: Yale University Press, 1980); Dworkin, *Justice for Hedgehogs*, chs 9 and 17; G. Klosko and S. Wall (eds), *Perfectionism and Neutrality: Essays in Liberal Theory* (Lanham, MD: Rowman & Littlefield, 2003). For a nuanced discussion of alternative conceptions, including a defence of her own distinctive account, which I lack the space to discuss, see C. Laborde, *Liberalism's Religion* (Cambridge, MA: Harvard University Press, 2017).

11. Rawls runs a different, complementary, argument for anti-perfectionism, which I shall not discuss. That argument rests on the value of social unity. For commentary on that argument, see A. Williams, 'Incentives, Inequality, and Publicity', *Philosophy & Public Affairs* 27 (1998): 225–47; A. Gosseries and T. Parr, 'Publicity', *The Stanford Encyclopedia of Philosophy* (Summer 2022 Edition), E. N. Zalta (ed.), https://plato.stanford.edu/archives/sum2022/entries/publicity/ (accessed 13 November 2023).

12. Rawls, *Political Liberalism*, 68.

13. By contrast, *non-directive* education involves teachers imparting to students an understanding of the different answers to religious or evaluative questions without aiming to get them to endorse any particular answer. For discussion of the distinction between directive and non-directive teaching, see M. Hand, *A Theory of Moral Education* (London: Routledge, 2018), ch. 3. John Tillson offers a related distinction between promotional and non-promotional teaching in his *Children, Religion and the Ethics of Influence* (London: Bloomsbury, 2019).

14. Note, however, that in certain societies, such as England, these arrangements are qualified by a parental right to exempt their child from participating in collective worship and religious education classes.

15. Rawls, *Political Liberalism*, Lecture VI; and 'The Idea of Public Reason Revisited', in *Collected Papers*, ed. S. Freeman (Cambridge, MA: Harvard University Press, 1999), particularly 601–4.

16. For this kind of anti-perfectionist view, albeit with constraints on parental choice to protect their children's personal autonomy and interests in acting justly, see I. MacMullen, *Faith in Schools? Autonomy, Citizenship, and Religious Education in the Liberal State* (Princeton, NJ: Princeton University Press, 2007).

17. Dworkin, *Justice for Hedgehogs*, 354–5.

18. For a review of different accounts of interpersonal comparison for the purposes of achieving justice, see Matthew Clayton and Andrew Williams' introduction to *The Ideal of Equality* (London: Palgrave Macmillan, 2002), 8–15.

19. For this view, see W. Galston, *Liberal Pluralism: The Implications of Value Pluralism for Political Theory and Practice* (Cambridge: Cambridge University Press, 2002); M. Moschella, *To Whom Do Children Belong? Parental Rights, Civic Education, and Children's Autonomy* (Cambridge: Cambridge University Press, 2016), particularly ch. 2.

20. MacMullen, *Faith in Schools?*, 186 and ch. 8.
21. In addition to MacMullen's discussion, see M. Levinson, *The Demands of Liberal Education* (Oxford: Oxford University Press, 1999), 133–5; T. H. McLaughlin, 'Parental Rights and the Religious Upbringing of Children', *Journal of Philosophy of Education* 18 (1984): 75–82.
22. For this argument, which I discuss in Section 5, see M. Merry, 'Indoctrination, Islamic Schools, and the Broader Scope of Harm', *Theory and Research in Education* 16 (2018): 162–78.
23. J. S. Mill, *On Liberty*, ch. II.
24. M. Clayton and D. Halliday, 'Big Data and the Liberal Conception of Education', *Theory and Research in Education* 15 (2018): 290–305.
25. The imagined citizen voucher scheme resembles schemes run by various supermarkets, which give customers tokens to choose between various good causes with the store's funding those causes in proportion to the customer support they receive.
26. See M. Clayton, *Justice and Legitimacy in Upbringing* (Oxford: Oxford University Press, 2006), ch. 3; and *Independence for Children* (Oxford: Oxford University Press, forthcoming).
27. Rawls, *Political Liberalism*, 67–8.
28. See, for example, P. Bou-Habib and S. Olsaretti, 'Autonomy and Children's Well-Being', in A. Bagattini and C. Macleod (eds), *The Nature of Children's Well-Being* (Dordrecht: Springer, 2015); N. Richards, 'Raising a Child with Respect', *Journal of Applied Philosophy* 35 (2018): 90–104.
29. Here I summarize the longer argument provided in Clayton, *Independence for Children*, particularly ch. 3.
30. C. Macleod, 'Liberal Equality and the Affective Family', in D. Archard and C. Macleod (eds), *The Moral and Political Status of Children* (Oxford: Oxford University Press, 2002); H. Brighouse and A. Swift, *Family Values: The Ethics of Parent-Child Relationships* (Princeton, NJ: Princeton University Press, 2014).
31. For more detail as to how I envisage intimate anti-perfectionist family life, see Clayton, *Independence for Children*, ch. 6.
32. J. Feinberg, 'The Child's Right to an Open Future', in his *Freedom and Fulfillment* (Princeton, NJ: Princeton University Press, 1992).
33. For this argument, see D. Weinstock, 'How the Interests of Children Limit the Religious Freedom of Parents', in C. Laborde and A. Bardon (eds), *Religion in Liberal Political Philosophy* (Oxford: Oxford University Press, 2017).
34. I defend this view at greater length in Clayton, *Independence for Children*, ch. 7.
35. We might also note that some argue for the abolition of all religious schools while defending the right of parents to raise their child in a religious tradition. For this view, see D. Weinstock, 'A Freedom of Religion-Based Argument against Religious Schools', in B. Berger and R. Moon (eds), *Religion and the Exercise of Public Authority* (Oxford: Hart, 2016).
36. Quoted in 'Church Schools Move towards Open Door Selection', *BBC News*, 6 May 2015, https://www.bbc.co.uk/news/education-32587694 (accessed 13 November 2023).
37. As an example, in 2013 the Catholic Bishops' Conference of England and Wales urged its dioceses not to establish so-called "free" schools—schools funded largely by the taxpayer—unless the government relaxed its rule that allows free schools to select only up to 50% of their pupils on the basis of religious affiliation. In its statement the Conference asserts: "in the circumstances prevailing in England and Wales, the conditions required to ensure a distinctive Catholic education remain the ownership of the school or college site, the appointment of the majority of governors, admissions arrangements, the RE curriculum and its inspection, worship, and the employment of staff." See Catholic Bishops' Conference of England and Wales, 'Statement: Admissions to Catholic Schools', 15 November 2013, https://www.cbcew.org.uk/home/the-church/catholic-bishops-conference-of-england-and-wales/plenary-meetings/plenary-november-2013/statement-admissions-to-catholic-schools/ (accessed 13 November 2023).
38. These issues, as they pertain to the relationship between religion and public schooling in nineteenth–century US education, are nicely explored in B. Justice and C. Macleod, *Have*

a Little Faith: Religion, Democracy, and the American Public School (Chicago, IL: University of Chicago Press, 2016). They discuss resource issues specifically at 75–7.

39. F. Millar, *The Best for My Child: Did the Schools Market Deliver?* (Woodbridge: John Catt Educational, 2018), 89.

40. A. Spielman, *The Annual Report of Her Majesty's Chief Inspector of Education, Children's Services and Skills 2017/18* (2018), https://assets.publishing.service.gov.uk/media/5c0692f 6ed915d7460c9dba9/29523_Ofsted_Annual_Report_2017-18_041218.pdf (accessed 13 November 2023), 50; J. E. Ryan, 'The Perverse Incentives of the No Child Left Behind Act', *New York University Law Review* 79 (2004): 969–70.

41. In Chapter 2, we reviewed various distributive principles that need considering in debates about religious schools. The discussion here shows how the design of a schooling system can generate unintended injustices. We don't need to pick between egalitarian, prioritarian, or adequacy views of distributive justices to see that educational markets as they are currently structured in most societies are unjust, because all three views converge on the view that worsening the educational outcomes of the least advantaged is wrong.

42. For example, Millar focuses on an Anglican school in the English county of Kent, St Olave's Grammar School, which captured the attention of the British press in 2017 for off-rolling students who were likely not to achieve the very highest grades in their final exams. See Millar, *The Best for My Child*.

43. The evidence I have for this is testimony from teachers. It is very difficult to get quantitative data to verify or falsify the facts I describe, because schools that try to game the system in the ways I mention tend to hide their activities, not least because they are illegal.

44. H. Brighouse, *School Choice and Social Justice* (Oxford: Oxford University Press, 2002).

45. A. Gutmann, *Democratic Education* (Princeton, NJ: Princeton University Press, 1987), ch. 3.

46. Merry, 'Indoctrination, Islamic Schools, and the Broader Scope of Harm', 162–78.

47. J. Rawls, *A Theory of Justice* (Cambridge, MA: Harvard University Press, 1971), Section 67.

48. M. Hewstone, A. Al Ramiah, K. Schmid, C. Floe, M. van Zalk, R. Wölfer, and R. New, 'Influence of Segregation versus Mixing: Intergroup Contact and Attitudes among White-British and Asian-British Students in High Schools in Oldham, England', *Theory and Research in Education* 16 (2018): 179–203.

49. For example, in England, the so-called "Fundamental British Values" that teachers are required to teach directively in schools include respect for the rule of law and democratic institutions, religious toleration, and anti-discrimination, but omit moral norms relating to socio-economic matters, such as the moral duty to sustain the National Health Service and other arrangements of the welfare state. See UK Department for Education, *Promoting Fundamental British Values as Part of SMSC in Schools: Departmental Advice for Maintained Schools* (2014), https://assets.publishing.service.gov.uk/government/uploads/ system/uploads/attachment_data/file/380595/SMSC_Guidance_Maintained_Schools. pdf (accessed 13 November 2023).

50. For a nice discussion of these issues in the context of education in Canada, see A. Cormier, 'Must Schools Teach Religions Neutrally? The Loyola Case and the Challenges of Liberal Neutrality in Education', *Religion & Education* 45 (2018): 308–30. The relationship between religious instruction and the development of an individual's sense of justice has been a key debate in the history of US education. For a nuanced discussion of that history, see Justice and Macleod, *Have a Little Faith*.

Notes to Chapter 5

1. Cf. Rawls' capacity to "frame, revise and pursue" a conception of the good.

2. See, for example, M. Clayton, *Justice and Legitimacy in Upbringing* (Oxford: Oxford University Press, 2006); and *Independence for Children* (Oxford: Oxford University Press, forthcoming).

3. H. Brighouse and A. Swift, *Family Values: The Ethics of Parent-Child Relationships* (Princeton, NJ: Princeton University Press, 2014).

4. See M. Clayton, A. Mason, A. Swift, and R. Wareham, 'The Political Morality of School Composition: The Case of Religious Selection', *British Journal of Political Science* 51 (2021): 827–44.
5. For the role that schools can play in promoting intergroup contact, see R. Wölfer, M. Hewstone, and E. Jaspers, 'Social Contact and Inter-Ethnic Attitudes: The Importance of Contact Experiences in Schools', in F. Kalter, J. O. Jonnson, F. van Tubergen, and A. Heath (eds), *Growing up in Diverse Societies: The Integration of the Children of Immigrants in England, Germany, the Netherlands, and Sweden* (Oxford: Oxford University Press, 2018).
6. S. Gerhardt, *Why Love Matters: How Affection Shapes a Baby's Brain* (London: Routledge, 2004).
7. A. C. Dailey, 'Developing Citizens', *Iowa Law Review* 91 (2006): 432–503, at 460.
8. C. Overall, *Why Have Children? The Ethical Debate* (Cambridge, MA: MIT Press, 2012).
9. Y. Reshef, 'Rethinking the Value of Families', *Critical Review of Social and Political Philosophy* 16 (2013): 130–50.
10. E. Page, 'Parental Rights', *Journal of Applied Philosophy* 1 (1984): 187–203; C. MacLeod, 'Liberal Equality and the Affective Family', in D. Archard and C. Macleod (eds), *The Moral and Political Status of Children* (Oxford: Oxford University Press, 2002).
11. For an attempt that fails for this reason, see F. Schoemann 'Rights of Children, Rights of Parents, and the Moral Basis of the Family', *Ethics* 91 (1980): 6–19.
12. J. Locke, *Two Treatises of Government*, ed. P. Laslett (Cambridge: Cambridge University Press, 1988. First published 1689 by A. Churchill, London).
13. For Rawls, we need to distinguish between "the point of view of people as citizens and their point of view as members of families and of other associations. As citizens we have reasons to impose the constraints specified by the political principles of justice on association; while as members of associations we have reasons for limiting those constraints so that they leave room for a free and flourishing internal life appropriate to the association in question" (J. Rawls, *Justice as Fairness: A Restatement* (Cambridge, MA: Harvard University Press, 2001), 165).
14. S. Burtt, 'The Proper Scope of Parental Authority: Why We Don't Owe Children an "Open Future"', in S. Macedo and I. M. Young (eds), *Nomos XLIV: Child, Family, and State* (New York: New York University Press, 2003), 243–70, at 253.
15. W. Galston, *Liberal Pluralism: The Implications of Value Pluralism for Political Theory and Practice* (Oxford: Oxford University Press, 2002), 102.
16. C. Fried. *Right and Wrong* (Cambridge, MA: Harvard University Press, 1976), 152.
17. Reshef, 'Rethinking the Value of Families', 132.
18. J. Rawls, 'The Sense of Justice', *Philosophical Review* 72 (1962): 281–305; also in his *Collected Papers*, ed. S. Freeman (Cambridge, MA: Harvard University Press, 1999), 96–116.
19. N. Richards, 'Raising a Child with Respect', *Journal of Applied Philosophy* 35 (2018): 90–104.
20. For views that emphasize the value of familial relationships' continuing into adulthood, see Reshef, 'Rethinking the Value of Families'; and especially, L. Ferracioli 'Why the Family?', *Law, Ethics and Philosophy* 3 (2015): 205–19.
21. See A. Cormier, 'On the Permissibility of Shaping Children's Values', *Critical Review of Social and Political Philosophy* 21 (2018): 333–50, for the related suggestion that children might retrospectively consent to parents' deliberate shaping of their values where that was necessary for the kind of relationship needed to develop autonomy.
22. Brighouse and Swift, *Family Values*, 142.
23. For more on discontinuity, see H. Brighouse, 'Channel One, the Anti-Commercial Principle, and the Discontinuous Ethos', *Education Policy* 19 (2005): 528–49.
24. Daniel Weinstock optimistically suggests that schools' "not simply being extensions of the values around which the familial domain is organized" would suffice to enable parents to avoid "the juggling act between intimacy and autonomy" (D. Weinstock, 'For a Political Philosophy of Parent-Child Relationships', *Critical Review of Social and Political Philosophy* 21 (2018): 351–65, at 363–4). This paragraph draws on the reply in H. Brighouse and A. Swift, 'Family Values Reconsidered', *Critical Review of Social and Political Philosophy* 21 (2018): 385–405, at 396–7.

25. I. MacMullen, *Faith in Schools? Autonomy, Citizenship and Religious Education in the Liberal State* (Princeton, NJ: Princeton University Press, 2007), ch. 8.
26. I discuss this distinction, and various views about what it means for a school to be "good enough", in *How Not to Be a Hypocrite: School Choice for the Morally Perplexed Parent* (London: Routledge, 2003) and, bite-sized, in 'The Morality of School Choice', *Theory and Research in Education* 2 (2004): 7–21. There the context is primarily economic inequality, and the issue concerns not parents' rights to shape their children's values but their rights to make choices that unfairly confer advantage on them.
27. See M. Merry, 'Indoctrination, Islamic Schools, and the Broader Scope of Harm', *Theory and Research in Education* 16 (2018): 162–78, for the argument that Islamic schools' ability to protect their students from stigmatic harms justifies parents' choosing such schools despite the risk of indoctrinatory harms.

Notes to Chapter 6

1. A. Hamlin and Z. Stemplowska, 'Theory, Ideal Theory, and the Theory of Ideals', *Political Studies Review* 10 (2012): 48–62.
2. See H. Brighouse, H. F. Ladd, S. Loeb, and A. Swift, 'Good Education Policy Making: Data-Informed but Values-Driven', *Phi Delta Kappan* 100 (2018): 36–9.
3. J. Rawls, *A Theory of Justice* (Cambridge, MA: Harvard University Press, 1971), 48–51; C. Knight, 'Reflective Equilibrium', in A. Blau (ed.), *Methods in Analytical Political Theory* (Cambridge: Cambridge University Press, 2017), 46–64.
4. H. Brighouse and A. Swift, *Family Values: The Ethics of Parent-Child Relationships* (Princeton, NJ: Princeton University Press, 2014).
5. A. Swift, *How Not To Be A Hypocrite: School Choice for the Morally Perplexed Parent* (London: Routledge, 2003).
6. N. Cartwright, 'Are RCTs the Gold Standard', *Biosocieties* 2 (2007): 11–20; A. Deaton and N. Cartwright, 'Understanding and Misunderstanding Randomized Controlled Trials', *Social Science & Medicine* 210 (2018): 2–21.
7. For an accessible introduction to democratic theory, see A. Swift, *Political Philosophy: A Beginners' Guide for Students and Politicians*, fourth edition (Cambridge: Polity Press, 2019), ch. 2.

Notes to Chapter 7

1. J. Raz, *The Morality of Freedom* (Oxford: Oxford University Press, 1986); I. MacMullen, *Faith in Schools: Autonomy, Citizenship, and Religious Education in the Liberal State* (Princeton, NJ: Princeton University Press, 2007).
2. See, for example, J. J. Rousseau, *On the Social Contract*, trans. D. A. Cress, second edition (Indianapolis, IN: Hackett, 2019. First published 1762 by M. M. Rey, Amsterdam), particularly Book 1, ch. 4; R. Dworkin, *Justice for Hedgehogs* (Cambridge, MA: Harvard University Press, 2011), ch. 9.
3. M. Hand, 'A Philosophical Objection to Faith Schools', *Theory and Research in Education* 1 (2003): 89–99; and 'The Problem with Faith Schools: A Reply to My Critics', *Theory and Research in Education* 2 (2004): 343–53; J. Tillson, *Children, Religion and the Ethics of Influence* (London: Bloomsbury, 2019).
4. Clarke and Woodhead distinguish religious instruction, which "does not involve critical questioning or consideration of alternative religious or non-religious options", from religious formation, which "form[s] children 'within a particular religious tradition'" and "imbue[s] them with certain beliefs and values" (C. Clarke and L. Woodhead, *A New Settlement: Religion and Belief in Schools* (London: Westminster Faith Debates, 2015), 33).
5. For Andrew Mason, whether directive religious teaching should be permitted in practice depends on the risk that it will close the minds of a sufficiently high number of children who are exposed to it, a risk that varies across time and place. In Chapter 3 he emphasizes the compatibility in principle between directive religious teaching and respect for each child's right to autonomy, but he judges the risk that this form of teaching poses in England in the present day to be high enough to warrant the prohibition.

6. See The Education (School Inspection) Regulations, 2005, part 3 (England), https://www.legislation.gov.uk/uksi/2005/2038/made (accessed 13 November 2023).

7. P. Chadwick, *Shifting Alliances: Church and State in English Education* (London: Cassell, 1997), cited in Richard Pring, *The Future of Publicly Funded Faith Schools: A Critical Perspective* (London: Routledge, 2018), 69.

8. For example, Clarke and Woodhead, *A New Settlement*; Commission on Religious Education, *Religious Education for All. Final Report. Religion and Worldviews: The Way Forward. A National Plan for RE (2018)*, https://www.commissiononre.org.uk/wp-content/uploads/2018/09/Final-Report-of-the-Commission-on-RE.pdf (accessed 13 November 2023); Commission on Religion and Belief in Public Life, *Living with Difference: Community, Diversity, and the Common Good* (2015), https://corablivingwith-difference.files.wordpress.com/2015/12/living-with-difference-community-diversity-and-the-common-good.pdf (accessed 13 November 2023).

9. In their amended recommendations, Clarke and Woodhead emphasize the need to draw on the expertise of professionals in the subject as well as faith communities. See C. Clarke and L. Woodhead, *A New Settlement Revised: Religion and Belief in Schools* (London: Westminster Faith Debates, 2018), 15–17.

10. In Wales, the option for parents to withdraw their children from Religious Education was recently removed when Religion, Values, and Ethics was introduced as a replacement. That option, and indeed parents' freedom to withdraw their children from communal worship, had apparently been introduced, in both England and Wales, to respect the right, enshrined by Article 2 Protocol 1 to the European Convention for the Protection of Human Rights and Fundamental Freedoms (Council of Europe. Publication date, 20 March 1952, last amendment 2021, https://www.echr.coe.int/documents/d/echr/convention_ENG), that "prevents states from pursuing an aim of indoctrination that might be considered as not respecting parents' religious and philosophical convictions". However, case law shows that, as long as the state avoids "indoctrination", parents who educate their children in state schools have no demonstrable legal right to exempt their children from classes of the kind we envisage. Most notably, in *Bernard et al. v. Luxembourg* (1993) the European Commission on Human Rights ruled in favour of the state's view that children could not be withdrawn from a course in moral and social education on the grounds that "no allegation of indoctrination had been made" and "the course aimed at equipping the child with the rules of life requisite for safeguarding democratic societies" (O. Jawoniyi, 'Children's Rights and Religious Education in State-Funded Schools: An International Human Rights Perspective', *International Journal of Human Rights* 16 (2012): 337–57, at 348).

11. In recent years there has been some movement towards recognizing this more explicitly in law. In 2015, the High Court ruled that, by issuing guidance claiming that the statutory duty to provide RE for pupils in Key Stage 4 (age 14–16) could be met solely via the GCSE Religious Studies syllabus—a syllabus which may not cover non-religious world views—the government had acted unlawfully. See R. Wareham, 'Achieving Pluralism? A Critical Analysis of the Inclusion of Non-Religious Worldviews in RE Policy in England and Wales after *R (Fox) v Secretary of State for Education*', *British Journal of Religious Education* 44 (2022): 455–71. In 2023, Kent County Council was deemed to have acted unlawfully when it refused to include a humanist on the SACRE on the grounds that humanism isn't a religion. The judgment maintained that, under human rights law, references to "religion" include non-religious belief—at least those beliefs that are analogous to religion—and must therefore be understood to embrace humanism. See *Bowen v Kent City Council* [2023], https://www.casemine.com/judgement/uk/6474564aca5ce06a4b2cc16f (accessed 13 November 2023).

12. For fuller discussions of political education, see A. Gutmann, *Democratic Education*, revised edition (Princeton, NJ: Princeton University Press, 1999); E. Callan, *Creating Citizens: Political Education and Liberal Democracy* (Oxford: Oxford University Press, 1997).

13. It is notable—and in our view lamentable—that the so-called Fundamental British Values guidance introduced in 2014 omits these political ideals that are so central to liberal democratic society.

14. J. Rawls, *Political Liberalism*, paperback edition (New York: Columbia University Press, 1996), Lecture VII.
15. See J. Rawls, *A Theory of Justice* (Cambridge, MA: Harvard University Press, 1971), Sections 53–9; Rawls, *Political Liberalism*, 427–9.
16. See M. Hand, *A Theory of Moral Education* (London: Routledge, 2018); Tillson, *Children, Religion and the Ethics of Influence*.
17. The idea that science is special in the sense that, notwithstanding the fact that some people are sceptical of its value and the veracity of its findings, we ought to promote it in schools has received many different defences. For example, in 'Science as Public Reason: A Restatement', *Res Publica* 24 (2018): 415–32, Cristóbal Bellolio Badiola argues that science should be promoted because it is relevantly like liberal reasoning about politics. Our argument for directive science education is somewhat different because we tie the importance of science to our two prominent educational goods.
18. For objections to the current rules that allow faith schools in England to teach Relationships and Sex Education according to their "distinctive religious character", see R. Wareham, 'The Problem with Faith-Based Carve-Outs: RSE Policy, Religion and Educational Goods', *Journal of Philosophy of Education* 56 (2022): 707–26.
19. Excerpt from the Vision of Trinity Christian School, https://trinitychristianschool.org.uk/about/vision/ (accessed 26 March 2024).
20. Some limits might nevertheless need to be placed here to prevent schools from raising money or providing gifts for charities involved in religious proselytization in other countries. See the discussion of *Operation Christmas Child*: 'Humanists UK Warns Parents to Be Wary of Operation Christmas Child', Humanists UK, 2 December 2022, https://humanists.uk/2022/12/02/humanists-uk-warns-parents-of-to-be-wary-of-operation-christmas-child/ (accessed 13 November 2023).
21. The Catholic Education Service argues that the rule "prevents the Church from meeting the demand from Catholic parents for Catholic places and could cause schools to turn Catholic families away on the grounds that they are Catholics", a state of affairs which they claim "contravenes not only Canon Law but also common sense". See Catholic Education Service, 'Press Statement: Catholic Church Welcomes Prime Minister's Removal of the Cap on Faith Admissions', 9 September 2016, http://www.catholiceducation.org.uk/component/k2/item/1003609-catholic-church-welcomes-prime-minister-s-removal-of-the-cap-on-faith-admissions (accessed 13 November 2023).
22. The Conservative and Unionist Party, *Manifesto: Forward, Together. Our Plan for a Stronger Britain and a Prosperous Future* (2017), https://ucrel.lancs.ac.uk/wmatrix/ukmanifestos2017/localpdf/Conservatives.pdf (accessed 13 November 2023).
23. UK Department for Education, *Schools That Work for Everyone: Government Consultation Response* (2018), https://assets.publishing.service.gov.uk/government/uploads/system/uploads/attachment_data/file/706243/Schools_that_work_for_everyone-Government_consultation_response.pdf (accessed 13 November 2023).
24. M. Hewstone, A. Al Ramiah, K. Schmid, C. Floe, M. van Zalk, R. Wölfer, and R. New, 'Influence of Segregation versus Mixing: Intergroup Contact and Attitudes among White-British and Asian-British Students in High Schools in Oldham, England', *Theory and Research in Education* 16 (2018): 179–203; M. Hewstone, M. van Zalk, A. Al Ramiah, K. Schmid, R. New, R. Wölfer, B. Fell, C. Floe, and C. Wigoder, *Diversity and Social Cohesion in Mixed and Segregated Secondary Schools in Oldham* (2017), https://assets.publishing.service.gov.uk/government/uploads/system/uploads/attachment_data/file/634118/Diversity_and_Social_Cohesion_in_Oldham_schools.pdf (accessed 13 November 2023).
25. Brighouse suggests 30 per cent (H. Brighouse, 'Faith Schools, Personal Autonomy and Democratic Competence', in G. Haydon (ed.), *Faith in Education: A Tribute to Terence McLaughlin* (London: Institute of Education, 2009), 78–93, at 90). John Pritchard, the former Bishop of Oxford suggested 10 per cent. See 'C of E Opens School Gates to Non-Believers', *TES Magazine*, 22 April 2011, https://www.tes.com/news/c-e-opens-school-gates-non-believers (accessed 13 November 2023).

26. Nigel Genders, quoted in 'Faith Schools Welcome 100% Faith-Based Admissions', *Schools Week*, 16 September 2016, https://schoolsweek.co.uk/faith-schools-welcome-100-faith-based-admissions/ (accessed 13 November 2023).

27. Accord Coalition for Inclusive Education, *Mixed Signals: The Discrepancy between What the Church Preaches and What It Practises about Religious Selection in Its State-Funded Schools* (2017), https://drive.google.com/file/d/1i5ImrZIpgoFkC7QrkRUdr1tTvCruqhHe/view (accessed 13 November 2023).

28. This could take the form of a nationally recognized award similar to the Investors in Diversity for Schools Award. See National Centre for Diversity, 'Investors in Diversity – Schools', http://www.nationalcentrefordiversity.com/home/services/investors-diversity-schools/ (accessed 13 November 2023).

29. R. Taylor, 'Parental Responsibility and Religion', in R. Probert, S. Gilmore, and J. Herring (eds), *Responsible Parents and Parental Responsibility* (Oxford: Hart Publishing, 2009), 123–41; and 'Responsibility for the Soul of the Child: The Role of the State and Parents in Determining Religious Upbringing and Education', *International Journal of Law, Policy and the Family* 29 (2015): 15–35.

30. Protocol 1 to the European Convention for the Protection of Human Rights and Fundamental Freedoms (1952), art. 2.

31. The government proposed its own legislation on this as part of the 2022 Schools Bill (see House of Lords, UK Parliament, *Schools Bill (Bill 49)*, https://bills.parliament.uk/publications/47514/documents/2173 (accessed 13 November 2023)), but, for reasons unrelated to the relevant sections of the Bill, this was dropped. See Humanists UK, 'Government Fails Most Vulnerable Children by Dropping Schools Bill', 7 December 2022, https://humanists.uk/2022/12/07/government-fails-most-vulnerable-children-by-dropping-schools-bill/ (accessed 13 November 2023).

32. UK Department for Education, 'Schools, Pupils and their Characteristics. January 2023', https://explore-education-statistics.service.gov.uk/find-statistics/school-pupils-and-their-characteristics (accessed 13 November 2023).

33. House of Lords, UK Parliament, 'Private Education: Charities. Private Education: Charities', https://questions-statements.parliament.uk/written-questions/detail/2022-05-16/HL279 (accessed 13 November 2023).

34. This suggestion mirrors the 'Shared Education' programme in Northern Ireland, on which see Department for Education of Northern Ireland, *Advancing Shared Education. 3rd Report to the Northern Ireland Assembly* (2022), https://www.education-ni.gov.uk/sites/default/files/publications/education/Advancing%20Shared%20Education%203rd%20Report%20to%20Assembly%20-%2025%20MARCH%202022%20%28amended%2022%2005%202023%29.PDF (accessed 13 November 2023).

35. Association of Directors of Children's Services (ADCS), *Elective Home Education Survey 2021* (2021), https://adcs.org.uk/assets/documentation/ADCS_EHE_Survey_2021_Report_FINAL.pdf (accessed 13 November 2023), 1. Because registration of home education is not a legal requirement in England, that number is an underestimate: see R. Long and S. Danechi, *Home Education in England* (2023), https://researchbriefings.files.parliament.uk/documents/SN05108/SN05108.pdf (accessed 13 November 2023).

36. UK Department for Education, *Elective Home Education: Departmental Guidance for Local Authorities* (2019), https://assets.publishing.service.gov.uk/media/5ca21e0b40f0b625e97ffe06/Elective_home_education_gudiance_for_LAv2.0.pdf (accessed 13 November 2023), 30–2.

37. See the Education Select Committee's report on home education: House of Commons Education Committee, *Strengthening Home Education. Third Report of Session 2021–22* (2021), https://committees.parliament.uk/publications/6974/documents/72808/default/ (accessed 13 November 2023).

38. Here, for ease of exposition, we classify home education as a form of "schooling".

Bibliography

Ackerman, B., *Social Justice and the Liberal State* (New Haven, CT: Yale University Press, 1980).

Allen, R. and A. West, 'Religious Schools in London: School Admissions, Religious Composition and Selectivity', *Oxford Review of Education* 35 (2009): 471–94.

Allen, R. and A. West, 'Why Do Faith Secondary Schools Have Advantaged Intakes? The Relative Importance of Neighbourhood Characteristics, Social Background and Religious Identification Amongst Parents', *British Educational Research Journal* 37 (2011): 691–712.

Allport, G. W., *The Nature of Prejudice* (Cambridge, MA: Addison-Wesley, 1954).

Andrews, J. and R. Johnes, *Faith Schools, Pupil Performance and Social Selection* (London: Education Policy Institute, 2016).

Avery, P., D. Hoffman, J. L. Sullivan, and K. Thalhammer, 'Exploring Political Toleration with Adolescents', *Theory and Research in Social Education* 20 (1992): 386–420.

Bellolio Badiola, C., 'Science as Public Reason: A Restatement', *Res Publica* 24 (2018): 415–32.

Bou-Habib, P. and S. Olsaretti, 'Autonomy and Children's Well-Being', in A. Baggatini and C. Macleod (eds), *The Nature of Children's Well-Being: Theory and Practice* (Dordrecht: Springer, 2015), 15–33.

Brennan, S., 'The Goods of Childhood and Children's Rights', in F. Baylis and C. Mcleod (eds), *Family-Making: Contemporary Ethical Challenges* (Oxford: Oxford University Press, 2014).

Brighouse, H., *School Choice and Social Justice* (Oxford: Oxford University Press, 2002).

Brighouse, H., 'Channel One, the Anti-Commercial Principle, and the Discontinuous Ethos', *Education Policy* 19 (2005): 528–49.

Brighouse, H., 'Faith Schools, Personal Autonomy and Democratic Competence', in G. Haydon (ed.), *Faith in Education: A Tribute to Terence McLaughlin* (London: Institute of Education, 2009), 78–93.

Brighouse, H., H. F. Ladd, S. Loeb, and A. Swift, 'Educational Goods and Values: A Framework for Decision-Makers', *Theory and Research in Education* 14 (2016): 3–25.

Brighouse, H., H. F. Ladd, S. Loeb, and A. Swift, *Educational Goods: Values, Evidence and Decision Making* (Chicago, IL: Chicago University Press, 2018).

Brighouse, H., H. F. Ladd, S. Loeb, and A. Swift, 'Good Education Policy Making: Data-Informed but Values-Driven', *Phi Delta Kappan* 100 (2018): 36–9.

Brighouse, H. and A. Swift, 'Educational Adequacy versus Educational Equality', *Journal of Applied Philosophy* 26 (2009): 117–28.

Brighouse H. and A. Swift, *Family Values: The Ethics of Parent-Child Relationships* (Princeton, NJ: Princeton University Press, 2014).

Brighouse, H. and A. Swift, 'Family Values Reconsidered', *Critical Review of Social and Political Philosophy* 21 (2018): 385–405.

Brighouse, H. and A. Swift, 'The Place of Educational Equality in Educational Justice', in K. Meyer (ed.), *Education, Justice and the Human Good* (Abingdon: Routledge, 2014), 14–33.

Burtt S., 'The Proper Scope of Parental Authority: Why We Don't Owe Children an "Open Future"', in S. Macedo and I. M. Young (eds), *Nomos XLIV: Child, Family, and State* (New York: New York University Press, 2003), 243–70.

Callan E., *Creating Citizens: Political Education and Liberal Democracy* (Oxford: Oxford University Press, 1997).

Cartwright N., 'Are RCTs the Gold Standard?', *Biosocieties* 2 (2007): 11–20.

Chadwick, P., *Shifting Alliances: Church and State in English Education* (London: Cassell, 1997).

Clarke, C. and L. Woodhead, *A New Settlement: Religion and Belief in Schools* (London: Westminster Faith Debates, 2015).

Clarke, C. and L. Woodhead, *A New Settlement Revised: Religion and Belief in Schools* (London: Westminster Faith Debates, 2018).

Clayton, M., 'Education', in S. Olsaretti (ed.), *The Oxford Handbook of Distributive Justice* (Oxford: Oxford University Press, 2018).

Clayton, M., *Independence for Children* (Oxford University Press, forthcoming).

Clayton, M., *Justice and Legitimacy in Upbringing* (Oxford: Oxford University Press, 2006).

Clayton, M. and D. Halliday, 'Big Data and the Liberal Conception of Education', *Theory and Research in Education* 15 (2018): 290–305.

Clayton, M., A. Mason, A. Swift, and R. Wareham, 'The Political Morality of School Composition: The Case of Religious Selection', *British Journal of Political Science* 51 (2021): 827–44.

Clayton, M. and A. Williams, *The Ideal of Equality* (London: Palgrave Macmillan, 2002).

Colburn, B., *Autonomy and Liberalism* (London: Routledge, 2013).

Cooper, B., 'Schools with a Religious Character and Social Cohesion: A Study of Faith Based Approaches to Educational Environments and Aims' (PhD thesis, University of Southampton, 2015).

Cormier, A., 'Must Schools Teach Religions Neutrally? The Loyola Case and the Challenges of Liberal Neutrality in Education', *Religion & Education* 45 (2018): 308–30.

Cormier, A., 'On the Permissibility of Shaping Children's Values', *Critical Review of Social and Political Philosophy* 21 (2018): 333–50.

Cormier, A. and M. Rossi, 'Is Children's Wellbeing Different from Adults' Wellbeing', *Canadian Journal of Philosophy* 49 (2019): 1146–68.

Craig, W. L., 'Five Reasons God Exists', in W. L. Craig and W. Sinnott-Armstrong, *God? A Debate between a Christian and an Atheist* (New York: Oxford University Press, 2004), 17–21.

Dailey, A. C., 'Developing Citizens', *Iowa Law Review* 91 (2006): 432–503.

Deaton, A. and N. Cartwright, 'Understanding and Misunderstanding Randomized Controlled Trials', *Social Science & Medicine* 210 (2018): 2–21.

Dericquebourg, R., 'Religious Education in France', in D. H. Davis and E. Miroshnikova (eds), *The Routledge International Handbook of Religious Education* (Abingdon: Routledge, 2013), 113–21.

Dhont, K., A. Van Hiel, and M. Hewstone, 'Changing the Ideological Roots of Prejudice: Longitudinal Effects of Ethnic Intergroup Contact on Social Dominance Orientation', *Group Processes & Intergroup Relations* 17 (2014): 27–44.

Diamond, C., *The Birmingham Book: Lessons in Urban Educational Leadership and Policy from the Trojan Horse Affair* (Carmarthen: Crown House Publishing, 2022).

Dreissen, G., A. Orhan, and M. S. Merry, 'The Gross and Net Effects of Primary School Denomination on Pupil Performance', *Educational Review* 68 (2016): 466–80.

Duckett, J. and C. Sibley, 'A Dual-Process Motivational Model of Ideology, Politics and Prejudice', *Psychological Inquiry* 20 (2009): 98–109.

Dworkin, R., *A Matter of Principle* (Oxford: Oxford University Press, 1985).

Dworkin, R., *Justice for Hedgehogs* (Cambridge, MA: Harvard University Press, 2011).

Dworkin, R., *Religion without God* (Cambridge, MA: Harvard University Press, 2013).

Dworkin, R., *Sovereign Virtue* (Cambridge, MA: Harvard University Press, 2000).

Dworkin, G., *The Theory and Practice of Autonomy* (Cambridge: Cambridge University Press, 1988).

Dwyer, J., 'Regulating Child Rearing in a Culturally Diverse Society', in E. Brake and L. Ferguson (eds), *Philosophical Foundations of Children's and Family Law* (Oxford: Oxford University Press, 2018).

Easton, C., 'LGBT-Inclusive Education in Liberal Pluralist Societies', *Journal of Applied Philosophy* 40 (2023): 550–68.

Ehman, L. H., 'The American School in the Political Socialization Process', *Review of Educational Research* 50 (1980): 99–119.

Feinberg, J., 'The Child's Right to an Open Future', in *Freedom and Fulfillment* (Princeton, NJ: Princeton University Press, 1992).

Ferracioli, L., 'Why the Family?', *Law, Ethics and Philosophy* 3 (2015): 205–19.

Fowler, T., *Liberalism, Childhood and Justice* (Bristol: Bristol University Press, 2020).

Fried, C., *Right and Wrong* (Cambridge, MA: Harvard University Press, 1976).

Galston, W., *Liberal Pluralism: The Implications of Value Pluralism for Political Theory and Practice* (Cambridge: Cambridge University Press, 2002).

Gerhardt, S., *Why Love Matters: How Affection Shapes a Baby's Brain* (London: Routledge, 2004).

Gheaus, A., 'The "Intrinsic Goods of Childhood" and the Just Society', in A. Bagattini and C. Macleod (eds), *The Nature of Children's Well-Being* (Dordrecht: Springer, 2015).

Gosseries, A. and T. Parr, 'Publicity', *The Stanford Encyclopedia of Philosophy* (Summer 2022 edition), ed. E. N. Zalta, https://plato.stanford.edu/archives/sum2022/entries/publicity/.

Greenawalt, K., *Does God Belong in Public Schools?* (Princeton, NJ: Princeton University Press, 2005).

Gutmann, A., *Democratic Education* (Princeton, NJ: Princeton University Press, 1987. Revised edition 1999).

Hamlin, A. and Z. Stemplowska, 'Theory, Ideal Theory and the Theory of Ideals', *Political Studies Review* 10 (2012): 48–62.

Hand, M., 'A Philosophical Objection to Faith Schools', *Theory and Research in Education* 1 (2003): 89–99.

Hand, M., *A Theory of Moral Education* (London: Routledge, 2018).

Hand, M., 'The Problem with Faith Schools: A Reply to My Critics', *Theory and Research in Education* 2 (2004): 343–53.

Hand, M., 'Towards a Theory of Moral Education', *Journal of Philosophy of Education* 48 (2014): 519–32.

Hand, M., 'What Should We Teach as Controversial: A Defense of the Epistemic Criterion', *Educational Theory* 58 (2008): 213–28.

Hewstone, M., A. Al Ramiah, K. Schmid, C. Floe, M. van Zalk, R. Wölfer, and R. New, 'Influence of Segregation versus Mixing: Intergroup Contact and Attitudes among White-British and Asian-British Students in High Schools in Oldham, England', *Theory and Research in Education* 16 (2018): 179–203.

Hollis, M., 'The Pen and the Purse', *Journal of Philosophy of Education* 5 (1971): 153–69.

Holmwood, J. and T. O'Toole, *Countering Extremism in British Schools? The Truth about the Birmingham Trojan Horse Affair* (Bristol: Policy Press, 2017).

Jawoniyi, O., 'Children's Rights and Religious Education in State-Funded Schools: An International Human Rights Perspective', *International Journal of Human Rights* 16 (2012): 337–57.

Jencks, C., 'Whom Must We Treat Equally for Educational Opportunity to be Equal?', *Ethics* 98 (1988): 518–33.

Justice, B. and C. Macleod, *Have a Little Faith: Religion, Democracy and the Public School* (Chicago, IL: Chicago University Press, 2016).

Klosko, G. and S. Wall (eds), *Perfectionism and Neutrality: Essays in Liberal Theory* (Lanham, MD: Rowman & Littlefield, 2003).

Knight, C., 'Reflective Equilibrium', in A. Blau (ed.), *Methods in Analytical Political Theory* (Cambridge: Cambridge University Press, 2017).

Kramer, M., *Liberalism with Excellence* (Oxford: Oxford University Press, 2017).

Kymlicka, W., *Contemporary Political Philosophy: An Introduction*, second edition (Oxford: Oxford University Press, 2002).

Kymlicka, W., 'Liberal Individualism and Liberal Neutrality', *Ethics* 99 (1989): 883–905.

Laborde, C., *Liberalism's Religion* (Cambridge, MA: Harvard University Press, 2017).

Levinson, M., *The Demands of Liberal Education* (Oxford: Oxford University Press, 1999).

Locke, J., *Two Treatises of Government*, ed. P. Laslett (Cambridge: Cambridge University Press, 1988. First published 1689 by A. Churchill, London).

McLaughlin, T. H., 'Parental Rights and the Religious Upbringing of Children', *Journal of Philosophy of Education* 18 (1984): 75–82.

Macleod, C., 'Liberal Equality and the Affective Family', in D. Archard and C. Macleod (eds), *The Moral and Political Status of Children* (Oxford: Oxford University Press, 2002).

Macleod, C., 'Primary Goods, Capabilities and Children', in H. Brighouse and I. Robeyns (eds), *Measuring Justice: Primary Goods and Capabilities* (Cambridge: Cambridge University Press, 2010).

MacMullen, I., *Faith in Schools: Autonomy, Citizenship, and Religious Education in the Liberal State* (Princeton, NJ: Princeton University Press, 2007).

Mason, A., 'Autonomy, Liberalism, and State Neutrality', *The Philosophical Quarterly* 40 (1990): 433–52.

Mason, A., 'Egalitarianism and the Levelling Down Objection', *Analysis* 61 (2001): 246–54.

Mason, A., 'Faith Schools and the Cultivation of Tolerance', *Theory and Research in Education* 16 (2018): 204–25.

Mason, A., 'Justice, Feasibility, and Ideal Theory: A Pluralist Approach', *Social Philosophy and Policy* 33 (2016): 32–54.

Mason, A., *Levelling the Playing Field: The Idea of Equal Opportunity and Its Place in Egalitarian Thought* (Oxford: Oxford University Press, 2006).

Mason, A., 'The Critique of Multiculturalism in Britain: Integration, Separation, and Shared Identification', *Critical Review of International Social and Political Philosophy* 21 (2018): 22–45.

Merry, M., *Equality, Citizenship, and Segregation: A Defense of Separation* (Basingstoke: Palgrave Macmillan, 2013).

Merry, M., 'Indoctrination, Islamic Schools, and the Broader Scope of Harm', *Theory and Research in Education* 16 (2018): 162–78.

Mill, J. S., 'On Liberty', in M. Warnock (ed.), *Utilitarianism* (London: Collins, 1962).

Millar, F., *The Best for My Child: Did the Schools Market Deliver?* (Woodbridge: John Catt Educational Ltd, 2018).

Moschella, M., *To Whom Do Children Belong? Parental Rights, Civic Education and Children's Autonomy* (Cambridge: Cambridge University Press, 2016).

Moulin, D., 'Religious Identity Choices in English Secondary Schools', *British Educational Research Journal* 41 (2015): 489–504.

Mullin, A., 'Children, Paternalism and the Development of Autonomy', *Ethical Theory and Moral Practice* 17 (2014): 413–26.

Nozick, R., *The Examined Life: Philosophical Meditations* (New York: Simon and Schuster, 1989).

Overall, C., *Why Have Children? The Ethical Debate* (Cambridge, MA: MIT Press, 2012).

Page, E., 'Parental Rights', *Journal of Applied Philosophy* 1 (1984): 187–203.

Pettigrew, T. F. and L. R. Tropp, 'A Meta-Analytic Test of Intergroup Contact Theory', *Journal of Personality and Social Psychology* 90 (2006): 751–83.

Pettigrew, T. F. and L. R. Tropp, 'Allport's Intergroup Contact Hypothesis: Its History and Influence', in J. F. Dividio, P. Glick, and L. A. Rudman (eds), *On the Nature of Prejudice: Fifty Years after Allport* (Oxford: Blackwell, 2005).

Pring, R., *The Future of Publicly Funded Faith Schools: A Critical Perspective* (London: Routledge, 2018).

Quong, J., *Liberalism without Perfection* (Oxford: Oxford University Press, 2011).

Quong, J., 'The Scope of Public Reason', *Political Studies* 52 (2004): 233–50.

Rawls, J., *A Theory of Justice* (Cambridge, MA: Harvard University Press, 1971).

Rawls, J., *Collected Papers*, ed. S. Freeman (Cambridge, MA: Harvard University Press, 1999).

Rawls, J., *Justice as Fairness: A Restatement* (Cambridge, MA: Harvard University Press, 2001).

Rawls, J., *Political Liberalism*, paperback edition (New York: Columbia University Press, 1996).

Rawls, J., 'The Sense of Justice', *Philosophical Review* 72 (1962): 281–305.

Raz, J., *Practical Reason and Norms*, second edition (Princeton, NJ: Princeton University Press, 1990).

Raz, J., *The Morality of Freedom* (Oxford: Oxford University Press, 1986).

Reshef, Y., 'Rethinking the Value of Families', *Critical Review of Social and Political Philosophy* 16 (2013): 130–50.

Richards, N., 'Raising a Child with Respect', *Journal of Applied Philosophy* 35 (2018): 90–104.

Rousseau, J. J., *On the Social Contract*, trans. D. A. Cress, second edition (Indianapolis, IN: Hackett, 2019. First published 1762 by M. M. Rey, Amsterdam).

Ryan, J. E., 'The Perverse Incentives of the No Child Left Behind Act', *New York University Law Review* 79 (2004): 932–89.

Satz, D., 'Equality, Adequacy, and Education for Citizenship', *Ethics* 117 (2007): 623–48.

Schoemann, F., 'Rights of Children, Rights of Parents, and the Moral Basis of the Family', *Ethics* 91 (1980): 6–19.

Short, G., 'Faith Schools and Social Cohesion: Opening Up the Debate', *British Journal of Religious Education* 25 (2003): 129–41.

Stemplowska, Z. and A. Swift, 'Ideal and Nonideal Theory', in D. Estlund (ed.), *The Oxford Handbook of Political Philosophy* (New York: Oxford University Press, 2012), 373–90.

Sullivan, A., S. Parsons, F. Green, R. D. Wiggins, G. Ploubidis, and T. Huynh, 'Educational Attainment in the Short and Long Term: Was there an Advantage to Attending Faith, Private and Selective Schools for Pupils in the 1980s?', *Oxford Review of Education* 44 (2018): 806–22.

Swift, A., *How Not to Be a Hypocrite: School Choice for the Morally Perplexed Parent* (London: Routledge, 2003).

Swift, A., *Political Philosophy: A Beginners' Guide for Students and Politicians*, fourth edition (Cambridge: Polity Press, 2019).

Swift, A., 'The Morality of School Choice', *Theory and Research in Education* 2 (2004): 7–21.

Tadros, V., 'Wrongful Intentions without Closeness', Philosophy and Public Affairs 43 (2015): 52–74.

Tausch, N. and M. Hewstone, 'Intergroup Contact', in J. F. Dividio, M. Hewstone, P. Glick, and V. M. Esses (eds), The Sage Handbook of Prejudice, Stereotyping and Discrimination (London: Sage, 2010), 544–60.

Taylor, R., 'Parental Responsibility and Religion', in R. Probert, S. Gilmore, and J. Herring (eds), Responsible Parents and Parental Responsibility (Oxford: Hart Publishing, 2009), 123–41.

Taylor, R., 'Responsibility for the Soul of the Child: The Role of the State and Parents in Determining Religious Upbringing and Education', International Journal of Law, Policy and the Family 29 (2015): 15–35.

Thomsen, L., E. Green, and J. Sidanius, 'We Will Hunt Them Down: How Social Dominance Orientation and Right-Wing Authoritarianism Fuel Ethnic Persecution of Immigrants in Fundamentally Different Ways', Journal of Experimental Social Psychology 44 (2008): 1455–64.

Tillson, J., Children, Religion and the Ethics of Influence (London: Bloomsbury, 2019).

Tomlin, P., 'The Value of Childhood', in A. Gheaus, G. Calder, and J. Wispelaere (eds), The Routledge Handbook of the Philosophy of Childhood and Children (London: Routledge, 2019).

Turner, R., T. Tam, M. Hewstone, J. Kenworthy, and E. Cairns, 'Contact between Catholic and Protestant Schoolchildren in Northern Ireland', Journal of Applied Social Psychology 43 (2013): E216–E228.

Uslaner, E. M., Segregation and Mistrust: Diversity, Isolation and Social Cohesion (Cambridge: Cambridge University Press, 2012).

Vogt, W. P., Tolerance and Education: Learning to Live with Diversity and Difference (Thousand Oaks, CA: Sage, 1997).

Wall, S., Liberalism, Perfectionism and Restraint (Cambridge: Cambridge University Press, 1998).

Wareham, R., 'Achieving Pluralism? A Critical Analysis of the Inclusion of Non-Religious Worldviews in RE policy in England and Wales after R (Fox) v Secretary of State for Education', British Journal of Religious Education 44 (2022): 455–71.

Wareham, R., 'The Problem with Faith-Based Carve-Outs: RSE Policy, Religion and Educational Goods', Journal of Philosophy of Education 56 (2022): 707–26.

Watson, B., 'Why Religious Education Matters', in L. Philip Barnes (ed.), Debates in Religious Education (London: Routledge, 2012), 13–21.

Weinstock, D., 'A Freedom of Religion-Based Argument against Religious Schools', in B. Berger and R. Moon (eds), Religion and the Exercise of Public Authority (Oxford: Hart, 2016).

Weinstock, D., 'For a Political Philosophy of Parent-Child Relationships', Critical Review of Social and Political Philosophy 21 (2018): 351–65.

Weinstock, D., 'How the Interests of Children Limit the Religious Freedom of Parents', in C. Laborde and A. Bardon (eds), Religion in Liberal Political Philosophy (Oxford: Oxford University Press, 2017).

Williams, A., 'Incentives, Inequality, and Publicity', Philosophy & Public Affairs 27 (1998): 225–47.

Williams, K., 'Republic of Ireland', in L. Philip Barnes (ed.), Debates in Religious Education (London: Routledge, 2012), 45–51.

Wölfer, R., M. Hewstone, and E. Jaspers, 'Social Contact and Inter-Ethnic Attitudes: The Importance of Contact Experiences in Schools', in F. Kalter, J. O. Jonnson, F. van Tubergen, and A. Heath (eds), Growing up in Diverse Societies: The Integration of the Children of Immigrants in England, Germany, the Netherlands, and Sweden (Oxford: Oxford University Press, 2018).

Other Sources

(i) Case Law (Rulings)

Bowen v Kent City Council [2023], https://www.casemine.com/judgement/uk/6474564aca5ce06a4b2cc16f.

(ii) Legislation

Protocol 1 to the European Convention for the Protection of Human Rights and Fundamental Freedoms. Publisher, Council of Europe. Publication date, 20 March 1952, available at https://www.echr.coe.int/documents/d/echr/convention_ENG.

The Education (School Inspection) Regulations, 2005, part 3 (England), available at https://www.legislation.gov.uk/uksi/2005/2038/made.

Universal Declaration on Human Rights (adopted 10 December 1948), available at https://www.un.org/en/about-us/universal-declaration-of-human-rights.

(iii) Official UK Reports and Guidance

Department for Education of Northern Ireland, Advancing Shared Education. 3rd Report to the Northern Ireland Assembly (2022), available at https://www.education-ni.gov.uk/sites/default/files/publications/education/Advancing%20Shared%20Education%203rd%20Report%20to%20Assembly%20-%2025%20MARCH%202022%20%28amended%2022%2005%202023%29.PDF.

Hewstone, M., M. van Zalk, A. Al Ramiah, K. Schmid, R. New, R. Wölfer, B. Fell, C. Floe, and C. Wigoder, Diversity and Social Cohesion in Mixed and Segregated Secondary Schools in Oldham (2017), available at https://assets.publishing.service.gov.uk/government/uploads/system/uploads/attachment_data/file/634118/Diversity_and_Social_Cohesion_in_Oldham_schools.pdf.

House of Commons Education Committee, Strengthening Home Education. Third Report of Session 2021–22 (2021), available at https://committees.parliament.uk/publications/6974/documents/72808/default/.

Long, R. and S. Danechi, Home Education in England (2023), available at https://researchbriefings.files.parliament.uk/documents/SN05108/SN05108.pdf.

Spielman, A., The Annual Report of Her Majesty's Chief Inspector of Education, Children's Services and Skills 2017/18 (2018), available at https://assets.publishing.service.gov.uk/media/5c0692f6ed915d7460c9dba9/29523_Ofsted_Annual_Report_2017-18_041218.pdf.

UK Department for Education, Promoting Fundamental British Values as Part of SMSC in Schools: Departmental Advice for Maintained Schools (2014), available at https://assets.publishing.service.gov.uk/government/uploads/system/uploads/attachment_data/file/380595/SMSC_Guidance_Maintained_Schools.pdf.

UK Department for Education, Schools that Work for Everyone: Government Consultation Response (2018), available at https://assets.publishing.service.gov.uk/government/uploads/system/uploads/attachment_data/file/706243/Schools_that_work_for_everyone-Government_consultation_response.pdf.

UK Department for Education, Elective Home Education: Departmental Guidance for Local Authorities (2019), available at https://assets.publishing.service.gov.uk/media/5ca21e0b40f0b625e97ffe06/Elective_home_education_gudiance_for_LAv2.0.pdf.

UK Department for Education, Establishing a New Academy: The Free School Presumption Route. Departmental Guidance for Local Authorities and New School Proposers (2023), available at https://assets.publishing.service.gov.uk/government/uploads/system/uploads/attachment_data/file/706171/Academy_and_free_school_presumption_departmental_advice.pdf.

UK Home Office, Community Cohesion: A Report of the Independent Review Team Chaired by Ted Cantle (2001), available at https://tedcantle.co.uk/pdf/communityco-hesion%20cantlereport.pdf.

(iv) Parliamentary Bills and Debates

Private Education: Charities, question for department for Education, https://questions-statements.parliament.uk/written-questions/detail/2022-05-16/HL279.

Schools Bill [HL], https://bills.parliament.uk/publications/47514/documents/2173.

Secretary of State for Education, debate on departmental responsibilities, https://hansard.parliament.uk/Commons/2018-01-29/debates/4F2A0469-2F29-4E94-8337-474108AD25AA/TopicalQuestions.

(v) News Articles

'C of E Opens School Gates to Non-Believers', *TES Magazine*, 22 April 2011, https://www.tes.com/news/c-e-opens-school-gates-non-believers.

Cameron, D., 'British Values Aren't Optional, They're Vital. That's Why I Will Promote Them in EVERY School', *Daily Mail*, 15 June 2014, http://www.dailymail.co.uk/debate/article-2658171/DAVID-CAMERON-British-values-arent-optional-theyre-vital-Thats-I-promote-EVERY-school-As-row-rages-Trojan-Horse-takeover-classrooms-Prime-Minister-delivers-uncompromising-pledge.html.

'Church Schools Move towards Open Door Selection', *BBC News*, 6 May 2015, https://www.bbc.co.uk/news/education-32587694.

'Faith Schools Welcome 100% Faith-Based Admissions', *Schools Week*, 16 September 2016, https://schoolsweek.co.uk/faith-schools-welcome-100-faith-based-admissions/.

'"Socially Selective" Faith Schools Must Introduce Fairer Admissions to Increase Poorer Students, Charity Says', *Independent*, 25 March 2019, https://www.independent.co.uk/news/education/education-news/faith-schools-sutton-trust-admissions-secondary-places-poorer-students-social-mobility-a8839236.html.

'U.S. Supreme Court Backs Public Money for Religious Schools', *Reuters*, 21 June 2022, https://www.reuters.com/legal/government/us-supreme-court-backs-public-money-religious-schools-maine-case-2022-06-21/.

'"We Can't Give In": The Birmingham School on the Frontline of Anti-LGBT Protests', *The Guardian*, 26 May 2019, https://www.theguardian.com/uk-news/2019/may/26/birmingham-anderton-park-primary-muslim-protests-lgbt-teaching-rights.

(vi) Other Web Sources

Accord Coalition for Inclusive Education, Mixed Signals: The Discrepancy between What the Church Preaches and What It Practises about Religious Selection in Its State-Funded Schools (2017), https://drive.google.com/file/d/1i5ImrZIpgoFkC7QrkRUdr1tTvCruqhHe/view.

Association of Directors of Children's Services (ADCS), Elective Home Education Survey 2021 (2021), https://adcs.org.uk/assets/documentation/ADCS_EHE_Survey_2021_Report_FINAL.pdf

Cameron, D., 'Prime Minister's Speech at Munich Security Conference', 5 February 2011, https://www.gov.uk/government/speeches/pms-speech-at-munich-security-conference.

Catholic Bishops' Conference of England and Wales, 'Statement: Admissions to Catholic Schools', 15 November 2013, https://www.cbcew.org.uk/home/the-church/catholic-bishops-conference-of-england-and-wales/plenary-meetings/plenary-november-2013/statement-admissions-to-catholic-schools/.

Catholic Education Service, 'Press Statement: Catholic Church welcomes Prime Minister's Removal of the Cap on Faith Admissions', 9 September 2016, http://www.

catholiceducation.org.uk/component/k2/item/1003609-catholic-church-welcomes-prime-minister-s-removal-of-the-cap-on-faith-admissions.

Commission on Religion and Belief in Public Life, Living with Difference. Community, Diversity, and the Common Good (2015), available at https://corablivingwithdifference.files.wordpress.com/2015/12/living-with-difference-community-diversity-and-the-common-good.pdf.

Commission on Religious Education, Religious Education for All. Final Report. Religion and Worldviews: The Way Forward. A National Plan for RE (2018), available at https://www.commissiononre.org.uk/wp-content/uploads/2018/09/Final-Report-of-the-Commission-on-RE.pdf.

Government of the Netherlands, 'Public Authority and Private Schools', https://www.government.nl/topics/freedom-of-education/public-authority-and-private-schools.

Humanists UK, 'Government Fails Most Vulnerable Children by Dropping Schools Bill', 7 December 2022, https://humanists.uk/2022/12/07/government-fails-most-vulnerable-children-by-dropping-schools-bill/.

Humanists UK, 'Humanists UK Warns Parents to Be Wary of Operation Christmas Child', 2 December 2022, https://humanists.uk/2022/12/02/humanists-uk-warns-parents-of-to-be-wary-of-operation-christmas-child/.

Humanists UK, 'Private Faith Schools', https://humanists.uk/campaigns/schools-and-education/faith-schools/private-faith-schools/.

May, T., 'Britain, the Great Meritocracy: Prime Minister's Speech', 9 November 2016, https://www.gov.uk/government/speeches/britain-the-great-meritocracy-prime-ministers-speech.

National Centre for Diversity, 'Investors in Diversity – Schools', http://www.nationalcentrefordiversity.com/home/services/investors-diversity-schools/.

The Conservative and Unionist Party, Manifesto: Forward, Together. Our Plan for a Stronger Britain and a Prosperous Future (2017), https://ucrel.lancs.ac.uk/wmatrix/ukmanifestos2017/localpdf/Conservatives.pdf.

Trinity Christian School, 'Vision', https://trinitychristianschool.org.uk/about/vision/.

UK Department for Education, 'Schools, Pupils and their Characteristics: Academic Year 2022/23' (2023), https://explore-education-statistics.service.gov.uk/find-statistics/school-pupils-and-their-characteristics.

Workable, 'What Are Soft Skills?', https://resources.workable.com/hr-terms/what-are-soft-skills.

(vii) Video (Documentary)

Faith School Menace?, written and presented by Richard Dawkins, directed by Molly Milton, released 18 August 2010, https://documentaryheaven.com/richard-dawkins-faith-school-menace/.

Index

Since the index has been created to work across multiple formats, indexed terms for which a page range is given (e.g., 52–53, 66–70, etc.) may occasionally appear only on some, but not all of the pages within the range.